HAMPTON

e

Multilingualism and Sign Languages

Ceil Lucas, General Editor

Multilingualism and Sign Languages

From the Great Plains

to Australia

Ceil Lucas, Editor

GALLAUDET UNIVERSITY PRESS

Washington, D.C.

UNIVERSITY OF WOLVERHAMPTON
LEARNING & INFORMATION
SERVICES

ACC. NO.
2412253

CONTROL NO.
1563682966

CLASS
149

306.
446

DATE *H 95* SITE
16 MAY 2017 *WV*

MUL

Sociolinguistics in Deaf Communities

A Series Edited by Ceil Lucas

Gallaudet University Press
Washington, D.C. 20002

http://gupress.gallaudet.edu

© 2006 by Gallaudet University.
All rights reserved
Published in 2006
Printed in the United States of America

ISBN 1-56368-296-6
ISSN 1080-5494

♾ The paper used in this publication meets the minimum requirements of
American National Standard for Information Sciences—Permanence of Paper
for Printed Library Materials, ANSI Z39.48-1984.

Contents

Editorial Advisory Board

Robert Bayley
Department of Linguistics
University of California, Davis
Davis, California

Jeffrey E. Davis
College of Education, Deaf
  Studies and Educational
  Interpreting
University of Tennessee
Knoxville, Tennessee

Trevor Johnston
Department of Linguistics
Macquarie University
Sydney, Australia

Susan M. Mather
Department of Linguistics
Gallaudet University
Washington, D.C.

Carolyn McCaskill
Department of ASL and Deaf
  Studies
Gallaudet University
Washington, D.C.

Stephen M. Nover
New Mexico School for the Deaf
Santa Fe, New Mexico

Lourdes Pietrosemoli
University of the Andes
Merida, Venezuela

Claire L. Ramsey
Teacher Education Program
University of California, San
  Diego
La Jolla, California

John Rickford
Department of Linguistics
Stanford University
Stanford, California

Adam Schembri
Deafness, Cognition and
  Language Research Centre
  (DCAL)
University College London
London, United Kingdom

Laurene Simms
Department of Education
Gallaudet University
Washington, D.C.

Graham H. Turner
Translation and Interpreting
  Studies
School of Management and
  Languages
Heriot-Watt University
Edinburgh, Scotland

Elizabeth Winston
Educational Linguistics Research
  Center
Loveland, Colorado

Editor's Introduction

The papers in this twelfth volume of the Sociolinguistics in Deaf Communities series demonstrate very clearly how much the field has grown in the eleven years since the first volume in 1995. As can be seen in the title, the papers cover topics that range from the sign language used by American Indians in the Great Plains to variation and issues of interpretation in Auslan, with papers on Puerto Rican Sign Language, la Langue des Signes Québécoise (LSQ), Italian Codas and ASL discourse in between. The papers also represent all of the key areas of sociolinguistic study and continue the series tradition of data-based accounts of the use of sign languages in a wide variety of contexts all over the world. Sociolinguistic issues are clearly being noticed, analyzed and documented in many Deaf communities. It is a pleasure to welcome this volume to the series!

Ceil Lucas
Washington, D.C.

Part 1　Multilingualism

A Historical Linguistic Account of Sign

Language among North American Indians

Jeffrey E. Davis

Signed communication among various indigenous peoples has been observed and documented across the North American continent since fifteenth- and sixteenth-century European contact. Early scholars of this subject (e.g., Clark 1885; Mallery 1880; Scott 1931; Tomkins 1926) have made cases for the North American Indian[1] sign variety to justify its being considered a full-fledged language. Two predominant themes in the early writings about Indian signed languages are "universality" and "iconicity" — theoretical issues that signed language linguists continue to address even today. The study of such phenomena helps broaden our understanding of these issues and other linguistic questions. For example, the early research on Indian signed languages informed the seminal work of some of the first signed language linguists (e.g., Stokoe 1960; Battison 1978/2003). These historical linguistic data need to be reexamined in light of current linguistic theories, interdisciplinary perspectives, and current sign use among deaf and hearing North American Indians and other indigenous populations around the world.

I am grateful to the Office of the Chancellor and Dean of Graduate Studies at the University of Tennessee for their generous support to have digitized the documentary materials that are the focus of this paper. I would also like to acknowledge the support from a National Endowment for the Humanities and National Science Foundation Documenting Endangered Languages fellowship (FN-50002-06). Any views, findings, conclusions, or recommendations expressed in this paper do not necessarily reflect those of the University of Tennessee, National Endowment for the Humanities, National Science Foundation, or the Smithsonian Institution.

Observed and documented across several geographic locations and cultural areas, the historical varieties of indigenous signed language specific to North America are sometimes collectively referred to as "North American Indian Sign Language" (see Wurtzburg and Campbell, 1995). Historically, these varieties of signed language were named in various ways — Plains Indian Sign Language, Indian Sign Language, The Sign Language, Indian Language of Signs, and historical references in this paper will apply those names where appropriate.[2] Previous anthropological linguistic field research (Kroeber 1958; Voegelin 1958; West 1960) indicates that signed language was used in varying degrees within most of the language families of Native North America. The best documented cases of indigenous signed languages involved various Indian groups who once inhabited the Great Plains area of the North American continent (see table 1). This enormous geographic expanse stretched north to south for more than two thousand miles from the North Saskatchewan River in Canada to the Rio Grande in Mexico. The east-west boundaries were approximately the Mississippi-Missouri valleys and the foothills of the Rocky Mountains and encompassed an area of some one million square miles. Generally, twelve major geographic cultural areas of Native North America are identified in the literature with the Plains cultural area centrally located to all of these (cf. Campbell 2000, Mithun 1999). Historically, this large geographic area was one of extreme linguistic diversity, and hundreds of different languages were spoken among the native populace.[3]

The Plains tribes were geographically and culturally central to most of the other North American Indian cultural groups and a signed lingua franca appears to have evolved as a way to make communication possible among individuals speaking so many different mother tongues (Davis, 2005). Traditionally, the nomadic groups of the Great Plains used Plains Sign Language (PISL hereafter) as an alternate to spoken language. Beyond the Plains geographic area, fluent signers of PISL have been identified among native groups from the Plateau area — e.g., the Nez Perce (Sahaptian) and the Flathead (Salishan). In what remains the most extensive study of PISL to date, West (1960) reported dialect differences among these Indian groups, but found that these did not seriously impede signed communication. In the late 1950s, West found that PISL was still practiced, particularly on intertribal ceremonial occasions but also in storytelling and conversation, even among speakers of the same language. The historical ethnographic and linguistic documentary materials that are the focus of this paper support that PISL was used as a lingua franca among the Plains Indian tribes as well as between them and other American Indian linguistic groups (compare Campbell 2000; Davis 2005; Farnell 1995; Mithun 1999; Taylor 1978; Umiker-Sebeok and Sebeok 1978; Wurtzburg and Campbell 1995).

For example, Campbell (2000, 10) writes that "the sign language as a whole became the lingua franca of the Great Plains, and it spread from there as far as British Columbia, Alberta, Saskatchewan, and Manitoba." Evidently there was some variation from tribe to tribe, and not all individuals were equally proficient in signed language. Varying degrees of signed language use among some American Indian individuals and groups has been observed even today. However, the number of users has dramatically declined since the nineteenth century, leading several researchers to conclude that these traditional signed language varieties are endangered (Davis 2005; Farnell 1995; Kelly and McGregor 2003; McKay-Cody 1997). Contemporary and historical use of the signed language among Native American groups needs to be documented, described, and stabilized through language maintenance and education to prevent imminent language loss.

Researchers have proposed that the signed systems used by hearing Indians as an alternative to spoken language became a primary signed language when acquired natively by tribal members who are deaf (Davis and Supalla 1995; Kelly and McGregor 2003; McKay-Cody 1997).[4] These studies have reported the contemporary use of traditional PISL among both deaf and hearing Native American descendents of the Plains Indian cultural groups. Deaf and hearing individuals from other Native American groups, such as the Diné/Navajo (Davis and Supalla 1995) and the Keresan of the New Mexico Pueblo cultural area (Kelly and McGregor 2003) appear to sign a variety that is distinct from traditional PISL. Preliminarily, the available linguistic evidence suggests that these traditional ways of signing among Indian groups are distinct from American Sign Language (ASL). At the same time, striking similarities in linguistic structure between PISL and ASL (e.g., marked and unmarked handshapes, symmetry and dominance conditions, classifier forms, and nonmanual markers), have been documented (see Davis 2005, Davis and Supalla 1995, McKay-Cody 1997). In this paper, I report the documented cases of historical and contemporary signed language use among North

American Indian groups, present preliminary linguistic descriptions and findings, and offer readers a link to a prototype on-line digital archive of PISL documentary materials. I aim to expand this open access on-line linguistic corpus of PISL to include more documentary materials, translations, and analyses. This will encourage and facilitate language revitalization efforts, further research, and scholarship. The link to the on-line digital archive of PISL documentary materials is Plains Sign Language Digital Archive: http://sunsite.utk.edu/plainssignlanguage/.

PRE-EUROPEAN CONTACT

Clearly, there was (and still remains) an indigenous form of North American signed language, and its use has been historically documented as being widespread. Wurtzburg and Campbell (1995) make a compelling case for there having been a preexistent, well-developed indigenous signed language across the Gulf Coast-Texas-northern Mexico area *before European contact*. In their historical study of "North American Indian Sign Language," Wurtzburg and Campbell (1995, 160) define "sign language" as "a conventionalized gesture language of the sort later attested among the Plains and neighboring areas." Based on numerous early historical accounts, they report that the earliest and most substantive accounts is from the 1527 expedition for the conquest of Florida, lead by the Spanish conquistador Cabeza de Vaca who reported numerous occasions wherein native groups communicated with signs (1995, 154–55). According to the historical record, Cabeza de Vaca "also clearly distinguished which groups spoke the same language, which spoke different languages but understood others, and which groups did not understand others at all, except through the use of sign language" (1995, 155).[5] Similar accounts were made by Coronado in 1541 (reported in Taylor 1978), and subsequent reports were made in the eighteenth century (e.g., Santa Ana in 1740 [reported in Mithun 1999]). Goddard (1979), and Wurtzburg and Campbell (1995) published papers about the role served by signed languages and some spoken native languages as lingua francas, and have discussed the pidgins, trade languages and "mixed" systems used among native groups. The generally accepted hypothesis among scholars (see Campbell 2000; Mithun 1999) is that North American Indian Sign Language originated and spread from the Gulf Coast, became the intertribal lingua franca of the Great Plains, and spread throughout the northwest territories of the United States and Canada (compare Goddard 1979; Taylor 1978; Wurtzburg and Campbell 1995). Further research of these topics is needed, but presently beyond the scope of this paper. The historical linguistic documents and ethnographic accounts that are the focus of this paper support that signed language was used beyond the Great Plains area and was evident across most of the major American Indian cultural areas (e.g., Southeast and Gulf Coast, Southwest, Plateau and Basin, Subarctic, Mesoamerica, and Northeast).

Attention to the rich legacy of historical linguistic documents that remain (essays, descriptions, illustrations, films) is needed in light of new linguistic theories. The indigenous origins of contemporary signed language use among Native American deaf and hearing signers across different geographic and cultural contexts must be documented. Further consideration must be given to the intergenerational use of highly elaborate signed communication systems that have been documented for hearing signing communities, even when deaf people are not present (e.g., historically on Martha's Vineyard as well as currently and historically in some indigenous and monastic communities). In addition to signed language use in Deaf communities, this linguistic phenomenon (i.e., signing communities that are predominately hearing) has been and continues to be documented in several aboriginal communities around the world and is also evident in some occupational settings and monastic traditions (see, e.g., Davis and Supalla 1995; Farnell 1995; Johnson 1994; Kendon 1988, 2002; Kelly and McGregor 2003; Plann 1997; Umiker-Sebeok and Sebeok 1978; Washabaugh 1986a, 1986b).

More recently, some signed language linguists (Davis 2005; Davis and Supalla 1995; Johnson 1994; Farnell 1995; Kelly and McGregor 2003; McKay-Cody 1997) have documented contemporary signed language use among other North American linguistic groups — for example, Algonquian (Blackfeet) and Siouan (Assiniboine, Dakotan, Stoney) language groups as well as Navajo (Diné), Keresan Pueblo, Northern Cheyenne, Yucatan-Mayan, and others. In light of new field studies and linguistic theories, linguists have reexamined the documented occurrences of aboriginal signed language in North American and in other continents (e.g., Australia and South America). The evidence suggests that in addition to its documented history as an intertribal lingua franca, signed language was used intratribally for a variety of discourse purposes (e.g., storytelling, gender-specific activities, times when speech was taboo, and ritual practices).

In this paper, I examine the documented film and written ethnographic accounts of North American Indians signing an assortment of
topics, including different discourse types across a variety of settings and
participants. Furthermore, I consider some of the historical connections
between ASL and indigenous signed language varieties. Historic and contemporary uses of signed language have been documented in at least one
dozen distinct North American language families (phyla). Certainly, signing may have been used by even more groups than these, but at least
this many cases were documented in historical linguistic accounts. The
archived data reveal that regardless of hearing status, signing was used by
members from approximately thirty-seven distinct American Indian spoken language groups. Conventions for the classification of North American language families are followed (compare Campbell 2000; Mithun
1999). In each case, the published source is provided and documented
cases of current use are highlighted. These historical and contemporary
cases are presented in table 1.

HISTORICAL LINGUISTIC DOCUMENTATION AND DESCRIPTION

Throughout the 1800s, the earliest explorers, naturalists, ethnologists,
and even U.S. military personnel, extensively documented the use of Indian
Sign Language for a variety of purposes. Documentation of Indian Sign
Language continued through the 1900s, and the earliest anthropologists,
linguists, and semioticians studied and described its linguistic structures
(e.g., Boas 1890/1978; Kroeber 1958; Mallery 1880; Umiker-Sebeok and
Sebeok 1978; Voegelin 1958), most of whom, notably, also served terms
as presidents of the Linguistic Society of America. These early scholars
laid the groundwork for Indian Sign Language to be considered a preexistent, full-fledged language. Thus, there remains a rich linguistic and
ethnographic legacy in the form of diaries, books, articles, illustrations,
dictionaries, and motion pictures that document the varieties of signed
language historically used among native populations of North America.
The most extensive documentation of PISL was made by the first ethnologists to do fieldwork for the Bureau of Ethnology at the Smithsonian
Institution in Washington, D.C. (from approximately the 1870s–1890s).
Figure 1 shows some of the original pen and ink illustrations of the PISL
from the files of Garrik Mallery and his collaborators working with the
Smithsonian in the late 1880s. One of the richest sources for archival data

TABLE 1. *Documentation of Historic and Current Sign Language Use among North American Indians*

Language Phyla and Group	Published Sources
I. Algic = Algonquian family	Campbell (2000),Mithun (1999), McKay-Cody (1997)
1. Arapaho	Clark (1885), Mallery (1880), Scott (1931)
2. Blackfoot = Blood = Piegan	Davis, 2005; Mallery (1880), Scott (1931); Weatherwax (2002)
3. Northern Cheyenne	Burton (1862), Mallery (1880), McKay-Cody, 1997; Scott (1931), Seton (1918)
4. Cree	Long (1823), Mallery (1880), Scott (1931)
5. Fox = Sauk-Kickapoo	Long (1823), Mallery (1880)
6. Ojibwa = Ojibwe = Chippeway	Hofsinde (1956), Long (1823), Mallery (1880)
7. Shawnee	Burton (1862), Harrington (1938)
II. Athabaskan-Tlingit family	Campbell (2000), Mithun (1999)
8. Navajo = Diné	Davis and Supalla (1995)
9. Plains Apache = Kiowa-Apache	Fronvall and Dubois (1985), Hadley (1891), Harrington (1938), Mallery (1880), Scott (1931)
10. Sarcee = Sarsi	Scott (1931)
III. Siouan-Catawban family	Campbell (2000), Mithun (1999)
11. Crow	Burton (1862),Mallery (1880), Scott (1931)
12. Hidasta = Gros Venture	Mallery (1880), Scott (1931)
13. Mandan	Scott (1931)
14. Dakotan = Sioux = Lak(h)ota	Burton (1862),Farnell, 1995; Long (1823), Mallery (1880), Seton (1918), Tompkins (1926)
15. Assiniboine = Stoney = Alberta	Farnell (1995),Mallery (1880), Scott (1931)
16. Omaha-Ponca	Long (1823), Mallery (1880)
17. Osage = Kansa	Harrington (1938), Long (1823)
18. Oto = Missouri = Iowa	Long (1823), Mallery (1880)
IV. Caddoan family	Campbell (2000), Mithun (1999)
19. Caddo	Harrington (1938)
20. Wichita	Harrington (1938), Mallery (1880)
21. Pawnee	Burton (1862), Mallery (1880)

Language Phyla and Group	Published Sources
22. Arikara	Mallery (1880), Scott (1931)
V. Kiowan-Tonoan family	Campbell (2000), Mithun (1999)
23. Kiowa	Fronval and Dubois (1985), Hadley (1891), Harrington (1938), Mallery (1880)
24. Tonoan = Tewa = Hopi-Tewa = Tano	Goddard (1979), Mallery (1880)
VI. Uto-Aztecan family	Campbell (2000), Mithun (1999)
25. Shoshone = Shoshoni	Burton (1862), Mallery (1880), Scott (1931)
26. Comanche	Harrington (1938), Mallery (1880)
27. Ute = Southern Paiute	Burton (1862), Mallery (1880)
28. Northern Paitue = Bannock = Banak	Mallery (1880)
VII. Shahaptian family	Campbell (2000), Mithun (1999)
29. Nez Perce = Nimipu = Chopunnish	Scott (1931)
30. Sahaptian	Mallery (1880)
VIII. Salishan family	Campbell (2000), Mithun (1999)
31. Coeur d'Alene	Teit (1930)
32. Flathead = Spokane = Kalispel	Scott (1931)
33. Shuswap, British Columbia	Boas (1890/1978)
IX. Eskimo-Aleut family	Campbell (2000), Mithun (1999)
34. Inuit = Inupiaq-Inuktitut	Hoffman (1895)
X. Iroquoian family	Campbell (2000), Mithun (1999)
35. Huron-Wyandot	Mallery (1880)
XI. Zuni (isolate)	Campbell (2000)
36. Zuni	Mallery (1880)
XII. Keresan = Keres	Campbell (2000)
New Mexico Pueblo varieties	
37. Laguna Pueblo	Goldfrank (1923)
Keresan Pueblo	Kelly and McGregor (2003)

Note: For descriptions of current sign language use see McKay-Cody (1997), Davis (2005), Davis and Supalla (1995), Farnell (1995), Goff-Paris and Wood (2002), Kelly and McGregor (2003).

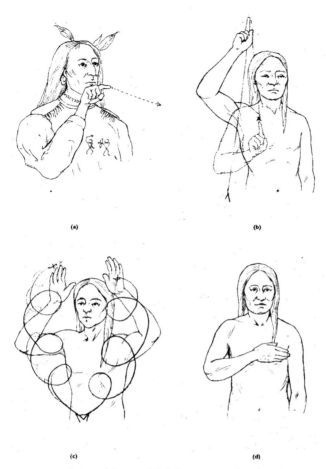

(a)   (b)

(c)   (d)

FIGURE 1. *Original Pen and Ink Drawings of Indian Signs (ca. 1880); Courtesy of the National Anthropological Archives, Smithsonian Institution (ms. 2372).*

comes from the motion pictures produced by Scott (1931) with support from a U.S. Act of Congress. The purpose of these films was to preserve signed language as a part of the North American Indian cultural and linguistic heritage. The source and content of these films will be described later in this paper.

Unfortunately, since the late 1800s, social, cultural, and historical factors have caused the population of native and secondary users of the signed languages to dramatically decrease, suggesting that PISL is an endangered language. Fortunately, some PISL varieties are still used today and need to be further documented and described. For example, current signed language use and maintenance programs have been documented for the Assiniboine, Stoney, Blackfeet, Piegan, Blood, Crow, and North Cheyenne (see Farnell 1995). Further, the National Multicultural Interpreting Project at El Paso Community College, the Intertribal Deaf Council, and the Department of Blackfeet Studies at Blackfeet Community College are involved in the revitalization of PISL.

Contemporary North American Indian Sign Language Studies

Davis and Supalla (1995) studied signed language in a contemporary Native American Indian linguistic community. For a period of two years (June, 1990–May, 1992) these researchers documented the signed language used in a Navajo (Diné) community with several deaf family members (i.e., six out of eleven siblings were deaf or hard of hearing). In that linguistic community, reminiscent of the historical case on Martha's Vineyard (Groce 1985), both deaf and hearing family members shared signed language. Note, however, that the members of the particular Navajo family having several deaf family members signed more fluently than most members of the larger hearing Navajo community.

Davis and Supalla documented the highly elaborate sign-based communication system that was used by the Navajo family and that was distinct from ASL. Apparently, the sign system used by the family has evolved intergenerationally because of several outstanding historical and sociolinguistic causes. The first of these influences was a reported history of sign communication in the larger hearing Navajo community (similar to the types evident in other North American indigenous communities). Second, the hearing Navajo parents of this family signed what was called "the Navajo way." Furthermore, a thirty-year age span separated the oldest deaf sibling and the youngest deaf sibling. Three younger sisters (two deaf and one hard of hearing) and a male cousin, who is also deaf, were educated at the Arizona School for the Deaf and Blind (ASDB) in Tucson. The three older deaf siblings, having never attended school, apparently never learned ASL. Although the younger deaf siblings and cousin were fluent in ASL, they continued to use what was called "the Navajo way" or "the family sign" with their deaf and hearing relatives living on the reservation.

The male cousin served as the primary consultant for the study.[6] He was fluent in the variety of signed language used by the family, fluent in the signed communication used within the larger hearing Navajo community, natively proficient in ASL, and able to communicate in written English.

He met with the researchers before and after each site visit and served as an interpreter. Ethnographic procedures were followed to enhance rapport, naturalness, and authenticity of the data collected. Approximately twenty hours of videotaped signed language data were documented for this family. The researchers described the nature of linguistic interaction (e.g., language functions and domains of use) between the deaf and hearing participants in this rarified situation. Davis and Supalla observed that both deaf and hearing family members maintained and recognized linguistic boundaries between these different varieties of signing.

The primary deaf Navajo consultant, hearing family members, and other deaf and hearing Navajo individuals described the different "ways of signing" used in the larger Navajo community. ASL was referred to as "English sign" or "the Anglo way of signing." The family sign system, which they called "our signs" or "family sign," was considered distinct from ASL. The signed language used by the larger Navajo community was called "the hearing Navajo way of signing," "signing the Navajo way," "Navajo Sign," and "Indian sign." The hearing Navajo way of signing was viewed as being related to their family signed language (i.e., shared lexicon), but distinct in other ways. When asked what makes the family sign different, the Navajo sources reported that the family sign is less transparent and environmentally dependent and is signed much faster than the hearing Navajo way of signing. Davis and Supalla observed that the following practices in both deaf and hearing Navajo family members:

- Consistently used the family sign system with one another (i.e., no observed use of ASL among the family members)
- Participated in signed conversations that spanned a range of topics and settings, past and present time periods, and conversations about daily routines (e.g., rug making and sheep herding)
- Interpreted between spoken Navajo, English, ASL, and the family sign system (depending on the hearing status and sociolinguistic background of the participant)
- Used name signs to identify each family member (present or absent)

Significantly, the so-called family sign appeared to be much more complex with linguistic features that are typically absent for various other home sign systems.

According to Frishberg (1987), home sign systems do share some features with natural languages (e.g., individual signs are segmentable, can be assigned to semantic categories, etc.). However, they also have specific characteristics that distinguish them from conventional signed languages. For example, signing space for home sign is larger; signs and sign sequences tend to be repeated; the number of distinct handshapes are fewer; eye gaze functions differently; signs are produced more slowly, awkwardly, and less fluently; and home sign systems are more environmentally dependent (e.g., requiring the signer to point to a color or object in the environment rather than make a sign for them). In contrast to the above features described for home sign, Davis and Supalla (1995) found that the Navajo family sign system had the following characteristics:

- More multilayered and complex than what is typically described for home sign (e.g., rich use of head and face nonmanual markers and classifier forms)
- Highly elaborated and conventionalized (e.g., a consistent meaning-symbol relationship for signs, including cultural concepts such as herding sheep, weaving, and performing Indian dancing)
- Developed in a historical context where signing has reportedly been used by some hearing members of the larger Navajo spoken language community (even when no deaf individuals were present)
- Used in this family cross-generationally for at least fifty years
- Signed with minimal ASL borrowing and codeswitching
- Distinct from ASL and spoken Navajo (i.e., languages kept separate by family members, depending on the language background of interlocutors)

Overall, Davis and Supalla (1995) observed minimal lexical borrowing from ASL (e.g., some ASL signs were used for family relations, food signs, and color terms, and ASL fingerspelling was used in token ways to convey some proper nouns). In contrast, home sign is usually not maintained cross-generationally and is typically replaced by the conventional sign language of the Deaf community. Davis and Supalla suggested that these combined sociolinguistic factors lead to a full-fledged (or at least emergent) language that is distinct from other types of signed communication (e.g., signs or gestures that accompany speech; home-based signing).

Davis and Supalla (1995) proposed a "Taxonomy of Signed Communication Systems" that was based on work with the Navajo family and on accounts from other aboriginal and indigenous signed language studies (e.g., Kendon 1988; Washabaugh 1986a, 1986b). In this taxonomy, they described the following types of visual-gestural communication:

- *Primary signed languages* that have evolved within specific historical, social, and cultural contexts and that have been used across generations of signers (e.g., ASL, French Sign Language, Danish Sign Language, etc.)
- *Alternate sign systems* developed and used by individuals who are already competent in spoken language (e.g., the highly elaborated and complex sign system used historically by the Plains Indians of North America)
- *Home sign systems* that are gestural communication systems developed when deaf individuals are isolated from other deaf people and need to communicate with other hearing people around them
- *Gestures* that accompany spoken language discourse

Naturally, these distinctions are not that cut and dried, and the different types of signed communications are interrelated. Although these categories are useful descriptively, Davis and Supalla noted overlap between the categories. For example, the family's home sign system was informed by the alternate signs used by some in the hearing Navajo community. Thus, the way of signing used by this Navajo family emerged as a primary signed language. Along similar lines, McKay-Cody's (1997, 10–11) study supported that the "alternate sign systems" used by hearing Indians became a "primary signed language" when acquired natively by Indians who are deaf. The linguistic evidence also suggests that alternate signs are used to varying degrees of proficiency, ranging from (a) signs that accompany speech to (b) signs that are used without speech to (c) sign use that functions similarly to primary signed language. Like other cases of sociolinguistic variation, these ways of signing are best considered along a continuum.

The National Archives

In 1993, Samuel Supalla and I received a small grant from the Laurent Clerc Cultural Fund from Gallaudet University Alumni Association to collect and organize film and literature on Native American Sign Language in North America. I traveled to Washington, D.C., and the day I was scheduled to do research at the National Archives, a snowstorm of unforecasted proportions descended on the city. The transit system was paralyzed for several hours, but finding safe refuge in the National Archives, I remained longer than expected. While waiting for the blizzard to subside, I met some researchers working on Ken Burns's upcoming

PBS special about the history of American baseball. When I shared my research agenda about Indian Sign Language, the researchers directed me to an area of the archives where there were numerous old films documenting Indian Sign Language.

Because Washington, D.C., was at a standstill, the National Archives remained open beyond the usual hours. Taking advantage of this opportunity, the archivists assisted me in making VHS copies of these old films to bring back to the signed language research lab at the University of Arizona. Since that time, I have shared these films with others who have also studied them periodically. However, a full-scale linguistic study of the phonology, morphology, and syntax of PISL is still forthcoming. A preliminary linguistic analysis of some of the data contained in these films and of the historical documents uncovered during the initial PISL project were the focus of an outstanding master's thesis completed by Melanie McKay-Cody (1997) at the University of Arizona. McKay-Cody compared a traditional narrative about buffalo hunting signed by one of the hearing Indian chiefs from the 1930s film with a similar narrative signed by a contemporary deaf Indian who was a native PISL user.[7] This study distinguished two major categories of signed language used by Indians: (1) as an alternative to spoken language by hearing tribal members; and (2) as a primary language (first language) for deaf tribal members (McKay-Cody 1997, 10). This finding was consistent with the patterns identified earlier by Davis and Supalla, and McKay-Cody observed that when signers who are deaf learn the signed language used by the larger hearing native community they "seem to gain a higher level of proficiency" than the hearing Indian signers (50). These findings suggest that alternate signed language used by hearing Indians become linguistically enriched when learned as a primary language by members of Indian communities who are deaf. McKay-Cody concluded that PISL was a full-fledged language.

McKay-Cody's study also demonstrated that the narrative structures and morphological complexities of historical and contemporary PISL are comparable with those found in ASL. For example, the sign types, marked and unmarked handshapes, and symmetry and dominance conditions described for ASL by Battison (1978/2003) are evident in the PISL lexicon, and the classifier form described for ASL by Ted Supalla (1978) are also clearly evident in the PISL data corpus. Remarkably, more than two-thirds of the signs used by the primary PISL deaf signer in his version of the buffalo hunting story were identical or similar (i.e., different in only one parameter, or signed with one hand instead of two) to the signs documented in the historical PISL lexicon. Though based on only the analysis of one signed narrative, these results were nonetheless significant. McKay-Cody's primary consultant learned PISL as a young deaf child on the Northern Cheyenne Reservation, and his Cheyenne ancestors were reported to be among the historical progenitors of traditional PISL.

Considering historical linguistic change, regional variation, and intensive language issues, the similarities that are evident between contemporary and historical PISL are striking. The fact that PISL has survived and continues to be used is remarkable, especially considering the pressures for linguistic and cultural assimilation that have been historically imposed on indigenous peoples. Further linguistic comparison, documentation, and description of historical and contemporary PISL use among deaf and hearing Indians are needed. Even more critical is the need for language maintenance and education because PISL is an endangered language. Unfortunately, programs to support the maintenance of the historical PISL variety and to educate users have been lacking. See Crystal (2000) for more information about the extreme urgency for language stabilization and maintenance.

The Historical Linguistic Database

The signs used by American Indians have been documented for a variety of purposes since the early 1800s, and I have identified over 8,000 lexical descriptions, illustrations, photographs, and films documented in archived sources that span three centuries (see table 1). Great care must be taken in classifying, preserving, analyzing, and describing these historical linguistic data documenting the Indians use of signs. Certainly, given the wide geographic expanse of the North American continent and the linguistic and cultural diversity that was evident, more than one native sign variety is represented in these historical linguistic documents. Describing, illustrating, and deciphering signs accurately is a challenge. Consequently, duplicate entries between dictionaries and instances of overlap (wherein the same sign is labeled differently) may have occurred, and some of the descriptions and illustrations may be erroneous.

Fortunately, a substantial amount of PISL has been filmed (historically and contemporarily), thus making possible further comparisons between the written, illustrated, and filmed historical linguistic documents. The sheer magnitude of these data, however, point to the need to establish an open-source database to provide access for others to study, teach, and research PISL and other Native American sign varieties. A history of language contact between North American Indian and Deaf American communities warrants further consideration, however, before any discussion about the content of the filmed documentation is presented here.

Historical Sign Language Studies

The first known description of Indian sign vocabulary was published in 1823 (Long 1823) after the Stephen Long expedition undertaken in 1820.[8] That account preceded by one hundred years the first published dictionary for the sign language used by Deaf Americans (J. S. Long 1918). In 1848, the first known article to be published by Thomas H. Gallaudet was an essay titled "On the Natural Language of Signs: And Its Value and Uses in the Instruction of the Deaf and Dumb." The first part of his essay appeared in the inaugural publication of *American Annals of the Deaf* (1848a) and the second part in the following issue (1848b). The essay was written following early nineteenth-century conventions that are archaic and patronizing by today's standards. Nonetheless, T. H. Gallaudet used the "Indian Language of Signs" to make a case for the value of "the natural language of signs" for teaching and communicating with deaf people.

In the published essay, Gallaudet did not propose that the Indian Language of Signs be used as the language of instruction, but that "The Natural Language of Signs" was the best method of instruction (1848a). In the second part of the essay (1848b), he proposed that the "originators of this language" are the deaf people themselves (93). Gallaudet discussed the "universality" of what he called the "the natural language of signs." His main point about "universality" was that signed language "naturally" occurs "when necessity exists" and "prompts the invention and use of this language of signs" (1848a, 59). As evidence, Gallaudet used examples from the Indian Language of Signs and included the detailed descriptions of signs used by the "aboriginal Indians" that he had taken in part from "Expedition from Pittsburgh to the Rocky Mountains," an account of the expedition led by Major Stephen H. Long that includes descriptions of a total of 104 "Indian signs" (Long 1823, 378–94).

The historical proximity of the first American deaf school having been established in 1817 and the fact that Gallaudet considered the sign language of the Indians significant enough to make that the central focus of his article in the inaugural edition of the *American Annals of the Deaf and Dumb,* makes its possible introduction to deaf students an intriguing question. However, the historic publications that are considered here do not exactly support this notion. For example, in 1848, Gallaudet wrote the following:

> Major Long's work contains an accurate description of many of these signs, and it is surprising to notice how not a few of them are almost identically the same with those which the deaf and dumb employ to describe the same things, while others have such general features of resemblance as to show that they originate from elements of this sign-language which nature furnishes to man wherever he is found, whether barbarous or civilized. (1848a, 59)

To support the hypothesis that signed language was a naturally occurring human phenomenon, Gallaudet (1848a) had selected eight examples from the previously published list of 104 Indian signs and descriptions (Long 1823). Specifically, he selected examples that he found were signed the same way by deaf people and by Indians. After the death of T. H. Gallaudet, the complete list of 104 Indian signs (Long 1823) was published as the "Indian Language of Signs" in the *American Annals of the Deaf and Dumb* (Gallaudet 1852) and included this note from the editor: "The points of resemblance between these signs and those in use among the educated deaf and dumb are numerous and striking" (157). The entire published list of the original 104 Indian sign descriptions (compare Long 1823) is too long to include here; however, the eight Indian sign descriptions from Gallaudet's 1848 article are presented in appendix A.

Other Historical Connections

It was not until 1918 that J. Schuyler Long (long-time principal at the Iowa School for the Deaf) published the first illustrated dictionary, *The Sign Language: A Manual of Signs,* which he described as "Being a descriptive vocabulary of signs used by the deaf of the United States and Canada" (Long 1918,). That statement [I mean the dictionary, not the statement] came almost one hundred years after S. H. Long's 1823 published descriptions of the "Indian Language of Signs." It should be noted that J. Schuyler Long corresponded with both Garrick Mallery and Hugh Scott, the two preeminent scholars of Indian Sign Language of the time. Additional research is needed to learn more about these collaborations and the historical relationships between the historical varieties of Indian Sign Language and ASL. Furthermore, linguistic comparisons must take into account iconicity, historical change, and variation.

Thus, the historical linguistic evidence in these earliest published accounts raises numerous questions such as the following:

- Did Gallaudet pick the eight signs from the 104 Indian signs as the most salient examples of how the Indians and deaf people signed the same (in an attempt to prove his claim about the universality of natural sign language)?
- Were Indian signs ever used to teach deaf students attending schools for the deaf (something not explicitly stated by Gallaudet in the 1848 *American Annals of the Deaf and Dumb* essay)?
- What about contact between the earliest European immigrants who were deaf and American Indians?
- What contact did deaf students attending the first American schools for the deaf have with American Indians who signed?
- Are there documented cases of American Indian children who were deaf attending schools for the deaf?
- Given the propensity for American Indians to use sign and the fact that Indians were reportedly inhabitants of Martha's Vineyard at the time of the first wave of European immigration (Groce 1985), what connection might there be between these historical facts and the subsequent emergence of a Martha's Vineyard sign language variety?

These questions are beyond the scope of the present study to address but are offered here for others to consider as possible topics for further investigation.

For this paper, I conducted a preliminary analysis of this 1823 published list of 104 Indian signs and compared them with subsequent sign descriptions contained in the historical PISL database. First, I compared the descriptions from the early 1800s with those made in the late 1800s and early 1900s (i.e., documented ethnographic accounts that spanned a one-hundred-year period). Then I compared the nineteenth and early twentieth century descriptions with 150 examples of Indian signs that were contemporarily signed and videotaped by Martin Weatherwax (2002), chair of Blackfeet Studies at Blackfeet Community College in Browning, Montana. Professor Weatherwax reported that he learned Indian Sign Language natively from his Blackfoot grandfather. Thus, the preliminary historical linguistic comparisons reported here span three centuries (i.e., from the very early 1800s until the 2000s).

Conservatively, I have estimated that at least 75 percent of the signs from the 1823 descriptions were identical or similar (i.e., differing in only a single parameter — handshape, movement, location, orientation) to the Indian signs that have been documented for subsequent generations. Although these results are preliminary and should be interpreted carefully, one must also consider the overwhelming historical linguistic evidence for there having been an intertribal and intergenerational signed lingua franca. The 1930s films produced by Hugh Scott remain the richest source of historical NASIL and provide the strongest evidence for a historical signed lingua franca.

THE 1930s FILM PRESERVATION PROJECT

Unfortunately, by the 1900s, the use of Indian Sign Language was greatly diminished and appeared endangered. Recognizing the endangered status of Indian Sign Language, in 1930, Hugh Scott proposed a motion picture preservation project that was funded and completed by an Act of the U.S. Congress.[9] This effort resulted in The Indian Sign Language Conference that was filmed September 4–6, 1930, in Browning, Montana. This event was the largest intertribal meeting of Indian chiefs, elders, medicine men, and other representatives ever filmed. There were eighteen official participants, including representatives from a dozen different tribes and language groups from the Plains, Plateau, and Basin cultural areas. A permanent monument to the Indian Sign Language Council signifying the importance of this gathering was established at the conference site, and each of the council members had their footprints placed in bronze as a part of the monument. Subsequently, the Museum of the Plains Indian was constructed on this site.

Council Participants and Tribal Affiliations

The original 1930 films documented that Indian Sign Language, without the accompaniment of speech, was the modus operandi for the conference. Following the opening signed remarks by General Scott, each representative signed their name, tribal affiliation, and introductory comments. The order of signed introductions was as follows: Dick Washakie,

Shoshone; Short Face, Piegan; Bitter Root Jim, Flathead; Night Shoots, Piegan; Drags Wolf, Hidasta; Deer Nose, Crow; James Eagle, Arikara; Foolish Woman, Mandan; Strange Owl, Cheyenne; Bird Rattler, Blood; Mountain Chief, Chief of the Piegans; Assiniboine Boy, Upper Gros Venture; Tom Whitehorse, Arapaho; Rides Black Horse, Assiniboine; Little Plum, Piegan; Fine Young Man, Sarcee; Big Plume, Sarcee; and General Scott, Anglo-American.

Notably, dozens of different spoken languages were represented among the participants. Thus, the so-called signed lingua franca was used by the participants, who were the chiefs and elders representing the various tribes. Because the location for the Indian Sign Language Council was in close proximity to the Blackfeet Reservation, several of the participants were from the Blackfeet nation (from both Piegan and Blood lineages). A few women and children were filmed entering the council lodge, but they were never formally introduced or shown signing. Two Blackfeet participants did not appear on the film. They were Jim White Calf, and Richard Sanderville.

Discourse Types

During the three-day Indian Sign Language Conference (September 4–6, 1930), the participants discussed a variety of topics and shared several anecdotes, stories, and discourse genres, all of which were documented in these films. In particular, the films included signed stories, titled "Sagas in Signs," which are summarized as follows:

- Introductions, signed names, signs for the twelve tribes (six minutes)
- Mountain Chief's Buffalo Signed Chant (two minutes) — The Piegan Chief tells a traditional buffalo hunting story. In the digitized copies of the films, it is possible to see much greater detail than it was previously with the old analog videotapes. It is clear in the film and from Scott's voiced translation that Mountain Chief is singing the Medicine Man chants in accompaniment with signing. In other words he is singing and signing simultaneously. Speech with sign accompaniment has been observed by others (e.g., Farnell 1995) but apparently, this practice was not a common occurrence in these films (there was only one example of a story told in sign with speech accompaniment, and that is noted below).
- Tom Whitehorse's Metaphorical Comparison (thirty seconds) — This Arapaho signer gives a metaphorical comparison of the radio (which he calls White Man's Medicine) and the ability to com-

municate in dreams (Red Man's Medicine). Part of the translation offered by Scott is "Thus the White Man, with his Mechanical Medicine, is also able to hear that which he cannot see."[10]

- Strange Owl's Anecdote (Cheyenne, forty-five seconds) — A story about how Strange Owl, when about fifteen years old, went hunting with his brother, and almost lost his life capturing a buffalo calf (speech with sign accompaniment was evident for this story).
- Bitter Root Jim's Bear Story (Flathead, five minutes and twenty-four seconds) — This narrative was the longest signed story filmed during the conference, and it was reportedly a "classic and renowned story." The translation of the story provided by Scott seems far-fetched. However, Martin Weatherwax, chair of Blackfeet Studies at Blackfeet Community College in Browning, Montana, told me that this narrative is a medicine story and should not be taken literally (Martin Weatherwax, personal communication, June 9, 2002).
- Intertribal Jokes in Sign Language (approximately two minutes) — This section of the film is titled "The formal features of the council over, the visitors relax." Here we see all of the participants engaged in lively signed language discourse.
- In outdated argot, the subsequent sections of the film are titled "Inter-tribal by-play," "Jokes and Wisecracks in Signs," and "The hoary conceit that the Indian does not laugh is left with not a leg to stand on."
- Closing Remarks in Sign Language (forty seconds)

These films show the participants engaged in natural and unrehearsed signed language discourse. For example, during these signed interactions, the interlocutors are frequently and consistently observed using a sign that appears to function as a discourse marker. This Indian sign was documented as early as 1823 and is translated as "Yes" or "It is so." The spontaneity and variety of discourse types captured in these films provide the most remarkable evidence that the Indians used a full-fledged natural signed language (see also figure 1 on page 11).

Further Historical Considerations

Hugh Scott was seventy-eight years old at the time of the conference and reportedly had been signing for more than fifty years. Though apparently fluent, his having lost several fingers because of frost bite in his younger days made it difficult to follow some of his signs. His proficiency, however, was evident in that he provided voice-over translation for all of the proceedings in 1931, which were professionally dubbed into the film during the subsequent production stages. No documentation has been uncovered showing that interpreters were used to assist in the translation process. Of course, the use of interpreters remains a possibility because one of the principle participants was Richard Sanderville (a Blackfeet tribal leader) who was reportedly present but who never appears in the 1930 films from the Council (suggesting that he was working behind the scenes and possibly helping with the translation).

Some participants at the Council were probably not fluent in PISL (e.g., the governor of Montana, and a congressman). Their presence suggests that an interpreter would have been needed, and Sanderville would have been a probable candidate. For example, he subsequently traveled to the Smithsonian in Washington, D.C., to complete the Indian Sign Language film dictionary project started by Scott before his death. Scott's contribution — a staggering 358 proper noun signs for tribes and geographic locations — were included with the 1930 films. While working in the National Archives in 2002, I finally came across Sanderville's contribution to Scott's "dictionary" that was filmed at the Smithsonian in the early 1930s. Unfortunately, the only preservation copies available were either poorly processed or produced in an outmoded format. After two years of painstaking analysis to decipher what remains of Sanderville's contribution, the results are more than 200 PISL signs and idioms signifying a variety of lexical categories (including abstract nouns, classifier predicates, and noun and verb modifiers). Thus, Sanderville's contributions represent a type of "Rosetta Stone." That is, the lexical inventories documented in these films combined with the basic voice-over translations provided by Scott in 1931 are the keys to translating what the original participants at the Council were signing.

The oldest participants on the film also appeared to be the most proficient in sign language. For example, Mountain Chief was reportedly eighty-two years old at the time, and Bitter Root Jim appeared to be in the same age range. The ages of the other participants were not reported, but the youngest participants appeared to be in their forties, with several of the others approaching their sixties and seventies. Age is significant because the older participants probably learned to sign in the mid-1800s, that is, before the decline of many Indian traditional ways that occurred in the late 1800s after the Civil War, brought on by the construction of the first cross-continental railroad and the rapid Western expansion by Anglo-Americans. This decline is reflected in one of the statements signed by Scott during the opening remarks: "The young men are not learning your sign language and soon it will disappear from this country. It is for us to make a record of it for those who come after us, before it becomes lost forever." Furthermore, Indian Schools were established during the post–Civil War reconstruction era, and it became commonplace for Indian children to be taken away from their families and placed in these residential schools. Native languages and cultural customs were forbidden in these schools, and the only language allowed was English. Certainly, such pressures affected the acquisition of PISL among subsequent generations.

DISCUSSION

The films produced from the 1930 Indian Sign Language Council have been preserved in the vaults of the National Archives. However, they are not easily accessible, except for researchers who know exactly what to look for. Preservation copies are not circulated, and the copies made available to researchers are second or third generation VHS analog format. The National Archives provides a list of private vendors who are authorized to digitize the preservation copies. In 2002, I obtained a small grant to have the original preservation copies of the 1930 films professionally digitized. The digitized copies of the original 8 mm films are extremely high quality, especially compared with the old analog copies.

The National Archives has preserved one dozen 8 mm films produced during the three-day Indian Sign Language Conference in Browning, Montana (September 4–6, 1930). The pristine condition of these films, the number of participants from a variety of backgrounds (linguistic and geographic), and the different types of discourse that were recorded provide an excellent source for PISL documentation and description. For this study, I have digitized many of the historical films described in this paper, and my goal is to have these digitized copies placed into an open-source PISL database so others can study these signed language varieties. While efforts are currently underway to establish an open-source database, some sample video clips of historical PISL use can be viewed on-line at this Web site http://sunsite.utk.edu/plainssignlanguage/.

In this paper, I have presented some of the results of preliminary historical sociolinguistic research of PISL, and I have found phonological, morphological, and syntactic patterns that are consistent with those evident for full-fledged conventional signed languages. For example, some of the phonological and morphological constraints in ASL described by Battison (1978/2003) — passive and dominant handshapes; marked and unmarked handshapes; symmetry and dominance conditions — were originally proposed for Indian Sign Language (compare Kroeber 1958; Voegelin 1958; West 1960). No phonological inventory or analysis of NAISL syntax has been completed since West's (1960) phonological analysis of PISL. Again, this type of effort represents a massive undertaking.

The present paper takes into account some of the historical and contemporary sociolinguistic contexts and describes some of the types of discourse that have been documented for PISL. This discourse includes hearing Indians using signed language for a variety of discourse functions such as making introductions, storytelling, making jokes, chanting, and naming practices. When viewed by native ASL signers, for example, they are astonished that these signers were hearing people (note that not one deaf person was reported present at the 1930 council gathering).

Richard Sanderville, Scott's chief collaborator and interpreter from the Blackfoot Nation returned to the Smithsonian Institution in 1934 (following Scott's death) and posed for 790 signs and signed narratives. The scope and discourse coherence of the signed narratives in the 1930 and 1934 films provides evidence of the use of a language, not a collection of gestures. The following sample translation is of a common joke signed by Richard Sanderville and was filmed in 1934. Sanderville provided the following written translation for the signed narrative.

A man asks a Chief's daughter: "Will you marry me?" She says: "No you're a poor man." The man is sad and goes to war. He steals ten horses and two guns. Man returns after ten days. He asks woman: "Will you marry me?" She says: "Yes!" He says: "No!! You love my horses, you love me not."

Additional translations of the narratives filmed during the 1930 council gathering and those of Richard Sanderville produced at the Smithsonian Institution in 1934 are currently underway. Restoration of the historical films in digitized formats with open captions will allow others to have access to the contact being conveyed. The leap to the pragmatic level is not intended to bypass the need for more comprehensive and current phonological or morphological descriptions. At this time, the variety of sociolinguistic contexts, participants and discourse types that are evident in these data, suggests that PISL was (and still remains) a full-fledged signed language. Many questions remain and much more linguistic research, documentation, and description are needed.

SOME ADDITIONAL QUESTIONS

Several additional research questions and linguistic issues are beyond the scope of the present study to address but are nevertheless important. Some of these are offered here for others to consider as possible research topics:

- Do the documented cases of PISL constitute one language variety or a variety of distinct languages?
- What happens when a child is born deaf into a community where there is historical or current use of signed communication by hearing individuals in the linguistic community? How do these instances compare with what happened historically on Martha's Vineyard?
- In what ways were the documented cases of signed language among indigenous populations in North American interrelated?
- What shared linguistic patterns and cognates do we find between these signed language varieties — between and within different groups of American Indian signers (deaf and hearing signers; families who speak and sign; groups differing by region, age, and gender)?
- How does current PISL use differ from its historical antecedents?
- What are the best ways to maintain and preserve these endangered signed language varieties?

CONCLUSION

There remains a linguistic and ethnographic legacy of diaries, books, articles, illustrations, dictionaries, and motion pictures documenting the varieties of signed language historically used among native populations of North America. These documents not only represent a vital part of American Indian cultures and heritages but also are a national treasure and source for invaluable historical linguistic information. Unfortunately, most people are not aware of this part of North American history. Even members of the scientific and academic communities, as well as many in the linguistic communities where these signed languages once flourished, are generally not cognizant that there once flourished a signed lingua franca and that these language varieties are currently endangered.

For example, I recently visited the National Museum of the American Indian in Washington, D.C., accompanied by a Ph.D. candidate in linguistics who is deaf and another graduate student in linguistics who is of Native American descent. We were inspired by the enormity of the building and quality of the collections. While enjoying all of the exhibits, we diligently searched for examples of the traditional signed language among the exhibits. We talked with various museum workers and curators who tried to help us, only to discover that there was no display of signed language that once had been so widespread and that is a major historical and linguistic part of American Indian culture. Sadly, even if these films were placed on exhibit, without accurate translations and open captions, the content would be incomprehensible to all but the few native PISL signers who remain. It was encouraging at least, to learn from one of my colleagues that a medicine man from the Northern Cheyenne nation, who also happens to be deaf and a native user of PISL, participated in the opening ceremonies for the National Museum of the American Indian.

Historically, with some exceptions, researchers of indigenous signed language were not fluent signers and were working from theoretical orientations and bases that were different from what we have available today. Fortunately, in the past few years, state of the art methods and techniques have emerged to assist the documentation and transcription processes for signed languages (see, e.g., Supalla 2001).

Finally, given new discoveries about PISL (both historical and current), we are better able to translate what the signers on these films were signing. Since the early studies were conducted, others have made new contributions in linguistic theory and ethnographic field practice. Interdisciplinary approaches informed by linguistic theory have brought new insights into the multiple dimensions of human language and cognition. Further PISL research as well as insights from native signers and linguistic researchers with native signed language proficiency can help broaden our understanding of these and other related linguistic phenomena.

NOTES

1. Many terms are commonly used to label the descendants of the first Americans — *Indian, American Indian,* and *Native American* — but the first

two are preferred by most members of these cultural groups (e.g., the National Museum of the American Indian in Washington, D.C.). In this article, these terms are used interchangeably depending on the historical context and source being cited. The term *North American Indian* is sometimes necessary to distinguish the indigenous peoples who inhabited the North American continent from those who inhabited Central and South America.

2. The historical linguistic documents that are the focus of the present study are based on North American fieldwork. Wurtzburg and Campbell (1995), among others, use *North American Indian Sign Language* to distinguish these sign varieties from those used by Central or South American indigenous populations. Historically, the most widely used signed language and the best documented was Plains Sign Language (PISL); however, earlier scholars alternately referred to this as Indian Sign Language (Clark 1885; Mallery 1880; Scott 1931). Some members of the Plains cultural groups referred to sign language as "hand talk" (Davis, 2005; Tomkins, 1926). Depending on the historical reference and cultural context, the uses of these different terms are included in the present paper. In cases where a specific or distinct signed language variety is known — such as Navajo or Keresan Pueblo sign varieties — those are referenced. Further research is needed to determine the number of distinct signed languages and dialects involved.

3. Waldman (2000, 32–33) explains that the modern cultural areas "are not finite and absolute boundaries, but simply helpful educational devices" and "that tribal territories were often vague and changing, with great movement among the tribes and the passing of cultural traits from one area to the next; and that people of the same language family sometimes lived in different cultural areas, even in some instances at opposite ends of the continent."

4. In this paper, uppercase Deaf refers to the larger cultural group or community; lowercase deaf refers to individuals who have a hearing loss regardless of cultural identity.

5. Wurtzburg and Campbell (1995, 155) cite that "Cabeza de Vaca's story was published in a 1542 edition (called *La Relación*) and in a 1555 second edition (entitled *Naufragios*), essentially the same as the earlier one with but minor differences."

6. In the Navajo matrilineal society (compare Witherspoon 1975) it was significant that the male cousin was on the mother's side. According to Navajo kinship terms, he was called a "brother-cousin."

7. The primary signer who was Deaf did not see the alternate signer's narrative before telling his version of the traditional buffalo hunting story. Furthermore, McKay-Cody reported that the primary signer did not use ASL signs in his rendition.

8. Long's 1820 expedition was the next official expedition after Lewis and Clark's initial expedition. Perhaps because of the extreme conditions encountered during that first expedition, there was a dearth of written documentation and no

documentation of Indian sign language uncovered. In contrast, Long's expedition was well documented, and he lived to an old age and lectured frequently about his expedition.

9. Hugh L. Scott had considerable political clout and diligently led the Indian Sign Language preservation effort until his death in 1934. He attended Princeton University, and graduated from West Point in 1876. He began his military career as a lieutenant in the U.S. Calvary, was promoted to major general in 1915, and served as secretary of war on Woodrow Wilson's cabinet. He was responsible for the passage of the Selective Service Act and the appointment of General Pershing as commander in chief. Even after he had officially retired from military and civil service, Scott remained extremely active as a member of the Board of Indian Commissioners and as chairman of the New Jersey Highway Commission, and he spent the remainder of his life studying, lecturing, and writing about Indian Sign Language. He received honorary doctorate degrees from both Princeton and Columbia Universities. In testimony to the respect held for him by tribal leaders, he was made an honorary member of various Indian tribes. Scott worked with the Indians for more than fifty years and was known as "Mole-I-Gu-Op," signifying "one who talks with his hands." Scott was a member of numerous learned societies including the American Philosophical Society and American Anthropological Association.

10. According to the National Multicultural Interpreting Curriculum (Mooney, Aramburo, Davis, Dunbar, Roth, and Nishimura, 2001, 27), "medicine is an array of spiritual practices, ideas, and concepts rather than only remedies and treatments as in *western medicine*" (emphasis in the original). Furthermore, "medicine men and women are viewed as the spiritual healers and leaders of the community. They have the role not only as a *doctor*, but they can be the diviner, rain-maker, prophet, priest, or chief" (27, emphasis in the original). Medicine is anything that brings one closer to the Great Spirit, to the Divine. In this tradition, all space is sacred space. Every place on the planet holds a specific energy connection to some living creature and is to be honored for that reason.

REFERENCES

Battison, R. 1978/2003. *Lexical borrowing in American Sign Language*. Repr. Burtonsville, Md.: Linstok Press.

Boas, F. 1890/1978. Sign language. In *Aboriginal Sign Language of the Americas and Australia*, Vol. 2, ed. D. J. Umiker-Sebeok and T.A. Sebeok, 19–20. Repr. New York: Plenum Press.

Burton, R. F. 1862. *The city of the saints and across the Rocky Mountains to California*. New York: Harper.

Campbell, L. 2000. *American Indian languages*. Oxford: Oxford University Press.

Clark, W. P. 1885. *The Indian sign language*. Philadelphia: L. R. Hamersly.

Crystal, D. 2000. *Language death*. Cambridge: Cambridge University Press.

Davis, J. E. 2005. Evidence of a historical signed lingua franca among North American Indians. *Deaf Worlds* 21 (3): 47–72.

Davis, J. E., and S. Supalla. 1995. A sociolinguistic description of sign language use in a Navajo Family. In *Sociolinguistics in Deaf communities*, ed. C. Lucas, 77–106. Washington, D.C.: Gallaudet University Press.

Farnell, B. M. 1995. *Do you see what I mean? Plains Indian sign talk and the embodiment of action*. Austin: University of Texas Press.

Frishberg N. 1987. Home sign. In *Gallaudet encyclopedia of Deaf people and deafness*, ed. J. V. Van Cleve, 128–31. New York: McGraw Hill.

Fronval, G., and D. Dubois. 1985. *Indian signals and sign language*. New York: Bonanza Books.

Gallaudet, T. H. 1848a. On the natural language of signs; and its value and uses in the instruction of the deaf and dumb. Part 1. *American Annals of the Deaf and Dumb* 1 (1): 55–60.

———. 1848b. On the natural language of signs; and its value and uses in the instruction of the deaf and dumb. Part 2. *American Annals of the Deaf and Dumb* 1 (2): 79–93.

———. 1852. Indian language of signs. *American Annals of the Deaf and Dumb* 4 (1): 157–71.

Goddard, I. 1979. The languages of South Texas and the lower Rio Grande. In *The languages of native America: Historical and comparative assessment*, ed. L. Campbell and M. Mithun, 355–89. Austin: University of Texas Press.

Goff-Paris, D., and S. Wood. 2002. *Step into the circle: The heartbeat of American Indian, Alaska native and First Nations Deaf communities*. Monmouth, Oreg.: AGO Publications.

Goldfrank, E. 1923. Notes on the two Pueblo feasts. *American Antiquity* 25: 193–95.

Groce, N. E. 1985. *Everyone here spoke sign language: Hereditary deafness on Martha's Vineyard*. Cambridge, Mass.: Harvard University Press.

Hadley, L. F. 1891. *Indian sign talk*. Chicago: Baker and Company.

Harrington, J. P. 1938a. The American Indian sign language. *Indians at Work* 5 (7): 8–15.

———. 1938b. The American Indian sign language. *Indians at Work* 5 (11): 28–32.

———. 1938c. The American Indian sign language. *Indians at Work* 5 (12): 25–30.

———. 1938d. The American Indian sign language. *Indians at Work* 6 (3): 24–29.

———. 1938/1978. The American Indian sign language. In *Aboriginal Sign Language of the Americas and Australia*, vol. 2, ed. D. J. Umiker-Sebeok and T.A. Sebeok, 109–56. Repr. New York: Plenum Press.

Hoffman, W. J. 1895. *The graphic arts of the Eskimos, 902–12; 948–58*. New York: AMS Press.

Hofsinde, R. 1956. *Indian sign language*. New York: William Morrow.

Johnson, R. E. 1994. Sign language and the concept of deafness in a traditional Yucatec Mayan village. In *The Deaf way: Perspectives from the international conference on Deaf culture*, ed. C. Erting, R. Johnson, D. Smith, and B. Snider, 102–9. Washington, D.C.: Gallaudet University Press.

Kelly, W. P., & McGregor, T. L. (2003). Keresan Pueblo Indian Sign Language. In *Nurturing native languages*, ed. J. Reyhner, O. Trujillo, R. L. Carrasco, and L. Lockard, 141–48. Flagstaff: Northern Arizona University.

Kendon, A. 1988. *Sign languages of aboriginal Australia: Cultural, semiotic, and communication perspectives*. Cambridge: Cambridge University Press.

———. 2002. Historical observations on the relationship between research on sign languages and language origins theory. In *Essays in honor of William C. Stokoe: The study of signed languages*, ed. D. Armstrong, M. A. Karchmer, and J. V. Van Cleve, 35–52. Washington, D.C.: Gallaudet University Press.

Kroeber, A. L. 1958. Sign language inquiry. *The International Journal of American Linquistics* 24: 1–19.

Long, J. S. 1918. *The sign language: A manual of signs*; Being a descriptive vocabulary of signs used by the Deaf of the United States and Canada. Washington, D.C.: Gallaudet College.

Long, S. H. 1823. *Account of an expedition from Pittsburgh to the Rocky Mountains*. Philadelphia: Edwin James, Co.

Mallery, G. 1880. The sign language of the Indians of the upper Missouri, in 1832. *American Antiquarian* 2 (3): 218–28.

McKay-Cody, M. 1997. *Plains Indian Sign Language: A comparative study of alternate and primary signers*. Master's thesis, University of Arizona, Tucson.

Mithun, M. 1999. *The languages of native North America*. Cambridge: Cambridge University Press.

Mooney, M., A. Aramburo, J. Davis, T. Dunbar, A. Roth, and J. Nishimura. 2001.*National multicultural interpreting project curriculum*. Stillwater: Oklahoma State University Clearinghouse for O.S.E.R.S. Training Materials.

Plann, S. 1997. *A silent minority: Deaf education in Spain, 1550–1835*. Berkeley: University of California Press.

Scott, H. L. 1931. *Film dictionary of the North American Indian Sign Language*. Washington, D.C.: National Archives.

Seton, E. T. 1918. *Sign talk: A universal signal code, without apparatus, for use in the Army, Navy, camping, hunting, and daily Life. The gesture language of the Cheyenne Indians*. New York: Doubleday, Page & Co.

Stokoe, W. C. 1960. *Sign language structure: An outline of the visual communication systems of the American Deaf*. Studies in Linguistics Occasional Papers 8. Buffalo, N.Y.: University of Buffalo.

———. 1972. *Semiotics and human sign languages*. The Hague: Mouton.

Supalla, T. 1978. Morphology of verbs of motion and location in American Sign Language. In *Proceedings of the second symposium on sign language research and teaching*, ed. F. Caccamise, 27–45. Silver Spring, Md.: National Association of the Deaf.

———. 2001. Making historical sign language materials accessible: A prototype data base of early ASL. *Sign Language and Linguistics* 4 (1/2).

Taylor, A. R. 1978. Nonverbal communication in aboriginal North America: The Plains sign language. In *Aboriginal sign languages of the Americas and Australia, the Americas and Australia*, vol. 2, ed. D. J. Umiker-Sebeok and T.A. Sebeok, 223–44. New York: Plenum Press.

Teit, J. A. 1930. *The Salishan tribes of the Western Plateau: 45th annual report of the Bureau of American Ethnology*. Washington, D.C.: U.S. Government Printing Office.

Tomkins, W. 1926/1969. *Universal Indian sign language of the Plains Indians of North America*. Repr. New York: Dover Press.

Umiker-Sebeok, J., and T. A. Sebeok. 1978. *Aboriginal Sign Languages of the Americas and Australia*. 2 vols. New York: Plenum Press.

Voegelin, C. F. 1958. Sign language analysis, on one lever or two? *International Journal of American Linguistics* 24: 71–77.

Waldman, C. 2000. *Atlas of the North American Indian*. New York: Facts on File.

Washabaugh, W. 1986a. The acquisition of communicative skills by the deaf of Providence Island. *Semiotica* 6 (2): 179–90.

———. 1986b. *Five fingers for survival*. Ann Arbor, Mich.: Koroma.

Weatherwax, M. 2002. *Indian Sign Language*. VHS. Department of Blackfeet Studies, Blackfeet Community College, Browning, Mont.

West, L. 1960. The sign language: An analysis. 2 vols. Ph.D. diss., Department of Anthropology, Indiana University, Bloomington.

Witherspoon, G. 1975. *Navajo kinship and marriage*. Chicago: University of Chicago Press.

Wurtzburg, S., and L. Campbell. 1995. North American Indian sign language: Evidence of its existence before European contact. *International Journal of American Linguistics* 61 (2): 153–67.

APPENDIX A

This appendix presents Indian sign descriptions that Gallaudet included in his first published essay titled "On the Natural Language of Signs: And

Its Value and Uses in the Instruction of the Deaf and Dumb" (1848a, 55–60).

To show how nature, when necessity exists, prompts to the invention and use of this language of signs, and to exhibit from another interesting point of view the features of its universality, a fact is worth mentioning, to be found in Major Stephen H. Long's account of an Expedition from Pittsburgh to the Rocky Mountains, in 1819. It seems, from what he tells us, that the aboriginal Indians, west of the Mississippi, consist of different tribes, having either different languages or dialects of the same language. Some are unable to communicate with others by speech; while they have fallen into a language of signs to remedy this inconvenience, which has been long used among them.

Major Long's work contains an accurate description of many of these signs, and it is surprising to notice how not a few of them are almost identically the same with those which the deaf and dumb employ to describe the same things, while others have such general features of resemblance as to show that they originate from elements of this sign-language which nature furnishes to man wherever he is found, whether barbarous or civilized. Such are the following:

Sun — The forefinger and thumb are brought together at tip, so as to form a circle, and held upwards towards the sun's track. To indicate any particular time of the day, the hand with the sign of the sun is stretched out towards the east horizon, and then gradually elevated, to show the ascent of that luminary, until the hand arrives in the proper direction to indicate the part of the heavens in which the sun will be at the given time.

Moon — The thumb and finger open are elevated towards the right ear. This last sign is generally preceded by the sign of the night or darkness.

Seeing — The forefinger, in the attitude of pointing, is passed from the eye towards the real or imaginary object.

Theft — The left forearm is held horizontally, a little forward of across the body, and the right hand, passing under it with a quick motion, seems to grasp something, and is suddenly withdrawn.

Truth — The forefinger is passed, in the attitude of pointing, from the mouth forward in a line curving a little upward, the thumb and other fingers being completely closed.

Love — The clenched hand is pressed hard upon the breast.

Now, or at present — The two hands, forming each a hollow, are brought near each other, and put in a tremulous motion upwards and downwards.

Done, or finished — The hands are placed, edge up and down, parallel to each other, the right hand without; which latter is drawn back as if cutting something.

[To Be Continued.]

The above descriptions as they appear here in this excerpt were taken out of order from the original list of descriptions first published by Long (1823). It was not until 1852 that the *American Annals of the Deaf and Dumb* editors published the "Indian Language of Signs" (Gallaudet 1852) that included the entire list of 104 Indian sign descriptions verbatim and in the same order as Long's original 1823 publication.

Part 2 Language Contact

Comparing Language Contact Phenomena

between Auslan–English Interpreters and

Deaf Australians: A Preliminary Study

Jemina Napier

This paper reports the findings of a study that explores the influence of language contact on the interpretations of Australian Sign Language (Auslan)–English interpreters and compares it with the influence of language contact on deaf Australians producing text[1] in Auslan. Inspired by the work of Davis (1990, 2003) on American Sign Language (ASL)/ English interpreters, this study presents first of all the analysis of data collected from two Auslan/ English interpreters, and their interpretation of university lectures from spoken English into Auslan. The key features discussed are the use of fingerspelling and mouthing in the context of interlingual transference and interlingual interference.

Referring to language contact phenomena between signed and spoken languages, as discussed by Lucas and Valli (1992) and Davis (1990, 2003), the paper discusses the sign language output of Auslan–English interpreters in relation to the influence of language contact on the Australian Deaf community. In addition, the paper presents analysis of data collected from two deaf Australians presenting university lectures in Auslan.[2] The linguistic features identified are compared with those of the interpreters.

I thank the four participants who willingly agreed to be filmed and to have their texts analyzed. In addition, I thank the reviewer who provided excellent constructive comments on an earlier version of this paper — and whose feedback has certainly led to a much tighter description and discussion of the study. My thanks go also to Jeff Davis, for many interesting conversations on the identification of language contact features in interpretation, and to Andy Carmichael, for being an inspiration to me as an interpreter and as a human being.

Using a functional approach to linguistic analysis (see Halliday 1994), a lexicogrammatical analysis of the texts focuses on the use of fingerspelling and mouthing. Discussion focuses on whether Auslan–English interpreters are incorporating language contact phenomena into their Auslan interpretations in the same way as Deaf people. Because the research focuses on the analysis of only four individuals, it should be considered as a preliminary study of such language contact phenomena with a view to a wider study at a later date.

LITERATURE REVIEW

The review of the literature is organized into four categories: features of language contact, lectures as a site of language contact, translation styles, and interpreting and language contact.

Features of Language Contact

When languages come into contact with one another, several possible outcomes can result. Language contact essentially involves transference of linguistic features from one language to another at different levels of language (Clyne 2003). One form of language contact involves codeswitching, common in bilinguals, wherein a bilingual person literally changes from one language to another during a conversation and makes a conscious and deliberate choice to do so (Kite 2001). The degree to which codeswitching occurs, however, depends on the theoretical standpoint of what is considered to be code 'switching' because the terminology used varies among authors (Clyne 2003). Codeswitching regularly occurs between bilingual users of more than one spoken language and can occur either intersententially or intrasententially at an individual or multiple lexical level (Clyne 2003). For example, an intersentential codeswitch might involve a person speaking one sentence in English, speaking the next in Spanish, and then reverting back to English in the next sentence. In an intrasentential codeswitch, however, a person would, for example, begin a sentence in English and finish it in Spanish. Intrasentential codeswitching is determined not only by the bilingual abilities and preferences of the speaker but also by those of the addressee (Shin 2002). Codeswitching is a strategy used by people sensitive to, and competent in, formal and functional aspects of language use (Grosjean 1982; Gumperz 1982; Romaine 1995).

For a sign language user, intersentential codeswitching occurs when someone who is signing stops, switches to speaking, and then switches back to signing again (Lucas and Valli 1992; Sofinski 2002). Alternatively, intersentential codeswitching could involve a hearing person vocalizing a nonmanual feature of a sign rather than using an English[3] lexical item, for example, "Pah! You've arrived!" This type of codeswitching is a common incidence among hearing bilinguals such as people who have grown up in deaf families (Codas — children of deaf adults) and interpreters when they are around other bilinguals (Banna 2004b; Bishop and Hicks 2005).

In a study of codeswitching between ASL and Cued English,[4] Hauser (2000) found that

> codeswitching functions ... are similar to those found in spoken language codeswitching. Cueing enables people to express English in a visual mode and to use English phonology, morphology, and syntax. . . . [W]hen used by a bilingual who is fluent in ASL, codeswitching between ASL and Cued English exhibits sociolinguistic characteristics similar to those found with people who are bilingual in spoken languages. (73)

Ann (1998) analyzed the extent of contact between a signed and a written language and identified the use of character signs in Taiwan Sign Language — where Chinese written characters were incorporated into the sign language — displaying similar language contact codeswitching patterns as spoken–sign language contact.

A more common form of language contact between a signed and spoken language is that of code-mixing, also known as code-blending (Emmorey, Borenstein, and Thompson 2003). Lucas and Valli (1992) describe code-mixing between ASL and English, whereby English words are mouthed on the lips or manually coded (fingerspelled) while the signer is still using linguistic features of ASL (e.g., spatial mapping and visual metaphor, constructed action and dialogue, nonmanual markers, etc.). Lucas and Valli refer to this phenomenon as contact signing and suggest a variety of sociolinguistic factors that influence the use of mixing between a signed and a spoken language, including lack of familiarity between participants, and the formality of a situation. Similar factors were found to influence deaf participants' code-mixing in their sign language production in a study of language contact between Italian Sign Language and spoken Italian (Fontana 1999).

Another influence on code-mixing is the phenomenon of "foreigner talk," which is the simplified register often identified as being appropriate for addressing foreigners or "outsiders" (Fontana 1999).[5] An example would be a situation in which deaf signers adapt their signing to be as "English-like" as possible when talking to a hearing person (Johnston 2002). Lucas and Valli (1992) found that deaf people adapt their signing to a more English-like style when signing to a hearing person, thus transferring features of English into ASL.[6] Sofinski (2002) corroborates these findings in his analysis of a deaf woman signing in ASL to a hearing man. Sofinski found that the narrative of the deaf woman contained a mix of English and ASL features, in particular, features of English not normally found in ASL (such as prepositions) and use of English mouthing.

Zimmer (1989) found that more English interference occurred in a formal ASL presentation when technical or specialized terms are used and incorporated into ASL in the form of mouth patterns or fingerspelling. Therefore, it can be hypothesized that a deaf academic, presenting a university lecture in Auslan, may produce similar language contact phenomena. (For a detailed overview of literature relating to language contact and codeswitching or code-mixing, see Davis 2003, 2005).

Lectures as a Site of Language Contact

For spoken languages, language contact has been identified as occurring in different "sites" or contexts: religious (Spolsky 2003), advertising (Piller 2003), business (Harris and Bargiela-Chiappini 2003), and education (Baker 2003). As mentioned earlier, Lucas and Valli (1992) and other researchers have identified formal situations, including lectures, as an environment that influences the production of contact features between a signed and spoken language. Goffman (1981) defines a lecture as

> an institutionalised extended holding of the floor in which one speaker imparts his views on a subject, these thoughts comprising what can be called his "text." The style is typically serious and slightly impersonal, the controlling intent being to generate calmly considered understanding, not mere entertainment, emotional impact, or immediate action. (165)

Lakoff (1982, cited in Cokely 1992) defined lectures in a similar way to Goffman (1981), stating that one participant in the interactive discourse is in control, selects the subject matter, and decides when the discourse should start and finish. Therefore lectures can be characterized as "expository monologues" (Cokely 1992). The focus of expository monologues tends to be on a theme or set of related themes, rather than on participants, such as in narratives. Expository texts convey new information and explain new topics to people (Black 1985) and rely less on inferential knowledge and text with causal plan or goal structures (Miller 1985). When scientific or technical in nature, expository texts can be cognitively demanding to comprehend (Britton, Glynn, and Smith 1985). Consequently, interpreting an expository lecture text can be far more challenging than producing that kind of text. Therefore, as expository texts, lectures tend to incorporate a formal register (Joos 1967), with use of technical terms, longer sentences, strategic pausing, and little interaction with the audience.

Studies have found that lectures delivered in a signed language are typically presented using particular discourse features. These studies are worth considering to frame the present study. Roy (1989) states that the linguistic elements of an ASL lecture are not part of the content, per se, but are used as a guide by listeners as to how they should interpret the information they are receiving. Words and phrases used as cohesive, structural devices can contribute to the listener's ability to distinguish between major and minor points, old and new information, and shifts in the flow of topics. After analyzing the discourse features of an ASL lecture, Roy found that naturally occurring segments of a lecture can be distinguished by the use of certain discourse markers. Among other things, Roy (1989) found that the sign NOW was most often used as a discourse marker because it was used to mark a shift into a new subtopic rather than simply indicate the present time in an ongoing discourse. The sign NOW THAT, however, was used to signify a shift into a group of episodes within the discourse. Constructed action and dialogue were also used very specifically during parts of the lecture.[7]

Drawing on Goffman's (1981) work, McKee (1992) found that particular eye-gaze and body posture cues (footing shifts) are used in ASL formal lectures in the same way that English speakers use other particular footing shifts such as pausing and intonation. Thus, these studies have shown that lectures produced in a signed language follow a similar structure to those presented in a spoken language because the expository goals are the same.

In addition to noting the use of certain discourse markers (such as spatial mapping and use of constructed action and dialogue), Zimmer

(1989) and Llewellyn Jones (1981) note differences in the signing style of deaf people using either ASL or British Sign Language (BSL) in formal lecture presentations compared with other less formal environments. Both researchers found that English mouthing and fingerspelling were prevalent, all of which adhered to similar patterns of linguistic transference. That finding demonstrates that lectures can be considered as a site of language contact. One could argue that language contact is an inherent feature of formal lectures in signed language and should be expected, in the same way that certain discourse features are expected.

Because of their inherent expository nature, university lectures are prime examples of sites of language contact. Interpreters working in university lectures therefore need to consider the typical discourse features of lectures for both spoken and signed presentations and, thus, incorporate language contact phenomena accordingly because their decisions will influence their choice of translation style.

Translation Styles

The signed language interpreting literature often discusses two key interpretation methods or "translation styles" (Napier 2002b): interpretation and transliteration. Interpretation has been defined as the process of immediately changing a message produced in one language into another language in real time (Frishberg 1990). This generic notion refers to the process of transferring the content of a message presented in "through the air" languages, a notion that spoken language interpreters also use to distinguish from the process of translation, which typically refers to transferring a message between written texts (Pöchhacker 2003).

The term *transliteration*, however, is used only by signed language interpreters and refers to the process of changing spoken English into a visual representation of the form and structure of English. Earlier definitions of transliteration were based on a mechanistic model that endorsed an exact sign-for-word (or vice versa) rendition of the source language message (Siple 1997). However, as a consequence of research studies, many authors have identified (a) that transliterators still incorporate the linguistic features of sign language (e.g., spatial mapping and pronominalization) into a signed transliteration and (b) that more effective transliterations are not produced word for word (Kelly 2001; Siple 1995; Sofinski 2003; Sofinski, Yesbeck, Gerhold, and Bach-Hansen 2001; Viera and Stauffer 2000; Winston 1989). These authors have discussed the merits of transliteration used in various settings so deaf consumers can access English, which may be the preferred option (Viera and Stauffer 2000).

Various studies (Livingston, Singer, and Abramson 1994; Locker 1990; Marschark, Sapere, Convertino, Seewagen, and Maltzen 2004; Winston and Monikowski 2003) have directly compared the effectiveness of interpretations and transliterations with varying results. But ultimately, those in the signed language interpreting profession accept that transliteration is an appropriate translation style if appropriate linguistic strategies are used.

More recently, authors have drawn on discussions of equivalence within the spoken-language interpreting and translation literature and have used alternative terminology to discuss concepts of "dynamic" and "formal" equivalence (Nida 1964), also known as "free" and "literal" interpretation (Banna 2004a; Conlon and Napier 2004; Leneham 2005; Metzger 1999; Napier 1998, 2000, 2002a, 2002b, 2005; Pollitt 2000b).[7] Free interpretation focuses on achievement of linguistic, cultural, pragmatic, and dynamic equivalence, where the message is "freed" from the form of the source language and the focus is on meaning. Literal interpretation involves retaining the form of the source message to some degree, providing a more formal equivalence in which either the original lexical items or syntactic structure are recognizable in the target language message. Spoken language translation and interpreting scholars endorse the use of both free and literal approaches as appropriate methods to use depending on the context.[8] Basically, literal interpretation and transliteration can be considered as being the same process (Cerney 2000).

Sign language interpreting authors have recognized that a free interpretation approach (a) focuses on conveying the message so it is linguistically and culturally meaningful and (b) gives consideration to the fact that discourse participants may bring different life experiences to an interaction, thus recognizing that interpreting takes place within a discourse process (Metzger 1999; Napier 1998). They have also recognized, however, that a literal interpretation approach is appropriate to use in some contexts — especially in higher education (Napier 2002b; Pollitt 2000a; Siple 1995; Winston 1989) — for example, to provide access to academic English or subject-specific terminology. Ultimately, the goal of an interpretation is to consider the intended outcome and adapt the translation style according to the people, place, purpose, and point of the interaction (Eighinger and Karlin 2003), thus, taking a functional approach to interpreting (Banna

2004a; Conlon and Napier 2004; Tate, Collins, and Tymms 2003). In other words, it is now acknowledged that interpreters can adopt strategies of language contact in their interpretations and can transfer features of English into the signed target text for specific purposes, particularly, if required by the consumer.

Interpreting and Language Contact

Research on spoken language interpreting "provides valuable insights about complex aspects of language contact" (Valdes and Angelelli 2003, 58). In relation to the language contact features of deaf sign language users, the ideal situation would be for sign language interpreters working in language contact situations such as university lectures to produce language contact phenomena that reflect similar patterns of use demonstrated by deaf people (as discussed earlier). Use of contact language in interpretations may occur for specific reasons, especially in relation to fingerspelling. An interpreter may fingerspell an English word to introduce or emphasize terminology or specialized vocabulary (Davis 2003; Napier 2002b). Even if a lexicalized sign exists, an interpreter might still choose to "borrow" the English word into Auslan and fingerspell the lexical item as well as paraphrase with explanation, to ensure that his or her target audience is accessing the subject-specific vocabulary and its meaning. In addition, an interpreter might mouth English words, although he or she may drop particular signs such as articles (Johnston 2002).

Davis (2003) adopts the same perspective on language contact as Lucas and Valli (1992), and refers to code-mixing between ASL and English as "interlingual" or "cross-linguistic" transference (97). He explored the use of these language contact phenomena in interpretations of spoken English into ASL and found that the mouthing of English words and the use of fingerspelling is patterned. Typically, he found that "English mouthing marks fingerspelled words," and "most lexicalized fingerspelling is used for emphasis, lists, numbers, and question words" (Davis 1989, 101) — all of which were identified as being appropriate to ASL. In relation to fingerspelling, Davis (1989) stated that an English word might be fingerspelled because an equivalent ASL sign does not exist. Alternatively, he observed that a "multi-meaning" ASL sign can be prefaced, or tagged, with a fingerspelled word. In such cases, Davis noted that fingerspelled words are flagged in very specific ways, for example, by the use of the sign QUOTATION MARKERS. In his later analyses, Davis (2003) found that "the forms of cross-linguistic transfer evident in bilingual discourse (namely, codeswitching, code-mixing, and lexical borrowing) are also characteristic features of ASL interpretation.... [Interpreters] utilize both oral and visual-gestural channels of communication and alternate between using ASL and English mouth movements" (118).

Winston (1989), in a study of English–ASL transliteration, and Detthow (2000), in a study of Swedish–Swedish Sign Language transliteration, also identified that interpreters used mouthing as a strategy to emphasize particular words in correlation with a generic ASL or Swedish sign (e.g., the same Auslan sign could be used to translate several different English words such as *nice, beautiful, lovely*).

Both Davis (1990, 2003) and Winston (1989) studied interpreters working in front of a live lecture audience, and they found that the interpreters used contact varieties of sign language appropriate to the situation in which they were interpreting. These findings thus agree with the conclusions of Lucas and Valli (1992) that the formality of a situation influences the use of language contact phenomena in sign language.

Davis (2003, citing the work of Lee 1983), states that the language contact phenomena demonstrated by the ASL interpreters in his study reflects the typical language use of Deaf people in this type of situation. Napier and Adam (2002), in a linguistic comparison of BSL and Auslan interpreters, drew similar conclusions. After comparing the sign language output of five BSL and five Auslan interpreters interpreting for the same formal presentation, they stated that the interpreters' use of language reflected the language use of the Deaf communities for whom they were interpreting, especially in relation to the use of fingerspelling. However, Napier and Adam did not analyze the sign language output of any deaf people, therefore their comments were based only on observations rather than on empirical evidence. When considering the notion of language contact and sign language variation, the discussion highlights the need for interpreters to appropriately reflect the language used by deaf people when participating in formal interactions, and to observe the norms of the discourse genres in which they are interpreting.

In a study of ten Auslan interpreters interpreting for a university lecture, Napier (2002b) borrowed the bilingualism–language contact terminology and applied it to interpreting in her discussion of translation styles. She found that interpreters tended to be more dominant in using a free or literal interpretation approach. Those who were extremely dominant in one style or another tended to stick to that style, but those who were less dominant had more tendency to codeswitch between free and literal methods to provide access to academic English or terminology; that is, they signed concepts in Auslan and used fingerspelling and mouthing to convey English words. Napier called this "translational contact," whereby two translation "styles" came together and interacted to ensure the successful outcome of the interpretation relative to the discourse environment. Napier stated that those interpreters who switched translation style, that is, introduced language contact, were producing the most appropriate interpretations for the university discourse environment. This statement was supported by a panel of Australian deaf university students. Four university students of differing language backgrounds were shown examples of free and literal Auslan interpretations of the same English lecture text and were asked questions about their perceptions and preferences of interpreting for university lectures. All the students confirmed that they would prefer interpreters to interpret concepts and meaning in Auslan but also to provide access to English terms through mouthing and fingerspelling (Napier and Barker 2004). These findings endorse the use of language contact features in the interpretation of spoken university lectures.

THE PRESENT STUDY

After reviewing the literature and finding several analyses of interpreters' and deaf people's use of language contact phenomena separately, I wanted to examine whether deaf people and interpreters use language contact in the same way in formal lectures by directly comparing university lecture texts produced by deaf people and interpreters. This study is the first time that both groups have been directly compared empirically. In designing the study, the key research questions were as follows:

- How do deaf Australians incorporate language contact features of mouthing and fingerspelling into their signed lectures?
- How do Auslan–English interpreters incorporate language contact features of mouthing and fingerspelling into their Auslan interpretations of a spoken English lecture?
- Are Auslan–English interpreters reflecting the language use of deaf people in this discourse environment?

- How do sociolinguistic factors influence the use of language contact phenomena among Auslan–English interpreters and deaf Australians?

Participants

Participants in the study comprised two interpreters and two deaf Auslan signers.

INTERPRETERS

Both of the interpreters were professionally accredited interpreters who had approximately fifteen years of interpreting experience, and who had accumulated substantial experience in the university setting. Each interpreter produced an English-to-Auslan interpretation of a lecture (a different lecture for each interpreter), short excerpts of which were analyzed. The English source texts were genuine lectures given to postgraduate students studying to become teachers of the deaf.

Interpreter 1 was a native signer and interpreted the lecture in front of an audience of students, one of whom was deaf. The lecture focused on issues in sign language assessment. Interpreter 2 was nonnative and had been signing for approximately twenty years. She interpreted from a videorecording of a lecture to a deaf person (which had been originally interpreted by another interpreter for a deaf student). The lecturer discussed signed language acquisition of deaf children.

Both interpreters had minimal preparation in that they knew the title of the lecture but had received no written preparation notes. Each interpreter was familiar with each lecturer, both having interpreted for these lecturers on several occasions.

DEAF AUSTRALIANS

Each of the two deaf Australians gave a university presentation in Auslan, of which a short excerpt from both were analyzed. The Auslan source texts were genuine lectures or presentations given to postgraduate students studying to become either teachers of the deaf or sign language interpreters. Signer 1 was a native signer, and the participant presented to a video camera and a hearing person (for the purpose of having the videotape shown to a class of hearing students at a later date). The presenter discussed the topic of Deaf community membership. The presenter had been specifically asked to prepare the presentation, which would be videotaped so hearing interpreting students taking a unit on Auslan discourse analysis could view it. The presenter was given a broad topic and asked to prepare a fifteen-minute presentation that would be recorded on video camera. Signer 2 was a nonnative signer, and that participant presented the lecture in front of an audience of hearing students. The lecture focused on Deaf identity and had been prepared as part of a series of lectures for postgraduate students taking a unit on Deaf culture. The same two interpreters had been present every week to voice over the lectures for the hearing students.

Procedure and Analysis

The four texts used in the analysis had been previously recorded for other purposes, and all of them involved presentations in the university discourse environment. Each source text was produced in a language contact environment where both Auslan users and English users were present. Because the recordings were made for other reasons, none of the participants were aware that their Auslan output would be analyzed for language contact features. Before analysis began, each of the participants was contacted and asked to give permission for the texts to be analyzed for research purposes. Each of the participants gave their permission for the texts to be used.

Excerpts of the introductory few minutes from each text were transcribed for analysis. Transcription conventions can be seen in appendix A, and full glosses and transcriptions of each text can be seen in appendix B.

A functional approach to the study of language requires categorizing texts within the context of situation, the parameters of the context of situation (i.e., field, tenor, and mode), and the structural elements of the texts (Butt et al. 2000), as seen in figure 1.

First, the researcher identified that the four texts had common contextual and structural features, which enabled a direct comparison of the content level and the lexicogrammatical features of each of the texts in terms of language contact phenomena. Contrastive analysis was used to directly compare the prevalence of fingerspelling and mouthing. The total number of signed lexical items produced by each participant were counted and compared with the number of fingerspelled items and English or Auslan mouthing. The analysis involved making particular note of any patterns of words that were mouthed, (i.e., nouns, verbs, etc.), noting any patterns of fingerspelling, and identifying marked and unmarked patterns.

```
┌──────────────────────────────────────────────────────────────┐
│                                                                │
│  Context of Situation: University lectures                     │
│                                                                │
│  Context of situation parameters:                              │
│      Fields: Deafness and sign language                        │
│      Tenor: Lecturer-student                                   │
│      Modes: Spoken (interpreted into sign) and signed          │
│                                                                │
│  Structural elements:                                          │
│      Register: Formal                                          │
│      Genre: Academic discourse                                 │
│          Sub-genres: Deafness, sign language                   │
│          Text type: Expository                                 │
│                                                                │
└──────────────────────────────────────────────────────────────┘
```

FIGURE 1. *Identifying the texts within context*

Noting that linguistic features are unmarked refers to the fact that the language use is normal, expected, and common in its usage. If the feature is marked, then it is unusual and stands out in some way because it is not typical usage (Butt et al. 2000). Comparisons were then made between the interpreters and the deaf signers. Consistency for coding was maintained by developing a system for counting the number of signed lexical items, as seen in figure 2. Instances of mouthing were coded when a full English lexical item was mouthed. Auslan-specific, nonmanual mouthing (e.g., ba-ba, pah) was coded as "Auslan mouthing."

Results

The results are presented here as a series of tables, contrasting the key linguistic features compared, that is, use of fingerspelling and mouthing. Table 1 shows the ratio of fingerspelling and mouthing to the total number of signed lexical items.

Note that Interpreter 2 and Signer 2 both produced more English items on the mouth than signed lexical items. This increased mouthing tended to occur because the participants were mouthing functional English words such as prepositions or determiners, which were mouthed but were not signed. This tendency is a feature of linguistic interference whereby both Interpreter 2 and Signer 2 produced signed sentences that adhered more closely to English syntactical structure. The English mouthing that was

1. One gloss = one sign = one lexical item (e.g., HAVE, SIGN)
2. Gloss of more than one English word for one Auslan sign = one lexical item (e.g., BOTH-OF-US).
3. Fingerspelled words = one lexical item (e.g., F-E-A-T-U-R-E-S)
4. Lexicalized initialization = one lexical item (e.g.,V-V = very, S-A = South Australia
5. Repetition of signs signified as: DIFFERENT+ = one lexical item (as normally repeated for emphasis and combined with one mouth pattern)
6. Repetition of signs signified as: DIFFERENT DIFFERENT DIFFERENT = separate lexical items
7. Beginning of sign or fingerspelled word signified as (P-R-O) or (PEOPLE) not counted as a complete lexical item — whereby person started to execute sign or fingerspelled word but did not complete the sign or fingerspelling.

FIGURE 2: *Coding system for counting signed lexical items*

Little bit	difficult		to know	which	readings		to start	with for this
LITTLE DIFFICULT KNOW WHICH READING START WITH THIS								

FIGURE 3: *Example sentence featuring more mouthing than signed lexical items*

produced, therefore, often reflected an English sentence. An example sentence from Signer 2 can be seen in figure 3.

Table 2 illustrates the percentage of signed lexical items that were produced with Auslan mouthing by each participant. The percentages show that Interpreter 1 and Signer 1 both matched signed lexical items with appropriate Auslan nonmanual features more often than Interpreter 2 and Signer 2. Because both Interpreter 2 and Signer 2 were nonnative signers, one possibility is that both participants were used to more English mouthing because they were more influenced by thinking in English rather than in Auslan.

Figure 4 provides an example of how Interpreter 1 used Auslan mouthing (puffed-cheeks) to accompany the sign for EXPAND. Figure 5 shows that Signer 1 used appropriate Auslan mouthing (pout) to accompany the signs for EXPLAIN and DISCUSS.

TABLE 1: *Ratio of Fingerspelling and Mouthing to Signed Lexical Items*

Participant	Total no. signed lexical items	Total no. fingerspelled items	Total no. mouthed English items
Interpreter 1	208	11	149
Interpreter 2	227	27	254
Signer 1	206	17	181
Signer 2	186	16	201

Fingerspelling is used for a range of reasons, primarily to borrow English words when no direct sign equivalent exists or to emphasize a particular English lexical item (Brennan 2001; Johnston 1998; Lucas and Valli 1992). Some English words have been assimilated into Auslan (e.g., do, so, if), and can be considered as "lexicalized fingerspelling" in which the fingerspelled item acts as a lexical sign (Johnston 2002; Schembri 1996). The number of fingerspelled items that are recognized as lexicalized signs in Auslan were counted to identify patterns of marked and unmarked fingerspelling that would enable the researcher to clearly categorize them as unmarked. For the purposes of this study, unmarked fingerspellings included lexicalized English items — v-v (very), D-O, S-O, O-F and I-F — and acronyms for Deaf-related organizations (e.g., Australian Association of the Deaf, or AAD) as well as established conventions such as hard of hearing (H-H). Table 3 shows the percentage of lexicalized fingerspelled words produced by each participant.

At an initial glance, the fact that Signer 1 produced a high number of lexicalized fingerspelled items seems surprising. However, on closer analysis, it can be seen that the production of lexicalized fingerspelling was heavily influenced by the content, which dictated which concepts would be repeated. The signer produced eighteen fingerspelled items, and a high proportion of them were identified as lexicalized for the purposes of this study (e.g., H-H). Table 4 breaks down the production of fingerspelled items by Signer 1, and figure 6 provides an example sentence from Signer 1.

DISCUSSION

When comparing the texts produced by the Auslan–English interpreters and deaf Australians, it does appear that there is some systematic

TABLE 2: *Percentage of Signed Lexical Items with Auslan Mouthing*

Participant	Percentage of signs produced with Auslan mouthing
Interpreter 1	34.5 %
Interpreter 2	9%
Signer 1	21%
Signer 2	16%

patterning to the language contact phenomena used as well as how and when it is used. The key distinction, however, is not necessarily between deaf and hearing people, but between native and nonnative sign language users.

The data revealed that both Interpreter 1 and Signer 1 often used the same Auslan and English features in similar ways and at comparable points in the text, demonstrating effective linguistic transference. Both Interpreter 1 and Signer 1 are native signers. Both Interpreter 2 and Signer 2 demonstrated more English interference, using more mouthing and fingerspelling than the other two participants. Both Interpreter 2 and Signer 2 are nonnative signers.

The analysis revealed that the nonnative signers generally mouthed more English words than the native signers. Interpreter 1 and Signer 1 tended not to produce English mouthing with verbs but, rather, used appropriate nonmanual features. However, they used plenty of English mouthing for nouns, as seen in figure 7. This evidence supports the findings of Schembri et al. (2000) and Johnston (2001) in their discussion of noun-verb pairs in Auslan. Both studies found that native Auslan users tend to use English mouthing for nouns and Auslan mouthing for verbs — for example, PLANE and FLY.

Signs that were coded as being produced with Auslan mouthing usually meant that the sign was accompanied by an appropriate nonmanual feature. An interesting note is that the participant who produced the highest percentage of signs with Auslan mouthing was Interpreter 1 (native), which highlights the fact that the difference is between native and nonnative signers rather than between deaf and hearing people.

Signer 2 (nonnative) produced 16 percent of signed lexical items with Auslan mouthing, but the majority of these were produced in concordance with the sign QUOTATION-MARKERS (see figure 8). The use of QUOTATION-MARKERS is a linguistic device often used by deaf people and interpreters

All these sorts of areas have grown quite dramatically in the last decade or so.				
So have	really	(puffcheeks)(puffcheeks)(puffcheeks)	maybe	ten	years
HAVE ONE TWO THREE FOUR REALLY EXPAND EXPAND EXPAND UNTIL-NOW TEN YEARS				

FIGURE 4: *Example of Interpreter 1 using Auslan mouthing.*

So	I	thought	worth	(pout)		over	what	difference	between	deaf	and
S-O ME THINK WORTH EXPLAIN DET POINTS OVER WHAT DIFFERENT BETWEEN DEAF AND											
hard-of-hearing	person		then	will	help	us	(pout)	what		Autralian	context
H-H		PERSON THEN WILL HELP PRO DISCUSS WHAT DET AUSTRALIA CONTEXT//									

FIGURE 5: *Example of Signer 1 using Auslan mouthing*

for the cross-linguistic transfer of information from English into a signed language (Davis 1990, 2003, 2005); the sign is used to flag a fingerspelled word or the signed representation of an English word or phrase. The sign can also be used to draw attention to a concept. In this context, Signer 2 used the sign QUOTATION-MARKERS in relation to the concepts for deaf, hearing, and attitude. So in this respect, she was not using the sign as a language contact device.

The nonnative participants (Interpreter 2 and Signer 2) produced more English mouthed words than actual lexical signs produced — mostly because of adding English lexical items on the mouth, including pronouns, determiners, auxiliary verbs, and prepositions. For example, Signer 2 produced 186 signed lexical items, but mouthed 201 English words. Figure 8 provides an illustration of how Signer 2 mouthed the English determiner 'the' twice in the phrases 'in the first presentation' and 'if the person'. One could speculate that the non-native signers were still thinking in English, and therefore still included a lot of function words which are not used in the same way in Auslan.

All the participants used mouthing for nominal groups, especially terminology and names of people or places. Some English mouthing was used by all participants for prepositions, pronouns, and determiners.

Fingerspelling for all participants was mostly limited to names, subject-specific terms, and cohesive discourse markers such as 'but' and 'so' or to lexicalized fingerspelling such as D-E-P-T (department). The native signers' fingerspelling tended to be unmarked. However, the nonnative

TABLE 3: *Percentage of Fingerspelled Items Recognized as Lexicalized Signs*

Participant	Percentage of fingerspelled words that are lexicalized
Interpreter 1	27%
Interpreter 2	22%
Signer 1	72%
Signer 2	19%

participants produced some marked fingerspelling choices where established signs existed and they apparently were trying to emphasize the English lexical item (e.g., users, relevant); even so, other visual strategies could have been used to convey the meaning. An example can be seen in figure 9.

It was difficult to directly compare the difference in fingerspelling between the native and nonnative signers in terms of amount of fingerspelled items produced because, coincidentally, both nonnative signers had more names occur in their texts, which required them to inevitably fingerspell these proper nouns. It was also difficult to compare between the interpreters and the deaf signers because Interpreter 2 and Signer 2 both produced marked fingerspelled items.

The native signers made more use of a topic-comment structure and often used rhetorical question strategy, which is common in sign language syntactic structure (e.g., WILL TALK ABOUT WHAT?). Comparatively, the nonnative signers tended to follow more of a typical English subject-verb-object grammatical structure (for example, see figure 9).

Overall, it was evident from the analysis that all participants used language contact features of English mouthing and fingerspelling, but that the patterns of linguistic transference were different according to whether the participant was a native or nonnative signer. These data demonstrate (a) that university lectures are in fact a site of language contact, as illustrated by the language use of both Auslan–English interpreters and deaf Australians and (b) that formal register of Auslan appears to incorporate English features in the same way as found in ASL and BSL.

LIMITATIONS OF THE STUDY

This study has limitations, which may lead some readers to question the validity of the research. However, I emphasize here that although the

TABLE 4: *Production of Fingerspelled Items by Signer* 1

Fingerspelled item	No. times produced
H-H*	5
A-A-D*	1
N-A-D*	2
W-W-W	1
S-O*	2
B-U-T	1
V-V*	2
O-F*	1
T-O	1
I-S	2

Note: *Items considered as lexicalized for the purposes of this analysis.

N.A.D their website have	information	over	what	is	difference	between	deaf	and
N-A-D DET W-W-W HAVE INFORMATION OVER WHAT I-S DIFFERENT BETWEEN DEAF AND								
hard-of-hearing hard	of	hearing	person hard-of-hearing person what's	the difference				
H-H	HARD O-F HEARING PERSON H-H PERSON		WHAT DIFFERENT REF REF?//					

FIGURE 6: *Example sentence from Signer 1 featuring lexicalized fingerspelling*

results and discussion do not provide conclusive evidence, they at least demonstrate the need for more research on this subject and especially the need for more research comparing native and nonnative signers as well as interpreters and deaf people. Nevertheless, this study (albeit preliminary) is needed to highlight relevant research questions and methods for more research on these language contact phenomena.

Because the study involved small numbers of participants, the findings cannot necessarily be extrapolated to the Deaf community and interpreting community at large. Another limitation is the small amount of text that was analyzed. Because of time constraints, only the first few minutes of each text was transcribed and analyzed. More text analysis may well lead to the identification of different patterns of linguistic transference.

Of note, too, is that each of the participants was involved in producing a different text with different subject matter, and each was recorded under dissimilar conditions to diverse audiences. Consequently, the texts

Interpreter 1

All these sorts of areas have grown quite dramatically in the last decade or so.

So have	really		maybe ten years
HAVE ONE TWO THREE FOUR REALLY EXPAND EXPAND EXPAND UNTIL-NOW TEN YEARS//			

But we still are a long way from . . . erm . . . having easy to use, readily accessible,

But still		Still	before
BUT STILL + THINK FINE EASY FIND+? NO [NEG]// STILL PROGRESS+BEFORE			

highly reliable, highly valid tests of sign language skill.

developed	test can use easy really	valid
ESTABLISH DEVELOP APPROPRIATE TEST CAN USE EASY REALLY VALUE V-A-L-I-D		

not yet
DIFFERENT + NOT-YET ESTABLISH//

Signer 1

So	I	thought worth		over	what	difference	between deaf and
S-O ME THINK WORTH EXPLAIN DET POINTS OVER WHAT DIFFERENT BETWEEN DEAF AND							

hard-of-hearing person	then will help us	what	Australian	context
H-H PERSON THEN WILL HELP PRO DISCUSS WHAT DET AUSTRALIA CONTEXT//				

FIGURE 7: *Native signers' use of English mouthing with nouns and verbs*

are difficult to compare directly. Another important point is that producing a text is a different process from interpreting a text. As stated earlier, expository texts can be cognitively demanding for a listener to comprehend, thus interpreters face a different challenge to convert that type of text into sign language from that of a signer who is authoring the text him- or herself.

Nonetheless, each participant was engaged in the same purpose in producing the texts. Each text had the same context of situation (university lecture); the same parameters within each context (field, tenor, and mode); and the same formal register, academic discourse genre, and expository text type, with the goal to introduce information and provide a point of view about an aspect of the Deaf community, its sign language, or its identity. Thus, the research is valid from a perspective of "inter-

We talked about	Humphries		in the first presentation	I think	at that	time
WE TALK ABOUT H-U-MP-H-R-I-E-S LONG-TIME-AGO FIRST LECTURE THINK DET TIME						
people		come up	again	When put	hearing	
PEOPLE NOT-UNDERSTAND POSTPONE COME-UP AGAIN// WHEN PUT HEARING						
in			because	a lot of the time you'll find	when	
QUOTATION-MARKERS IN QUOTATION-MARKERS BECAUSE A-LOT TIME YOU FIND WHEN						
you talk about hearing		and deaf		it's not related just to		
TALK HEARING QUOTATION-MARKERS DEAF QUOTATION-MARKERS DET NOT LINK ONLY						
if the person can hear	or	not	It's more		about attitude	
PERSON CAN HEAR OR NOT// MORE QUOTATION-MARKERS ATTITUDE//						
That's really what		we'll	talk about this	week		
DET REALLY DET QUOTATION-MARKERS WE WILL TALK ABOUT THIS WEEK//						

FIGURE 8: *Signer 2's use of mouthing*

textuality" because the texts are from a recognizable genre, they are thematically similar to the other texts, they make the reader or listener think of other texts, and they derive from and imply familiarity with other texts (Weiser 1988).

Further research is needed to determine whether what interpreters do is consistent with deaf signers or whether they are simply producing a form of "interpreter-ese." To minimize limitations of future research, I make suggestions at the end of this paper that could ensure a more robust study.

CONCLUSION

This paper has detailed the findings of a study that identified and compared the language contact phenomena used by Auslan–English interpreters and deaf Australians. Fingerspelling and English mouthing, the two key language contact features, were discussed within the context of university lectures, which served as a site of language contact. The study considered interpreters' use of different translation styles to incorporate language contact features into their interpretations. A lexicogrammatical analysis

And what they **did** was contrast the acquisition of these these features with the
Really   compare   how   people   learn   those   features
REALLY COMPARE HOW PEOPLE LEARN DET F-E-A-T-U-R-E-S

acquisition of the same types of grammatical features in English,
with   how   people   learn the same   grammar   features in English
WITH HOW PEOPLE LEARN SAME G-R-A-M-M-A-R F-E-A-T-U-R-E-S ENGLISH//

FIGURE 9: *Interpreter 2's use of fingerspelling*

of four texts was carried out using a functional linguistic approach that focused on the use of fingerspelling and English mouthing. Two Auslan texts and two English-to-Auslan interpreted texts, produced by a balance of native and nonnative signers, were analyzed and compared.

The analysis revealed evidence of code-mixing, rather than codeswitching, as linguistic features of English were transferred into Auslan and the two languages blended together. The findings also revealed that another sociolinguistic feature influenced the use of language contact phenomena — the fact that the distinction is not necessarily between interpreters and deaf people but, rather, between native and nonnative signers.

These findings are similar to those of Armstrong (2002), who analyzed the use of constructed action (CA) and constructed dialogue (CD)[9] in the interpretations of four ASL interpreters. She found that native and nonnative signers used these linguistic features differently, although the two native signers were consistent in their use of CA and CD and used them at the same points in the texts. Thus, the results of this study and Armstrong's analysis demonstrate that further research is needed comparing native and nonnative signers among deaf people and interpreters.

The analysis of linguistic transference in the form of English mouthing and fingerspelling showed not only that some patterning of features was more common to native signers (e.g., use of Auslan mouthing and unmarked fingerspelling) and other patterning was more common to nonnative signers (e.g., use of English mouthing and marked fingerspelling) but also that essentially all the participants used features of language contact — especially English mouthing. Because the Deaf community is made up of both native and nonnative signers and because interpreters also comprise both categories, it can be suggested that interpreters are incorporating language contact phenomena in the same way as deaf people.

Taking into account the limitations of this study, outlined earlier, especially the fact that few participants were involved, the primary recommendation from this study is for further research to be carried out comparing the use of language contact phenomena by deaf people and interpreters in Australia, the United States, and other countries.

A larger number of participants should be involved in future studies, and the deaf signers should be asked to produce a substantial text in sign language of at least fifteen minutes duration on the same topic. In addition, the interpreters should each be asked to interpret, for the same duration, the same English text on a topic identical to that of the deaf presenters. All participants should be required to either present or interpret to a mixed audience including equal numbers of deaf and hearing people, which will reduce problems of direct comparability and provide more robust data for further analysis and comparison with the findings of this study.

Deaf interpreters should also be included in the group of participants for any future study. Including this group would allow for analysis to focus on how much use of language contact features are influenced by the interpreting process and to further distinguish between native and nonnative signers and between deaf and hearing people.

A final research suggestion is to film deaf people and interpreters in informal contexts of situation and apply the same functional lexicogrammatical analysis to the texts, calculating the amount of fingerspelling and English mouthing used and then comparing the results with those found in the formal lecture contexts of situation. This approach would reveal whether the patterns identified here occur only in formal settings or whether native and nonnative signers, and whether deaf people and interpreters, use language contact features differently in alternate contexts.

NOTES

1. The term *text* is used here in a functional linguistic sense, whereby text is regarded as a piece of language that is functional and can be spoken, written, or signed (Halliday and Hasan 1985).

2. The convention of using the uppercase D is only used here with reference to the Deaf community or Deaf people as a group. When referring specifically to deaf individuals, the D-d convention is not adopted because the focus is on

the fact that both deaf people in this study choose to use Auslan as their first or preferred language, without any comment on whether they are culturally deaf.

3. When referring to English, the author is referring to spoken language in general and recognizes that it could be Spanish, French, German, etc., depending on the country in question. For the purposes of this paper, any references to spoken language will be to English because the author resides in an English-speaking country.

4. Cued English (also known as Cued Speech) is a system of combining handshapes, nonmanual signals, and locations to make spoken language visible through cues: "Cues are visual allophones that reference the phonemes of a traditionally spoken language" (Hauser 2000, 55).

5. Features of "foreigner talk" are also used by monolinguals to address another person of different intellectual status using the same language, for example, slowed down speech and louder volume.

6. There is a difference, however, between (a) transference of English features into ASL so the signed utterance is still cohesive and (b) interference from English, which makes the signed utterance difficult to understand.

7. Drawing on the work of Deborah Tannen and other discourse analysts, Metzger (1995) discusses the notions of constructed action, often referred to as role playing or role shifting, and constructed dialogue, previously thought of as "reported speech."

8. For example, see Bell (1991), Hatim and Mason (1990, 1997), Newmark (1988), Nida (1964), and Seleskovitch (1978).

9. *Constructed action* is another term for the use of classifiers to describe the action of people or objects or specific processes. Previously referred to as "role shift," constructed dialogue is when a signer takes on different characters in the first person and represents a conversation taking place. See Metzger (1995) for a discussion about the use of CA and CD in ASL.

REFERENCES

Ann, J. 1998. Contact between a sign language and a written language: Character signs in Taiwan Sign Language. In *Pinky extension and eye gaze: Language use in deaf communities*, ed. C. Lucas, 59–99. Washington, D.C.: Gallaudet University Press.

Armstrong, J. 2002. *Constructed action and constructed dialogue of ASL interpreters.* Master's thesis, English Department, Ball State University, Muncie, IN.

Baker, C. 2003. Education as a site of language contact. *Annual Review of Applied Linguistics* 23: 95–112.

Banna, K. 2004a. Auslan interpreting: What can we learn from translation theory? *Deaf Worlds* 20 (2): 100–119.

———. 2004b. *Codeswitching in Auslan/English interpreters*. Research report, Macquarie University, Sydney.

Bell, R. T. 1991. *Translation and translating: Theory and practice*. London: Longman.

Bishop, M., and S. Hicks. 2005. Orange eyes: Bimodal bilingualism in hearing adults from deaf families. *Sign Language Studies* 5 (2): 188–230.

Black, J. B. 1985. An exposition on understanding expository text. In *Understanding expository text: A theoretical and practical handbook for analyzing explanatory text*, ed. B. K. Britton and J. B. Black, 249–67. Hillsdale, N.J.: Lawrence Erlbaum.

Brennan, M. 2001. Making borrowings work in British Sign Language. In *Foreign vocabulary in sign languages*, D. Brentari, 49–86. Mahwah, N.J.: Lawrence Erlbaum.

Britton, B. K., S. M. Glynn, and J. W. Smith. 1985. Cognitive demands of processing expository text: A cognitive workbench model. In *Understanding expository text: A theoretical and practical handbook for analyzing explanatory text*, ed. B. K. Britton and J. B. Black, 227–48. Hillsdale, N.J.: Lawrence Erlbaum.

Butt, D., R. Fahey, S. Feez, S. Spinks, and C. Yallop. 2000. *Using functional grammar: An explorer's guide*. 2nd ed. Sydney, New South Wales: National Centre for English Language Teaching and Research, Macquarie University.

Cerney, B. 2000. The ten C's of effective target texts. *Journal of Interpretation* 131–50.

Clyne, M. 2003. *Dynamics of language contact*. New York: Cambridge University Press.

Cokely, D. 1992. *Interpretation: A sociolinguistic model*. Burtonsville, Md.: Linstok Press.

Conlon, C., and J. Napier. 2004. Developing Auslan educational resources: A process of effective translation of children's books. *Deaf Worlds* 20 (2): 141–61.

Davis, J. 1989. Distinguishing language contact phenomena in ASL. In *The sociolinguistics of the Deaf community*, ed. C. Lucas, 85–102. San Diego: Academic Press.

———. 1990. Linguistic transference and interference: Interpreting between English and ASL. In *Sign language research: Theoretical issues*, ed. C. Lucas, 308–21. Washington, D.C: Gallaudet University Press.

———. 2003. Cross-linguistic strategies used by interpreters. *Journal of Interpretation* 95–128.

———. 2005. Code choices and consequences: Implications for educational interpreting. In *Interpreting and interpreter education: Directions for research and practice*, ed. M. Marschark, R. Peterson, and E. A. Winston, 112-141. New York: Oxford University Press.

Detthow, A. 2000. Transliteration between spoken Swedish and Swedish signs. In *Bilingualism and identity in deaf communities*, ed. M. Metzger, 79–94. Washington, D.C.: Gallaudet University Press.

Eighinger, L., and B. Karlin. 2003. The feminist-relational approach: A social construct for event management. In *The critical link 3: Interpreters in the community*, ed. L. Brunette, G. Bastim, I. Hemlin, and H. Clarke, 37–50. Philadelphia: John Benjamins.

Emmorey, K., H. Borenstein, and R. Thompson. 2003. *Bimodal bilingualism: Code-blending between spoken English and American Sign Language*. San Diego: The Salk Institute and The University of California.

Fontana, S. 1999. Italian Sign Language and spoken Italian in contact: An analysis of interactions between Deaf parents and hearing children. In *Storytelling and conversation: Discourse in Deaf communities*, ed. E. Winston, 149–61. Washington, D.C: Gallaudet University Press.

Frishberg, N. 1990. *Interpreting: An introduction*. 2nd ed. Silver Spring, Md.: RID Publications.

Goffman, E. 1981. *Forms of talk*. Oxford: Basil Blackwell.

Grosjean, F. 1982. *Life with two languages: An introduction to bilingualism*. Cambridge, Mass.: Harvard University Press.

Gumperz, J., ed. 1982. *Discourse strategies*. Cambridge: Cambridge University Press.

Halliday, M. A. K. 1994. *An introduction to functional grammar*. London: Edward Arnold.

Halliday, M. A. K., and R. Hasan. 1985. *Language, context and text: Aspects of language in a social semiotic perspective*. Geelong, Victoria: Deakin University Press.

Harris, S., and F. Bargiela-Chiappini. 2003. Business as a site of language contact. *Annual Review of Applied Linguistics* 23: 155–69.

Hatim, B., and I. Mason. 1990. *Discourse and the translator*. London: Longman.

———. 1997. *Translator as communicator*. London: Routledge.

Hauser, P. C. 2000. An analysis of code-switching: American Sign Language and Cued English. In *Bilingualism and identity in deaf communities*, ed. M. Metzger, 43–78. Washington, D.C.: Gallaudet University Press.

Johnston, T. 1998. *Signs of Australia: A new dictionary of Auslan*. Sydney, New South Wales: North Rocks Press.

———. 2001. Nouns and verbs in Australian Sign Language: An open and shut case? *Journal of Deaf Studies and Deaf Education* 6 (4): 235–57.

———. 2002. The representation of English using Auslan: Implications for Deaf bilingualism and English literacy. *Australian Journal of Education of the Deaf* 8: 23–37.

Joos, M. 1967. *The five clocks.* New York: Harbinger Books.

Kelly, J. 2001. *Transliterating: Show me the English.* Alexandria, Vir.: RID Press.

Kite, Y. 2001. English/Japanese codeswitching among students in an international high school. In *Studies in Japanese bilingualism,* ed. M. Noguchi and S. Fotos, 313–28. Clevedon, United Kingdom: Multilingual Matters.

Leneham, M. 2005. The sign language interpreter as translator: Challenging traditional definitions of translation and interpreting. *Deaf Worlds,* 21 (1): 79–101.

Livingston, S., B. Singer, and T. Abramson. 1994. Effectiveness compared: ASL interpretation versus transliteration. *Sign Language Studies* 82: 1–54.

Llewellyn Jones, P. 1981. Target language styles and source language processing in conference sign language interpreting. Paper presented at the 3rd International Symposium on Sign Language Interpreting, Bristol.

Locker, R. 1990. Lexical equivalence in transliterating for deaf students in the university classroom: Two perspectives. *Issues in Applied Linguistics* 1 (2): 167–95.

Lucas, C., and C. Valli. 1992. *Language contact in the American Deaf community.* San Diego: Academic Press.

Marschark, M., P. Sapere, C. Convertino, R. Seewagen, and H. Maltzen. 2004. Comprehension of sign language interpreting: Deciphering a complex task situation. *Sign Language Studies* 4 (4): 345–68.

Mather, S., and E. Winston. 1998. Spatial mapping and involvement in ASL storytelling. In *Pinky extension and eye gaze: Language use in Deaf communities,* ed. C. Lucas, 170–82. Washington, D.C.: Gallaudet University Press.

McKee, R. L. 1992. *Footing shifts in American Sign Language lectures.* Ph.D. diss., Department of Applied Linguistics and TESL, University of California, Los Angeles.

Metzger, M. 1995. Constructed action and constructed dialogue in American Sign Language. In *Sociolinguistics in Deaf communities,* ed. C. Lucas, 255–71. Washington, D.C.: Gallaudet University Press.

———. 1999. *Sign language interpreting: Deconstructing the myth of neutrality.* Washington, D.C: Gallaudet University Press.

Miller, J. R. 1985. A knowledge-based model of prose comprehension: Applications to expository texts. In *Understanding expository text: A theoretical and practical handbook for analyzing explanatory text,* ed. B. K. Britton and J. B. Black, 199–226. Hillsdale, N.J.: Lawrence Erlbaum.

Napier, J. 1998. Free your mind—The rest will follow. *Deaf Worlds* 14 (3): 15–22.

———. 2000. Free Interpretation: What is it and does it translate into training? In *Deaf Studies, Sydney 1998: Selected papers from the Australasian Deaf Studies Research Symposium, Renwick College, Sydney, 22–23 August 1998,* ed. A. Schembri, J. Napier, R. Beattie, and G. Leigh, 21–33. Sydney, New South Wales: North Rocks Press.

———. 2002a. *Sign language interpreting: Linguistic coping strategies.* Coleford, United Kingdom: Douglas McLean.

———. 2002b. University interpreting: Linguistic issues for consideration. *Journal of Deaf Studies and Deaf Education* 7 (4): 281–301.

———. 2005. Linguistic features and strategies of interpreting: From research to education to practice. In *Sign language interpreting and interpreter education: Directions for research and practice,* ed. M. Marschark, R. Peterson, and E. Winston, 84–111. New York: Oxford University Press.

Napier, J., and R. Adam. 2002. A comparative linguistic analysis of BSL and Auslan interpreting. *Deaf Worlds* 18 (1): 22–31.

Napier, J., and R. Barker. 2004. Accessing university education: Perceptions, preferences and expectations for interpreting by deaf students. *Journal of Deaf Studies and Deaf Education* 9 (2): 228–38.

Newmark, P. 1988. *A textbook of translation.* London: Prentice Hall.

Nida, E. 1964. *Toward a science of translating with special reference to principles and procedures involved in Bible translating.* Leiden, The Netherlands: E. J. Brill.

Piller, I. 2003. Advertising as a site of language contact. *Annual Review of Applied Linguistics* 23: 170–83.

Pöchhacker, F. 2003. *Introducing interpreting studies.* London: Routledge.

Pollitt, K. 2000a. Critical linguistic and cultural awareness: Essential tools in the interpreter's kit bag. In *Innovative practices for teaching sign language interpreters,* ed. C. Roy, 67–82. Washington,, D.C: Gallaudet University Press.

———. 2000b. On babies, bathwater and approaches to interpreting. *Deaf Worlds* 16 (2): 60–64.

Romaine, S. 1995. *Bilingualism.* 2nd ed. Oxford: Blackwell.

Roy, C. 1989. Features of discourse in an American Sign Language lecture. In *The sociolinguistics of the Deaf community,* ed. C. Lucas, 231–52. New York: Academic Press.

Schembri, A. 1996. *The structure and formation of signs in Auslan (Australian Sign Language).* Sydney, New South Wales: North Rocks Press.

Schembri, A., G. Wigglesworth, T. Johnston, G. Leigh, R. Adam, and R. Barker. 2000. The test battery for Australian Sign Language morphology and syntax project: Noun-verb pairs in Auslan. In *Deaf Studies, Sydney 1998: Selected papers from the Australasian Deaf Studies Research Symposium,* ed. A. Schembri, J. Napier, R. Beattie, and G. Leigh, 99–118. Sydney, New South Wales: North Rocks Press.

Seleskovitch, D. 1978. *Interpreting for international conferences.* Washington, D.C: Pen and Booth.

Shin, S. J. 2002. Differentiating language contact phenomena: Evidence from Korean-English bilingual children. *Applied Psycholinguistics* 23 (3): 337–60.

Siple, L. 1995. *The use of additions in sign language transliteration.* Ph.D. diss., State University of New York, Buffalo.

———. 1997. Historical development of the definition of transliteration. *Journal of Interpretation* 77–100.

Sofinski, B. A. 2002. So, why do I call this English? In *Turn-taking, fingerspelling, and contact in signed languages,* ed. C. Lucas, 27–52. Washington, D.C.: Gallaudet University Press.

———. 2003. Adverbials, constructed dialogue, and use of space: Oh my!: Non-manual elements used in signed language transliteration. In *From topic boundaries to omission: New research on interpretation,* ed. M. Metzger, S. Collins, V. Dively, and R. Shaw, 154–86. Washington, D.C.: Gallaudet University Press.

Sofinski, B. A., N. A. Yesbeck, S. C. Gerhold, and M. C. Bach-Hansen. 2001. Features of voice-to-sign transliteration by educational interpreters. *Journal of Interpretation* 47–68.

Spolsky, B. 2003. Religion as a site of language contact. *Annual Review of Applied Linguistics* 23: 81–94.

Tate, G., J. Collins, and P. Tymms. 2003. Assessments using BSL: Issues of translation for performance indicators in primary schools. *Deaf Worlds* 19 (1): 6–35.

Valdes, G., and C. Angelelli. 2003. Interpreters, interpreting, and the study of bilingualism. *Annual Review of Applied Linguistics* 23: 58–78.

Viera, J. A., and L. K. Stauffer. 2000. Transliteration: The consumer's perspective. *Journal of Interpretation* 83–100.

Weiser, I. 1988. (Inter)textuality, semantics, and coherence. Paper presented at the Annual Meeting of the Conference on College Composition and Communication, St. Louis, Mo.

Winston, E. A. 1989. Transliteration: What's the message? In *The sociolinguistics of the Deaf community,* ed. C. Lucas, 147–64. Washington, D.C: Gallaudet University Press.

———. 1995. Spatial mapping in comparative discourse frames. In *Language, gesture and space,* ed. K. Emmorey and J. Reilly, 87–114. Hillsdale, N.J.: Lawrence Erlbaum.

Winston, E. A., and C. Monikowski. 2003. Marking topic boundaries in signed interpretation and transliteration. In *From topic boundaries to omission: New research on interpretation,* ed. M. Metzger, S. Collins, V. Dively, and R. Shaw, 187–227. Washington, D.C.: Gallaudet University Press.

Zimmer, J. 1989. Toward a description of register variation in American Sign Language. In *The sociolinguistics of the Deaf community,* ed. C. Lucas, 253–72. New York: Academic Press.

Transcription Conventions

Adapted from Napier (2002a)

Know (conventional orthography)	— spoken English words
Know	— emphasis in spoken intonation
KNOW	— English representation (gloss) of an Auslan sign
I-ASK-YOU	— English words separated by a hyphen when more than one English word needed to gloss meaning of an Auslan sign
T-R-U-E	— letters in the word separated by a hyphen when English word fingerspelled

<u>   faith</u>
BELIEVE   — indicates particular mouthing of English word (e.g., faith) in conjunction with sign

<u>   faith</u>
F-A-I-T-H   — indicates particular mouthing of word (e.g., faith) in conjunction with fingerspelled word

<u>   (pout)</u>
EXPLAIN   — indicates particular Auslan mouthing in conjunction with sign (e.g., pout or puffed cheeks)

KNOCK+   — plus symbol indicates that the sign is repeated to give emphasis

PRO/DET	— index/fist 'point' to indicate (a) pronouns or determiners or (b) possessive pronouns
REF	— index point to (a) establish placement of newly introduced concept or (b) refer back to established placement of concept
[NEG]	— indicates head shake at end of utterance to negate statement
(VERY)	— signer has started to execute a particular sign but has stopped and moved on to another sign
(P-R-O)	— signer has started to execute a particular fingerspelled word but has stopped and moved on to another sign or has begun to re-fingerspell
//	— indicates end of Auslan 'sentence'
...	— noticeable pause of less than five seconds
(pause)	— substantial pause of more than five seconds

Glosses and Transcripts of Texts

This appendix comprises four texts that have been glossed and transcribed as appropriate to reflect actual communication of the four participants in the study.

TEXT I — ENGLISH–AUSLAN INTERPRETATION: UNIVERSITY LECTURE ON SIGNED LANGUAGE ASSESSMENT (INTERPRETER I, NATIVE SIGNER)

OK, Hello. You'll have to excuse me if I look a little bit disorganised, that's because I

	Have to	if	look	little	
OK	APOLOGISE I-F LOOK	LITTLE PANIC+ WHY? TRUE ME

am! But I have an overview of what I want to talk about tonight. I was going to make an

But have	over	want	talk	over	tonight
PANIC+ DISORGANISE// ME HAVE OVERALL OVERHEAD OVER WANT TALK OVER TONIGHT

overhead, but... the interpreter will just have to look on... to the sheet. Where's Kate

what	Really	plan to make	but	have	Means	the interpreter
WHAT// REALLY PLAN MAKE OVERHEAD BUT BAD HAVE NOTHING// MEANS INTERPRETER

sitting? At the back? (pause) OK so the topic for tonight is "Issues in Sign Language

have to	Kate	will	sit	where
HAVE LOOK-AT+ READ //... K-A-T-E WILL SIT WHERE? SIT-DOWN SOMEWHERE SIT-DOWN-

Assessment". First of all, I want to say that the, erm, the handout I've just given you, the

at the back	topic	tonight	what	issues	with	sign	language	assessment
REF // (PAUSE) OK TOPIC TONIGHT WHAT ISSUE RELATE SIGN LANGUAGE ASSESSMENT//

overview of what I want to talk about tonight actually comes from a workshop that John

The first thing	want	handout	that	over	want
FIRST THING WANT ANNOUNCE WHAT FIRST DET HANDOUT LIST DET VISUALISE OVER WANT

Smith and I gave to a group of teachers and er.. various other people from the Department

talk	tonight	really that	from	workshop	John Smith
TALK TONIGHT WHAT// REALLY DET FROM WHERE? WORKSHOP BOTH-OF-US J-S BOTH-OF-

of Education in South Australia, in Adelaide. Erm, so this work has come from... work

to different	teacher	different	people	from	department of education
US FINISH TEACH DIFFERENT+ TEACHER DIFFERENT+ PEOPLE FROM D-E-P-T EDUCATION

that both John and I have done, erm... as a workshop last year. Erm... also I'd like to

   Adelaide   South Australia So really that   that from   John work

WHERE? ADELAIDE REF S-A REF// REALLY DET COPY DET FROM BOTH-OF-US J-S WORK

say that neither John nor I... er at all are experts in the question of language

    workshop last year   Also   also

INVOLVE WORKSHOP LAST-YEAR//(PAUSE) ALSO LET-YOU-KNOW STOP DOOR-OPEN... ALSO

assessment. I don't have a background in language testing and assessment itself, erm... I

       that myself   John   really   expert with   language

LET-YOU-KNOW MYSELF HIMSELF J-S BOTH REALLY EXPERT RELATE LANGUAGE

actually have a background in sign language research. But sign language assessment... is

    assessment   My background   with   language   testing

ASSESSMENT [NEG]// MY BACKGROUND RELATE LANGUAGE ASSESSMENT TEST NOTHING//

one of the... fastest growing areas I guess, in applied sign language linguistics, because

  Really my   background   sign   language   research But   sign   language

REALLY MY BACKGROUND SIGN LANGUAGE RESEARCH//BUT REF SIGN LANGUAGE

of the growth in bilingual programs, new interpreter training courses, er...the need for

   assessment that   now with   applied   sign   language

ASSESSMENT REF BECOME EXPAND NOW RELATE A-P-P-L-I-E-D SIGN LANGUAGE

some sort of assessment tools, er for psychometric, psychological testing of deaf adults to

  linguistics   like   bilingual program   new   interpreter   training

LINGUISTICS SAME EXPAND REF BILINGUAL PROGRAM REF NEW INTERPRETER TRAINING

find out what their language skills are like. All these sorts of areas have grown quite

  course   need   assessment   tool involve   psycho   metric

COURSE ONE TWO NEED TEST ASSESSMENT T-O-O-L RELATE PSYCHOLOGY M-E-T-R-I-C//

dramatically in the last decade or so. But we still are a long way from ...erm... having

  like psychological testing deaf adults   like   their language   skills

SAME PSYCHOLOGY TEST DEAF ADULT+ SAME RESEARCH FIND+ PRO LANGUAGE SKILL REF

easy to use, readily accessible, highly reliable, highly valid tests of sign language skill.

   So have   really   maybe   ten

WHAT// HAVE ONE TWO THREE FOUR REALLY EXPAND EXPAND EXPAND UNTIL-NOW TEN

  years But still   Still   before

YEARS// BUT STILL+ THINK FINE EASY FIND+? NO [NEG]// STILL PROGRESS+ BEFORE

| developed | | test | can | use | easy | really | | valid |

ESTABLISH DEVELOP APPROPRIATE TEST CAN USE EASY REALLY VALUE V-A-L-I-D

| not yet |

DIFFERENT+ NOT-YET ESTABLISH//

TEXT 2 — ENGLISH–AUSLAN INTERPRETATION: UNIVERSITY LECTURE ON SIGNED LANGUAGE ACQUISITION (INTERPRETER 2, NONNATIVE SIGNER)

And what they **did** was contrast the acquisition of these these features with the

| Really | compare | how | people | learn | those | | features |

REALLY COMPARE HOW PEOPLE LEARN DET F-E-A-T-U-R-E-S

acquisition of the same types of grammatical features in English, and came up with, as a

| with | how | people | learn | the same | grammar | | features | | in English |

WITH HOW PEOPLE LEARN SAME G-R-A-M-M-A-R F-E-A-T-U-R-E-S ENGLISH//

result of this study, with what seemed to me some quite consistent patterns of

| From that | that | | they found the same how people | learn | that one that one |

FROM DET DET (PAUSE) FIND SAME+ HOW PEOPLE LEARN DET OR DET

grammatical acquisition across the two languages. A little bit later on tonight, when we

| doesn't matter | which | language | | | | Later |

DOESN'T-MATTER WHICH LANGUAGE REF // (PAUSE) | LATER

share the readings, those of you who read the Petitto, erm, paper, we'll look specifically

| tonight | we will talk | over | the study | if you've finished read | | the Petpito | paper | If |

TONIGHT WILL TALK OVER RESEARCH I-F FINISH READ (P-E-T) P-E-T-P-I-T-O PAPER// I-F

at that paper, and er, - who did read the Petitto? Yeah, on pronouns...

| you look | specifically at that paper | who | finish | | read | that | paper | one | | Yep fine |

PRO LOOK SPECIFIC DET PAPER WHO FINISH PRO READ THAT PAPER? ONE PRO// YES FINE

yep... it should be two and two. I was saying Kate before you came in, I can't, I knew

| pronouns | | Yep | OK | Should be | two two | | Same | said | before | | you arrive |

P-R-O-N-O-U-N-S// YES ALRIGHT// SHOULD TWO TWO// SAME SAID BEFORE ARRIVE

there was something, when you asked the question last week and I said I'd copy those

| Kate | remember | you asked me a question | last week | I said | would copy | those articles | | but | can |

K-A-T-E REMEMBER ASK-ME QUESTION LAST-WEEK SAID WILL COPY DET ARTICLE BUT CAN articles, I remembered I can't copy more than one, one, one-tenth or one chapter from a

only   copy one   tenth or one   chapter   from one book   without   any trouble

ONLY COPY ONE DIVIDE TEN OR ONE C-H-A-P-T-E-R FROM ONE BOOK NOTHING TROUBLE

single book without getting into trouble with the photocopy, er, powers that be, so you've

from   authority   copyright

FROM REF (C-) POWER TARGET C-O-P-Y-R-I-G-H-T//

each got, er, one article. And I didn't do them, somebody else did. But when we talk...
(pause)

We'll come back to that after the break tonight, but what Petitto found, in a nutshell,

We will back to that after the break tonight

WILL BACK-TO AFTER BREAK TONIGHT

coming back to the study and look at it in a little more detail, was a very very similar

what   Petitto   found if   summarise we will   talk   (?)   more deep later   but really was very

WHAT P-E-T-T-I-T-O FIND I-F SUMMARY WILL TALK STORY DEEP LATER BUT REALLY V-V

pattern of acquisition of pronoun pro-nominalisation in, erm, sign language users and

similar   pattern   pattern   of how people learn   pronouns   in sign

SAME AREA P-A-T-E-R-N P-A-T-T-E-R-N HOW PEOPLE LEARN P-R-O-N-O-U-N-S IN SIGN

English language users. So that's a precursor for what we're going to talk about tonight.

language   users   and English   language   users   Before

LANGUAGE U-S-E-R-S REF AND ENGLISH LANGUAGE REF U-S-E-R-S REF // BEFORE

Let me quote to you from that study by Reilly, McIntire and Bellugi: 'Babyface'(pause).

what we will talk tonight   will   quote   from   the research from   Reilly

PROCEED WHAT WILL TALK TONIGHT WILL QUOTE FROM RESEARCH FROM R-E-I-L-L-Y

This is what they say: "despite radical differences in language modality, we find

Bell   Bellugi   and   McIntire   This is what they say three say

(B-E-L-L-O) B-E-L-L-L-U-G-I AND M-C-I-N-T-I-R-E// WHAT SAY THREE SAY

that deaf and hearing children show dramatically similar courses of development...What

Doesn't   matter   really   different   language mode   We see

DOESN'T-MATTER REALLY DIFFERENT REF LANGUAGE M-O-D-E REF (PAUSE) SEE

is impressive, they say, is the remarkable resilience of the mechanisms that children bring

deaf   hearing   children   really   similar   development   Really

DEAF HEARING CHILDREN REF REALLY SAME AREA DEVELOP REF REF// (PAUSE) REALLY to bear on language acquisition (pause), whether the input is in streams of linearly

| really | doesn't | matter | which language | they learn | children | use |

JAW-DROP (PAUSE) REALLY DOESN'T-MATTER WHICH LANGUAGE LEARN CHILDREN U-S-E

ordered sound or in complex simultaneously organised movements of the hands and

| the same | methods | | to | learn language | If | suppose | we're talking over |

SAME M-E-T-H-O-D-S REF T-O LEARN LANGUAGE// I-F SUPPOSE TALK OVER ONE-STEP-AT

arms" (pause). So what they're saying is, what Bellugi, erm, what Reilly, McIntire and

| sound | or | how | the hands move | | Really | what | three | | people say |

-A-TIME SOUND OR HOW HANDS MOVE+// (PAUSE) REALLY WHAT THREE PRO PEOPLE SAY

Bellugi are saying is what... summarises some if the issues we're going to look at tonight,

| the researcher s | say | | Really | summarise | some of the issues | of what we're talking over |

RESEARCHER SAY THREE (PAUSE) REALLY SUMMARY SOME I-S-S-U-E-S TALK OVER

as young language learners, kids are remarkably, erm, malleable, and resilient.

| tonight | Same as young | children | or young language | | learners | | learners | | really |

TONIGHT// SAME YOUNG CHILDREN YOUNG LANGUAGE L-E-A-R-N-E-R-S LEARNER REALLY

you can ver flexible | in how they learn language

CAN V-V FLEXIBLE WELL HOW LEARN LANGUAGE//

TEXT 3 — AUSLAN PRESENTATION: UNIVERSITY PRESENTATION ON THE DEAF COMMUNITY (SIGNER 1, NATIVE SIGNER)

| First of all I want to thank you all for inviting me to come | today | to talk over | | where | deaf |

GOOD FIRST WANT THANK PRO INVITE-ME COME TODAY TALK OVER WHERE DEAF

| community | is | now | what | Have a lot of | | in | Australian | Deaf |

COMMUNITY DET I-S NOW WHAT// HAVE A-LOT DISCUSSION IN AUSTRALIA DEAF

| community over | | disability | group | or | | deaf |

COMMUNITY OVER REALLY PRO DET DISABILITY GROUP OR SMALL-GROUP DEAF

| community | cultural | linguistic | what | Also | have | relationship |

COMMUNITY DET CULTURAL LINGUISTIC DET WHAT REF REF// ALSO HAVE RELATIONSHIP

| with | hard-of-hearing people | So | I thought | worth | what | information |

WITH WHAT REF H-H PEOPLE// WELL THINK WORTH RESEARCH WHAT INFORMATION

available   overseas I found   N.A.D   American same   A.A.D
AVAILABLE OVERSEAS// FIND REF N-A-D DET AMERICA SAME EQUIVALENT REF A-A-D//

N.A.D their website have   information   over   what is   difference   between deaf and
N-A-D DET W-W-W HAVE INFORMATION OVER WHAT I-S DIFFERENT BETWEEN DEAF AND

hard-of-hearing hard   of   hearing person hard-of-hearing person what's the difference
H-H   HARD O-F HEARING PERSON H-H PERSON   WHAT DIFFERENT REF REF?//

So   I   thought worth   over   what   difference between deaf and
S-O ME THINK WORTH EXPLAIN DET POINTS OVER WHAT DIFFERENT BETWEEN DEAF AND

hard-of-hearing person   then will help us   what   Australian context
H-H   PERSON THEN WILL HELP PRO DISCUSS WHAT DET AUSTRALIA CONTEXT//

Because   know really very little   over culture of Australian deaf
WHY UP-TILL-NOW KNOW REALLY V-V LITTLE PRINT+ OVER CULTURE O-F AUSTRALIA DEAF

community Any   Auslan student   want   over Deaf culture finds
COMMUNITY// ANY (STUDENT) AUSLAN STUDENT WANT SEARCH OVER DEAF CULTURE FIND

          British   information   American but   really   Australian
A-LOT BRITISH ENGLISH INFORMATION DET AMERICA B-U-T REALLY BELONG AUSTRALIA

      So worth good time for Deaf community to   now   Now will
[NEG]// S-O WORTH GOOD TIME FOR DEAF COMMUNITY T-O DISCUSS NOW// GOOD NOW WILL

talk over Deaf   hard-of-hearing community   very
TALK OVER DEAF WELL H-H   COMMUNITY LARGE-GROUP-TOGETHER? DET V-V

     really what   different different   different different depends on what
VARIETY REALLY WHAT DIFFERENT DIFFERENT DIFFERENT DIFFERENT FOLLOW ON WHAT?

    why hearing loss   hearing loss   age   hearing loss
ONE WHY HEARING LOST TWO DEGREE HEARING LOST THREE AGE HAPPEN HEARING LOST

    educational background   communication method plus   how   feel
FOUR EDUCATION BACKGROUND FIVE COMMUNICATION METHOD PLUS SIX HOW PRO FEEL

over   hearing   loss
OVER DET HEARING LOST//

TEXT 4 — AUSLAN PRESENTATION: UNIVERSITY LECTURE
ON DEAF IDENTITY (SIGNER 2, NONNATIVE SIGNER)

Little bit difficult   to know which   readings   to start with for this.   Which   readings   have   you

LITTLE DIFFICULT KNOW WHICH READING START WITH THIS// WHICH READING HAVE YOU

book   Padden   and   Humphries

ACCESS+ SEVERAL... BOOK P-A-D-D-E-N AND H-U-M-P-H-R-I-E-S QUOTATION-MARKERS

very   accessible good   introduction to the whole area   first   chapter   in

VERY ACCESSIBLE GOOD INTRODUCTION T-O WHOLE AREA// THIS FIRST CHAPTER COPY IN

your   readings   called   learning to   be deaf   read that one?

YOUR READING NAME QUOTATION-MARKERS LEARN T-O B-E DEAF. FINISH READ?//GOOD

That gives alot of interesting   stories   about   young   children   and   how   they

GIVES GOOD INTERESTING STORY ABOUT YOUNG CHILDREN   HOW PRO

work out   if   a person's deaf or hearing   article   by

LOOK-UP-DOWN+ WORK-OUT I-F PERSON DEAF HEARING... ONE// TWO... ARTICLE B-Y

Humphries   the same   Humphries   Padden   and   Humphries

H-U-M-P-H-R-I-E-S SAME H-U-M-P-H-R-I-E-S P-A-D-D-E-N AND H-U-M-P-H-R-I-E-S

by himself   his article   more   bit   more   heavy

PRO MOVE-OVER HIMSELF// HIS ARTICLE MORE DEEP LITTLE MORE HEAVY// PRO READ

Also in your   collection   little bit   A lot of that   maybe   American

WELL?//ALSO IN COLLECTION// LITTLE HEAVY //MANY DET MAYBE PRO AMERICA

so maybe not   relevant   here   but a lot of   interesting   things there   too.   Two

MAYBE NOT R-E-L-E-V-A-N-T HERE BUT BIG INTERESTING THING DET SAME// TWO

articles you don't have to   read   but   have   in   your collection   anyway

TWO-MORE ARTICLE NOT   HAVE-TO READ BUT HAVE IN COLLECTION ANYWAY

Mowe   Everyone   that one   Mowe   and   Napier   Napier   You all read that one

M-O-W-E?// ALL READ DET?// M-O-W-E AND N-A-P-I-E-R? N-A-P-I-E-R// ALL READ DET

will be   interesting   to talk about   that OK I'll   start   with

WILL INTERESTING TALK ABOUT DET// OK ME START WITH FOLLOW//

We talked about   Humphries   in the first presentation I think at that time

WE TALK ABOUT H-U-MP-H-R-I-E-S LONG-TIME-AGO FIRST LECTURE THINK DET TIME

people		come up	again	When put	hearing

PEOPLE NOT-UNDERSTAND POSTPONE COME-UP AGAIN// WHEN PUT HEARING QUOTATION-

in		because	a lot of the time you'll find	when	you talk about

MARKERS IN QUOTATION-MARKERS BECAUSE A-LOT TIME YOU FIND WHEN   TALK

hearing	and deaf		it's not	related just to if the person

HEARING QUOTATION-MARKERS DEAF QUOTATION-MARKERS DET NOT LINK ONLY PERSON

can hear or not	It's more	about attitude That's really	what

CAN HEAR OR NOT// MORE QUOTATION-MARKERS ATTITUDE//DET REALLY DET QUOTATION-

we'll	talk	about	this week

MARKERS WE WILL TALK ABOUT THIS WEEK//

Capitalizing on Simultaneity: Features

of Bimodal Bilingualism in Hearing Italian

Native Signers

Michele Bishop, Sherry Hicks, Antonella Bertone, *and Rita Sala*

Essentially three main groups of bimodal bilinguals need to be considered in bimodal bilingual research, each of which has its own range of bimodal bilingualism: deaf people who not only know a signed language but also have learned to read, write, and sometimes speak a spoken language; hearing people who come from deaf families and who often acquire both languages natively (hereafter referred to as Codas, or children of

This work was sponsored by Gallaudet Small Grants, awarded to Sherry Hicks and Michele Bishop in 2004, and by a Fulbright Scholarship awarded to Michele Bishop the same year through the Italian Fulbright Commission and the Mason Perkins Deafness Fund in Rome. We thank Elena Radutzky for her support as a liaison in Italy and her guidance during this project. We are very grateful for the insights of two Italian Codas, Antonella Bertone and Rita Sala, whose fluency in Italian and LIS (Lingua Italiana dei Segni) made this research possible. Ceil Lucas, Kendall King, and Karen Emmorey provided crucial comments on earlier drafts of this article for which we are very appreciative. We appreciate Sarah Taub for her ideas about the mouth as a "partitionable zone" in bilingual bimodal code-blending. We are also grateful for valuable input from Scott Liddell and Paul Dudis on real space and mapping. Susan Mather and Christopher Miller offered excellent insight into the function of bimodal codeswitching and code-blending in narrative discourse. We would like to extend special thanks to David Bishop for his help in salvaging the still shots from the compromised original videotaped data.

deaf adults);[1] and hearing people who are second-language learners of a signed language. A comparison of the bimodal bilingualism of these three groups of bilinguals will be left for future research.

This study focused on only one group, native users of both a signed and spoken language (the second group described above), to analyze their naturalistic discourse. Our goal was to characterize the nature of bimodal bilingualism within this group as a means to explore the effect bimodality has on language production and usage. The bimodal bilinguals in this group have an option that bilinguals using spoken language do not: they can either codeswitch or code-blend. *Code-blending,* a term coined by Emmorey (2003), also known as code-mixing in the literature, describes simultaneous speech and sign production. Our first set of questions asks, do bimodal bilinguals prefer code-blending to codeswitching? What communicative benefits are there in code-blending? Does the grammatical integrity of both languages remain intact in code-blended utterances?

Second, we ask, does having a strong "Coda identity" affect bimodal language usage? Codas grow up as a part of the Deaf community and often learn a signed language as their first language.[2] Linguistic interest in signed and spoken language bilingualism over the last few decades has led to a focus on mother-child dyads rather than adult bilingualism. Studies have found that deaf mothers not only sign but also speak to their deaf and hearing children (Meadow-Orlans, Erting, and Spencer 1987; Maestas y Moores 1980; Schiff and Ventry 1976; Mills and Coerts 1990; Moores and Moores 1982; Van den Bogaerde 2000; Rodriquez 2001; Petitto et al. 2001). Van den Bogaerde (2003) studied the mixed-language input of six deaf mothers with their hearing and deaf children and found that the hearing children were getting input from a "third system" that comprised both spoken Dutch and the signed language of the Netherlands. It remains to be seen the extent to which this type of mixed language input during childhood has shaped the bilingual bimodal output of adult bilinguals.

Anthropological studies, Coda autobiographies, and, to some extent, films about deaf families[3] have indicated that many Codas feel they are more culturally aligned with the Deaf community than with hearing society in general, in spite of their ability to hear (Preston 1994; Lane et al. 1996; Miller 2004). This literature also makes salient points about the understanding among these individuals that Deaf culture is indeed different from hearing culture and about the fact that hearing children do not see themselves as different from their deaf parents and siblings until they become older (Lane et al. 1996). From a deaf perspective, these hearing children are essentially deaf because they understand and assimilate to Deaf cultural norms. The one aspect missing for these children is the experience of not being able to hear (Lane et al. 1996).

Research on American Codas suggests that many find it impossible to separate their deaf identity from American Sign Language (ASL) and their hearing identity from English (Bishop and Hicks 2005). This deaf-hearing identity has often been referred to as a "third identity" in the Coda community and signifies having both Deaf and hearing parts (Jacobs 1992).[4] Understanding this bicultural and bilingual aspect of Coda identity[5] is important on a global level because Deaf people throughout the world often marry other Deaf people and have hearing children. One direction for future research is not only to examine the sociolinguistic functions of codeswitching and code-blending but also to gain a greater understanding of the relationship between those bimodal linguistic phenomena and the "third identity" development of these bilinguals.

To our knowledge, only several other studies have been done on the linguistic output of hearing, adult bimodal bilinguals (Emmorey, Borinstein, and Thompson 2003; Bishop and Hicks 2005, Emmorey and Pyers in press),[6] and those have been based on data from individuals who are aware of their Coda identity. These studies analyzed data taken from people involved with CODA events and who are consciously aware of their deaf and hearing "parts." Findings from Emmorey, Borinstein, and Thompson (2003) revealed a preference to code-blend rather than codeswitch (95 percent of ASL signs co-occurred with English words) and presented examples of spoken English that were clearly influenced by the accompanying ASL. Some code-blended utterances were a variant of English that bimodal bilinguals use among themselves, called "Coda-talk" by the Coda community[7] and "Coda-speak" or "Coda-speech" by linguists (Lucas and Valli 1992; Emmorey, Borinstein, and Thompson 2003).

In Bishop and Hicks (2005), an analysis of written Coda e-mails revealed ASL structural influence evidenced by a high frequency of sentences lacking copulas, auxiliaries, modals, prepositions, or some combination.[8] In many cases, these e-mails included no overt subjects or objects, especially when context rendered them unnecessary. The messages also contained linguistic features unrelated to ASL structure, for example, nonstandard verb inflections, overgeneralization of 's' (I speaks), and syntactic calquing (a calque is an expression introduced into one language

by translating it from another language [syn: _HYPERLINK"http://
dictionary.reference.com/search?q=loan%20translation"_loan translation_])
suggesting the regular usage of Coda-talk in the written and the spoken
form. In Coda-talk, Codas can use English words to describe an ASL sign
(Bishop and Hicks 2005). For example, the ASL sign STUCK is formed
with the index and middle fingertip (similar to the generic peace sign or a
V handshape) pressing against the throat, the palm facing the body. The
same handshape on the palm of the hand means FORK. Codas can play
with the visual nature of the sign in both written and spoken sentences
such as *My father fork-in-throat* (which literally means "My father is
stuck") by replacing the English lexical item 'stuck' with the description
of the ASL sign (note the absence of a copula) as a creative way to combine both languages.

Coda-talk sometimes includes using "deaf voice," the re-creation of
the sounds of certain deaf people, friends, or one's family members. A
cursory analysis of the phonology of deaf-voice characteristics includes
a pervasive nasalization, a distortion of prosody toward the extremes of
highs and lows, strong assimilation processes that lead to a loss of syllables, and nonlinguistic vocal gestures. This re-creation extends not only
to phonation patterns but also to signing styles. It would be similar to
the way hearing children from hearing families imitate parental speech
patterns or accents. This kind of language use indicates a direct relationship between language and identity, a sociolinguistic phenomenon that
has already been well documented for codeswitching among spoken language bilinguals (Gumperz 1972; Labov 1972; Grosjean 1982; Romaine
1989; Myers-Scotton 1993b; Zentella 1997; Winford 2003).

The CODA organization is strong in the United States and has enjoyed
the participation of international Codas for many years. The enthusiasm
to establish a CODA organization has spread to many countries around
the world and, as of this writing, Canada, Australia, Sweden, England,
Austria, Germany, Ireland, Japan, Sri Lanka, Denmark,[9] Greece, and
Holland (among others) have established their own versions of CODA.
However, to our knowledge, Italy has no local or national CODA organizations nor do Italian Codas participate in the predominantly English-
based CODA Internet forum. The absence of CODA in Italy provides an
opportunity to compare the language of Italian and American bimodal
bilinguals to determine whether a strong Coda identity (or lack of one)
has a direct effect on their linguistic output. Italy, therefore, provided a
unique context in which to study bimodal discourse phenomena by a

population relatively unaffected by formalized Coda identity: Do Italian hearing people from deaf families manifest the same patterns for bimodal language usage as were identified for American Codas?

Italian Sign Language (LIS, or Lingua Italiana dei Segni) and the majority of the world's signed languages have a concurrent relationship with a spoken language. Many phenomena result from the contact between signed and spoken languages, of which codeswitching and code-blending are only two. An extensive study of language contact in the American Deaf community identified certain features of contact signing: mouthing, whispering English words, ASL-like signs such as BECAUSE, the appearance of prepositions (e.g., ON) in sentences with English word order, and morphological changes in both ASL and English (see Lucas and Valli 1992). Parallel phenomena may also result from the contact between LIS and Italian.

Many people are unaware of the fact that LIS and ASL (as well as many other signed languages) are separate languages with their own grammatical structure unlike that of spoken languages. Both English and Italian mark tense morphologically on verbs whereas ASL and LIS express tense lexically by means of temporal adverbs. English and Italian also differ quite dramatically from ASL and LIS with respect to how spatial information is encoded. Like many spoken languages, English and Italian express locative information with prepositions such as *in*, *on*, or *under*. In contrast, ASL and LIS encode locative and motion information with verbal classifier constructions. In these constructions, handshape morphemes specify object type, and the position of the hands in signing space schematically represents the spatial relation between two objects. Movement of the hand specifies the movement of an object through space. Thus, both English and Italian are quite distinct from ASL and LIS within phonological, morphological, and syntactic domains.

Another feature of signed languages is the meaningful use of space. Signers frequently conceive of areas of the space around them, or even themselves, as if they were something else (Liddell 2003), a phenomenon labeled by Liddell as a *real-space blend*. A real-space blend[10] is created when the signer conceptualizes things as something other than what they are. Examples of real-space blends that will figure into this analysis are token blends, surrogate blends, depicting verbs, and list buoys. When the signer points to an area in signing space that represents a nonpresent entity, conceptual content is blended with that space, creating a token blend. Signers then direct pronouns or verbs toward that token blend. Alternatively, surrogate blends are created when the signer conceives of him or herself as someone other than who he or she is, or perhaps that person may be herself at a time in the past. Signers may "become" characters in their own narrative, talking and acting as though they were that person. Surrogate blends are different from token blends in that they are "life-size"; in other words, the signer uses his or her full body to represent either another person or him or herself in a different event space. Although people who use a spoken language also use strategy (especially in narratives), this discourse tool is indispensable in signed languages.

Although both surrogate and token blends are conceptualizations mapped onto physical space, in our everyday experience of the world, we treat real space as if it were our real, physical environment (see Liddell 2003 for further explanation of these concepts). Although both signed and spoken discourse make extensive use of real-space blends, signed languages require verbs and pronouns to be directed appropriately in space, suggesting that real-space blends are more tightly integrated into the grammatical structure for signed languages than they are for spoken languages (Liddell 2003). Consequently, real-space blends may be more frequent and systematic in signed languages than in spoken languages. A brief explanation of the theoretical framework behind real-space blends, including list buoys and depicting verbs, is provided in the section titled "Data."

Language contact phenomena between two spoken languages has benefited from extensive research on when and how bilinguals switch from one language to another (Gumperz 1982; Labov 1972; Grosjean 1982; Romaine 1989; Zentella 1997; King 2000; Muysken 2000). Codeswitching is defined as "the juxtaposition within the same speech exchange of passages of speech belonging to two different grammatical systems or subsystems" (Romaine 1989, 121). Switching can occur at different places in speech, either within the boundaries of a clause or sentence (e.g., *Yo quiero* water, I want *agua*) or at clause boundaries (e.g., *Yo quiero agua* because I'm thirsty). Zentella's (1997) ethnographic work with Puerto Rican children shows that the intermixing of two languages is a creative style of bilingual communication that accomplishes important cultural and conversational work. Codeswitching is fundamentally a conversational activity by which speakers negotiate meaning with each other. A "code switch" (Zentella 1997, 101) may better articulate a message by capturing a meaning or expressing a point more effectively. It also calls attention to the fact that the members are integrating the heritages of their two worlds into a reflection of both identities (Zentella 1997). Codeswitching speaks to how a person can use language to reflect dual cultural identities, especially when one of the cultures is marginalized. Grosjean (1982) argues that this mixed mode of speaking is not random but, rather, serves important functions in the communities where it is used.

Similar to the findings in the research on codeswitching, Codas can and do switch back and forth between a signed language and a spoken language as well as code-blend. The unique features of bimodality include the ability to use aspects of both languages simultaneously and the ability to choose whether to switch or blend. Continued research will undoubtedly expand and inform theories of bilingualism, codeswitching, and theoretical models such as Myers-Scotton's (1997) Matrix Language Frame model. To our knowledge, the majority of models that address the issues of constraints in codeswitching based on sequential rather than simultaneous language mixing. Although this article and that of Emmorey, Borinstein, and Thompson (2003) examine bimodal linguistic output, questions about the sociolinguistic functions that codeswitching and code-blending have in Coda communities remain relatively unexplored (see Bishop and Hicks, 2005, for a preliminary hypothesis on the role of Coda-talk and the development of Coda identity).

METHOD

Only hearing Italian adults who were native users of both a signed and spoken language were chosen for this study. Although deaf people are also bimodal bilinguals, most deaf children are born to hearing families. In many countries including Italy, these families support an oral approach to their child's education and rarely learn more than a few basic signs. This minimal signing mainly functions as support for the oral output. In many countries, the growing practice of putting a cochlear implant in young deaf children has also meant an emphasis on teaching the child to speak instead of sign. Subsequently, Deaf people are often exposed to signed language later in life, either socially through friendships with other deaf people or through educational programs for deaf students that may use both signed and oral communication in the classroom. Other bimodal bilinguals — hearing, second-language learners of a signed language — may be quite successful at attaining a high degree of fluency in a signed language, but they lack native intuition of the language and an insider's knowledge of Deaf culture. For these reasons, the latter two groups were not included in the study.

Ten hearing Italian native signers in two groups of five people each were videotaped for an hour and a half as they discussed their childhood, family, and relationship to the Deaf community. One session took place in a deaf school and the other in a building that houses a deaf school, an interpreting agency, and a school for interpreter training. The researchers set up the camera, provided *caffè e cornetti* (coffee and pastry), and instructed the group to talk about any topics that came to mind concerning their childhood, family, and work with the Deaf community. These topics were chosen to increase the possibility of a bimodal frame of mind (Emmorey, Borinstein, and Thompson 2003). The Italian facilitator, also a participant and included in the group of five Codas, was asked to facilitate the conversation by asking questions about childhood and to change the tape in the camera as needed. Before the group session, the American Coda researcher videotaped each participant in a one-on-one interview. Influenced by Preston's (1994) findings, the researchers considered it important that these one-on-one interviews be "Coda-only" to create a sense of shared identity. Preston interviewed 150 Codas throughout the United States (many had never been involved with the CODA organization) and found that, although many Codas were highly protective of their parents and reluctant to share family stories, they were willing to share important personal information with another Coda. The interviews with Italian Codas were used only to collect background information, and identifying details were not included in the data analysis. The participant was given a list of the interview questions in Italian, questions that covered the number of siblings, parents' educational level, language usage in the home, relationships with extended family, whether there were other deaf family members, whether the hearing children interpreted for their parents, and so forth.

Group I

The first group was comprised of five people (three women and two men, mean age thirty-two) who grew up together in a small town. Written permission was given to the researchers to videotape and to use both personal information and/or videoclips for publication or presentations. All participants had two deaf parents; these parents all knew one another as children from school (although they sometimes attended during different years) as well as through deaf associations and social events. Four out of five of these Coda participants had been brought up attending the

TABLE 1. *Participant Backgrounds for Both Groups*

Participant	Sex	Age	Deaf Parents	Siblings	Profession
S-1	F	39	M F both	Hearing	Teacher/Interpreter
S-2	F	34	Hearing	Interpreter	
S-3	F	30	M F both	Only child	Interpreter
S-4	M	29	M F both	Deaf sibling	Bank
S-5	M	36	M F both	Hearing	Bank
S-6	F	20	Father	Hearing	Student
S-7	F	46	Father	Hearing	Interpreter/Teacher
S-8	F	55	M F both	Hearing	Finance/Interpreter
S-9	M	30	M F both	Only child	Interpreter
S-10	F	29	M F both	Deaf siblings	Interpreter

same deaf functions as their parents, allowing them to meet other hearing children (Kodas or *Kids of deaf adults*). Three participants were working principally with the Deaf community as interpreters and teachers, one worked part-time as an interpreter and full-time outside the Deaf community in a bank, and one did not work in any way with the Deaf community but rather worked in a bank as well. Only one participant had a deaf sibling, making him the only hearing person in his family. One was an only child and the other three had hearing siblings. Because of the small town atmosphere and the even smaller Deaf community within that town, they had all grown up knowing one another and one another's families (see table 1).

Group 2

The second group also consisted of five people (one man and four women, mean age thirty-eight) from a much larger city. The man and three of the women were interpreters and knew one another through work. One woman was a full-time student and did not work. Of these five, one had deaf siblings, three had hearing siblings, and one was an only child (similar to the first group). All the fathers were deaf. Three mothers were deaf and two were hearing. The age range was much wider in this group (from twenty to fifty-five), covering two, possibly three generations. The student met the other four interpreters for the first time on the day of the videotaping. Although the interpreters worked together, there was no indication that they either socialized outside of work or grew up together. There was also no mention of whether or not their parents knew one another or had gone to school together. Of note in both groups is the high number of participants who work with the Deaf community, mostly as interpreters. It raises the question of whether the demands of interpreting might change the relationship one has to both languages and what effect that relationship has on how the languages are used. For future research, it would be interesting to compare the bimodal bilingualism of those Codas heavily involved with the Deaf community (especially if one's spouse is Deaf) with those whose daily lives do not include working or socializing with, or interpreting for, Deaf people.

Data

In the ninety minutes of discussion, the participants talked about their experiences growing up and the challenges they faced. They sometimes referred back to the one-on-one interview questions, for example, questions that asked whether they would rather have a deaf or a hearing child or to what degree they had to interpret for their parents. Several times, participants described mediating between parents and the outside hearing world at a very young age. One participant described having to buy a girdle for her mom but the pronunciation her mom used for that item was in reality a combination of two different words in Italian, *bustino* (corselet) and *panciera* (girdle). The mother instructed her daughter to ask for a *bacino*.[11] The daughter was unable to make anyone understand and recalled feeling terribly embarrassed. Other stories described interpreting parent-teacher meetings for a sibling and changing the bad news to protect that sibling. These kinds of narratives elicited laughter and affirmations that these events were familiar to the others. Yet, some topics were more serious, dealing with the burden of interpreting (often falling on the female child regardless of age), and how the participants do not feel like other hearing people. In spite of feeling this difference, the idea of creating an organization such as CODA in Italy seemed foreign and unnecessary (eliciting responses such as "What's there to talk about?" "What for?"). There was also discussion about rebellious behavior against one's parents. One participant recounted that from the age of fifteen until the age of twenty-one, he refused to sign with his parents, and they accepted his decision and communicated orally. Ironically, this participant is currently a full-time interpreter and well respected for his signing and interpreting skills.

Some commonalities in the two groups were related to refusing to do certain interpreting jobs (often occurring when teenagers) such as making phone calls for their parents or interpreting appointments and other interactions with hearing people. Other stories described taking advantage of being in the interpreter role by manipulating the interaction to achieve a desired outcome.

In general, the second group discussed less personal topics, possibly attributable to the presence of a new person and the co-worker relationships among the other four interpreters. This group spent more time asking the new person questions and exchanging background information with one another, effectively keeping the overall tone of their discussion more superficial than the first group. Both discussions lasted approximately an hour and a half and provided many instances of code switches, code blends, and other features that indicate influence from signed language (i.e., directing verbs and pronouns meaningfully in space as described earlier).

The data from the group sessions were reviewed to identify code-blending and codeswitching examples based on cases in which the speaker-signer alternated between Italian and LIS either (a) within the same speech event or (b) within a single turn or when the speaker-signer mixed elements from the two codes within the same utterance (Winford 2003). In addition, the researchers identified examples of signed language influence on spoken utterances, including some taken from prior research, and used these examples to "flag" similar occurrences in the data (Emmorey, Borinstein, and Thompson 2003; Preston 1994; Bishop and Hicks 2005). Table 2 shows a partial list of these examples.

The grammatical category of each code switch and code blend was also determined. The bimodal utterance was transcribed using a notation system that is standard in signed language studies for differentiating between signed and spoken speech. Signed utterances are written in small capital letters (glossing) and spoken utterances in lowercase. Because the data are in LIS and Italian, translations of the transcriptions are provided in ASL and English (however, the participants did not use English or ASL at any time). Simultaneous signed and spoken utterances follow the same transcription method but are written with the spoken utterance over the signed one. Analyzing only a relatively small number of salient features of bimodal discourse allowed the researchers to consider all the data without having to provide a complete transcription for each participant.

TABLE 2. *Partial List of Bimodal Discourse Features Pre-Data Collection*

1. Missing copula	Father very sick, hospital, heart (Preston 1994)
2. Missing subject	Not ask questions
3. Missing determiners	Me sit by phone
4. Missing auxiliaries	I not know how
5. Atypical verb inflections	So I am think
6. Novel lexicon	Me 'F' to chin (speaking the description of how the ASL sign for 'expert" is formed
7. Code blend sites (i.e. on verb)	The cat jumped JUMP
9. Semantic non-equivalency	He's like hmm [all of a sudden] Ack! LOOK-AT-ME (Emmorey et al.ibid)

RESULTS AND ANALYSIS

For the entire conversation, in both groups, spoken Italian was the dominant language. When the participants in both groups were talking before the session officially began, they asked the facilitator (who was also one of the participants) whether they were expected to speak or sign. In both groups, the facilitator did as instructed and told the group that the researchers wanted them to communicate in whatever way they were comfortable. From the two groups, a total of 178 bimodal utterances were documented (both sequential and simultaneous). These utterances fell into three categories: "code-blends," "code switches," and "other" (this last category consisted of idiomatic expressions and LIS-influenced spoken utterances). Figure 1 shows that, of the 178 bimodal utterances, 57 percent were blends (simultaneously spoken and signed) 36 percent were switches (sequentially spoken and signed), and 7 percent were other (LIS-influenced speech).

Grammatical Categories

The syntactic aspects of code blends and code switches were examined to determine the grammatical category and revealed a slightly higher frequency in code-blended verbs than code-blended nouns (34 percent compared with 33 percent). (Fig. 2.) The margin was larger between codeswitched verbs and codeswitched nouns (45 percent compared to

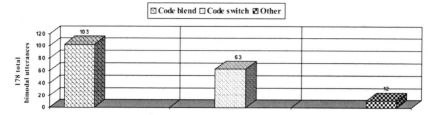

FIGURE 1. *Comparison of frequency of code-blends versus code-switches*

30 percent). This finding contrasts with spoken language bilingualism in which nouns are more frequently code-switched than verbs (Muysken 2000). Nouns, as opposed to verbs in many spoken languages, are not encumbered by complicated morphology and they often appear with higher frequency than verbs, making a one-to-one nominal switch comparatively easy and potentially more frequent.

The finding that verbs are more readily switched or blended in bimodal utterances is not so unexpected. Emmorey, Borinstein, and Thompson (2003) point out that an ASL verb (e.g., JUMP) can contribute additional information such as the manner in which the action happened (speed, height, direction). This capability makes a bimodal utterance an attractive option compared with simply speaking without signing. They also explain that verb tense inflections in the spoken utterance can be maintained while simultaneously incorporating a signed verb that is not inflected for tense or person morphologically. For example, in example 1 (shown in the next section), the spoken verb is inflected for both the past tense and the first person singular in Italian (*ho capito*) whereas the LIS verb does not inflect for tense morphologically but relies instead on a temporal adverb. The requirement to use a temporal adverb to mark tense is nullified when tense is simultaneously carried by the spoken utterance.

Code Switches

The following section provides a description of the different kinds of code switches found in the data. The base language in both groups was spoken Italian with rather frequent switches into LIS. In some instances, the reason for the switch was rather obvious and therefore was not included in the data analysis, for example, switching to signing when one's mouth is full of food (not included here).

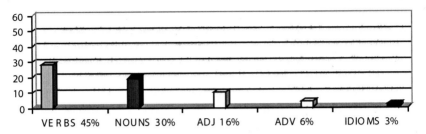

FIGURE 2: *Grammatical categories for code-switches*

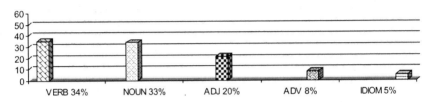

FIGURE 3: *Grammatical categories for code-blends*

Cases of switching that occurred in an effort to keep a communication private were also noted. In example 1, the researchers are busy collecting papers and getting ready to leave the room before starting the session, and a participant switches from speaking to signing to double-check with other group members whether the researchers understood what the participants had just been discussing. The response from another participant is completely in LIS.[12]

(1)   A: *Qui l'unica 'single'*[13] *sono io* ....VERO, NON CAPISCONO. HANNO CAPITO?
Translation: I am the only single one here.... THEY DON'T UNDERSTAND, RIGHT? DO THEY UNDERSTAND?

        B: NON CREDO NO
Translation: I DON'T THINK SO

The following are examples of intrasentential code switches that illustrate the notion that switches can, and often do, express a particular idea better (Zentella 1997). In example 2, the participant is summing up the trials and tribulations of childhood by saying that it is hard to define everything in terms of positive and negative experiences, that it is really one and the same thing. Quite likely, LIS expressed the idea more to her satisfaction than the spoken equivalent. The translation from LIS to Italian proved to be quite challenging, and ultimately, we were hard-pressed to find a satisfying equivalent as evidenced by the awkwardness of the translation.

(2)   *Non esistono lati positivi o negativi, è lo stesso* ELENCO
        There are no positive or negative sides; it's all the same AGENDA.

In example 3, the participant completes her spoken utterance by demonstrating in LIS how several people turned to look at her when she stopped talking mid-sentence. (This example is a surrogate blend as defined by Liddell [2003] and will be discussed in the section titled "Data.")

(3)   *Come dico una mezza parola,* TUTTI-MI-GUARDONO
        Since I stopped midway, THEY-ALL-LOOKED-AT-ME.

When speaking, the participants often preferred to refer to LIS itself by codeswitching to the sign GESTI instead of saying *LIS* or *Lingua dei Segni*. In example 4, GESTI refers to the language of the Deaf community and does not intend to convey that it is gesture as opposed to a full, natural signed language. However, in example 5, the meaning of GESTI is literally "gesture" and refers to the fact that the researcher and the interviewee had to resort to using some gesture during the background interview to understand each other.

(4)   *Gliel'ho spiegato ai* GESTI.
        I explained it to them in SIGN.

(5)   *Ci scappa l'intervista a* GESTI.
        We managed to get through the interview by GESTURE.

In the majority of intrasentential code switches, a sign was inserted in a spoken utterance. However, we also found signs appearing first, followed by the same word in Italian, perhaps suggesting that the lexical item had been accessed first in LIS. In figure 4, the participant signed DARKNESS and followed that with the spoken word *dark*. Figure 4 shows the participant expressing example 6.

(6)   *Mio padre non poteva parlarci perchè,* BUIO, *c'era il buio totale.*
        My father couldn't talk to us because, DARK, it was completely dark.

FIGURE 4. *Illustration of (6), intrasentential code-switch from Italian to LIS*

This insertion of LIS may have two possible motivations, both or either of which may be the case: (a) to emphasize the main point of the story (the darkness prohibited the use of signed communication — the reason for the narrative) and (b) to intensify through repetition in two different modalities. Analysis of bimodal narrative structure may reveal that switching between modalities adds an extra sensory stimulation by allowing the other participants to see and then to hear (or vice versa) a key element of the story. It is precisely in these particular key narrative segments that many examples of code switches and code blends occur, making the analysis of bimodal narrative structure an essential next step.

In example 7, the participant signs CURIOUS and then adds the subject and verb in Italian. The spoken utterance in isolation would not make any sense, but the combination of signed and spoken information completes the communication.

(7)   CURIOSE *perchè siamo*
       CURIOUS because we are

In example 8, the participant uses a sign name but, because a newcomer was in the group, adds the spoken name to clarify that person's identity, a nod to Deaf cultural norms in which a sign name is further clarified when necessary. In Deaf culture, a person would normally fingerspell the full name, provide identifying information about that person, or both.

(8)   *I figli di* SIGN NAME, *Giancarlo*
       The children of SIGN NAME, Giancarlo

The participants also used intersentential code switches not only between turns (see example 9) but also contained within one person's turn (see example 10), labeled by Poplack (1980) as "tag-switching" because the majority of the utterance is in one language:

(9)   A: *Ma parliamo o segniamo?*
       B: MI SCOCCIO, COSA VUOI?

A: But are we speaking or signing?

B: I'M ANNOYED, WHAT DO YOU WANT FROM ME?

(10)   *Siamo anche interpreti* ... LO SAI
        We are also interpreters ... YOU KNOW

The abovementioned examples of code switches provide evidence that bimodal bilinguals exercise their ability to switch between their two languages as a natural part of their expression, and they do so for a variety of reasons, as preliminarily described above. The data suggest that bimodality itself does not cause codeswitching phenomena to differ greatly from that determined for spoken language (Myers-Scotton 1993a). What sets bimodal bilingualism apart is that it offers *options* to either codeswitch or code-blend, however, motivations for choosing one over the other are as of yet unexplored. Of particular interest is the dual sensory aspect of bimodal bilingualism. Does being able to both see and hear an utterance affect discourse structure? How does a bimodal bilingual capitalize on this simultaneous expressive capability?

Code-Blending

Code-blending, also known as code-mixing in the literature, describes simultaneous speech and sign production. Bimodal output when two languages are structurally very different (for a review on the structure of ASL, see Emmorey 2002; Liddell 2003) offers linguists the opportunity to analyze discourse phenomena that are impossible in spoken language bilingualism (one cannot speak Japanese and Arabic simultaneously). In this study, each occurrence of simultaneous speech and sign output was transcribed and analyzed on both a semantic and structural level. Examples that follow illustrate blending on verbs (example 11) and on nouns (example 12). Brackets indicate the spoken word co-occurring with the sign. English translations are provided immediately below the examples.

(11)   *Io l'ho [capito] bene*
        CAPITO
        I [understood] it well.
        UNDERSTAND

(12)   *non é un [problema]*
        PROBLEMA
        It's not a [problem]
        PROBLEM

In the majority of the code blends, as illustrated in examples 11 and 12, the signed and spoken utterances present semantically equivalent information. Of the 103 code blends analyzed in this study, all but five were equivalent in meaning to the spoken Italian word or words. A semantically nonequivalent code blend is illustrated in example 13 below. This code blend occurred when the speaker was describing an accident and the resulting bruises on his face. The arrows indicate that the spoken and signed utterances were temporally aligned. Figure 5 shows the participant signing the location of the bruises while simultaneously speaking. The verb and its morphological inflection for tense and person is carried by the spoken utterance while the location is indicated through sign (similar to findings in Emmorey, Borinstein, and Thompson 2003).

(13)   [*Ero viola*] → (arrows indicate the spoken and signed utterances were
       TUTTA-LA-FACCIA   temporally aligned)

       [I was purple]
       (MY) ENTIRE-FACE

In example 14, the signed utterance includes both the topic (40 EURO) and the verb (GIVE-ME) but the spoken utterance includes only the topic.

(14)   [*quaranta euro*] ⟶
       40 EURO   DAMMI

       [forty euros] ⟶
       40 EURO   GIVE-ME

In example 15, the participant's spoken utterance, "a cute low," is incomplete, but the co-occurrence of the LIS sign HEEL provides a complete, comprehensible bimodal utterance.

(15)   *un bel* [*bassi*]
       TACCHI
       a cute [low]
       HEEL

In examples 13 to 15, the speaker takes advantage of being able to express different but complementary information in each modality. Klima and Bellugi (1979) explain that manual articulation as a rule is slower than oral articulation, saying "Grosjean (1977) has studied the rate of signing and speaking in memorized narratives and reports results comparable to ours, namely, that the mean duration of signs is twice the duration

FIGURE 5. *Illustration of (13), semantically non-equivalent code-blend of LIS and Italian*

of words" (185). The difference in time to produce a signed and spoken utterance requires phonological changes in either the spoken or the signed utterance when they are produced simultaneously. The tight temporal correspondence between the spoken and signed utterances in examples 13 to 15 suggests that the utterance is conceptualized as a single unit. More detailed phonological work is required to understand how simultaneity affects production of the sign and the speech signal. The data, however, raise critical questions about why this kind of communicative and expressive efficiency is relatively rare — 6 percent in Emmorey, Borinstein, and Thompson (2003) and roughly 4 percent in this study. Code-blending of this nature seems to be rather expedient, supporting a prediction for a higher rather than a lower frequency of use. Are the cognitive demands too great in producing nonequivalent code blends?

Sign Influence on Spoken Utterances

In his book, MOTHER FATHER DEAF, Preston (1994) writes of one Coda's traumatic experience when her deaf father was hospitalized far from home in another state. In retelling the story to other Codas, "the carefully crafted balance of shifting between two worlds crumbled under the strain of her father's illness and the different patterns of response from the Deaf and Hearing worlds" (222). The story, spoken and signed in the original and later transcribed, shows the natural code-blending of a bimodal bilingual and was labeled as the beginning of Coda-talk by the Coda community. Many ASL features are present in Coda-talk such as verb reduplication (*ask ask ask*), verb stringing (*We sit down, discuss, group-together*), copula omission (*Father very sick*), subject omission (*Not ask questions*), and so forth. This spoken "style" is quite similar to the written style found in Coda e-mails analyzed in Bishop and Hicks (2005). In that study, 275 lines from 100 e-mails were analyzed to determine grammatical structure. The study revealed evidence of ASL grammatical influence on the writing. Some examples of syntactic calquing included the frequent absence of the following: overt subjects, overt objects, determiners, copulas, and prepositions as well as unique structures such as nonstandard verb inflections, overgeneralization of 's' on verbs, and innovative verb manipulation (irregular infinitives and inflections). Emmorey, Borinstein, and Thompson (2003, 668) also found one Coda's narrative of a Tweety and Sylvester cartoon episode was spoken almost entirely in Coda-talk:

a.   "[An] [old] [woman] [seem] [her] [bird] [she] [protect]."
       A-N OLD WOMAN SEEM POSS BIRD. PRO PROTECT[14]

This example is a word-for-sign translation of grammatical ASL. The ASL phrases could be translated into English as "There's this old woman, and it seems it's her bird. She protects it." Emmorey, Borinstein, and Thompson observe that "for this participant, it may be that ASL was actually the base language of production, not English" (2003, 6). The data in this study also revealed code-blended utterances that effectively rearranged the spoken utterance to fit LIS grammatical requirements. In other words, only the signed utterance is grammatically correct whereas the spoken utterance is missing key grammatical elements for Italian (missing words in Italian are indicated between parentheses). In example 16, the participant is talking about helping her father to exhibit his paintings in various art shows.

(16)   *[con papa] (lo) [accompagno] (per) [fare] (le) [mostre]. [Ama fare] (le) [mostre insieme]*
       CON PAPÀ ACCOMPAGNO FARE MOSTRE. AMA FARE MOSTRE INSIEME

       (ai) [sordi] (per) [parlare], [sapere nuovo], [io insieme] (ai) [sordi] ci sto.
       SORDI PARLARE SAPERE NUOVO, IO INSIEME SORDI

       Translation:
       [with] [dad] [I go] [put on art exhibit]. [He loves] [to exhibit] [together] [deaf]
       WITH DAD GO SHOW ART. HE LOVE SHOW ART TOGETHER DEAF

       [talk] [know] [new] … [I] [together] [deaf], [I'm there].
       TALK   KNOW NEW…PRO-1 TOGETHER DEAF AM

In example 16, it is clear that the base language of production is LIS and the grammatical requirements for the spoken utterances in Italian have been "loosened" to some degree.

In examples 17 and 18, the copula is missing in the spoken utterance, creating a grammatically correct utterance in LIS but not in Italian.

(17)   [Io], quando (ero) [piccola]
       PRO-1 PICCOLA

       [I], when (I was) [small]
       PRO-1 SMALL

(18)   [Tu] (sei) [separata], [tu] (sei) [separata]?
       PRO SEPARATA PRO SEPARATA

       You (are) separated.... you (are) separated?
       PRO SEPARATED... PRO SEPARATED?

In examples 16 to 18, the evidence suggests that the base language of production is LIS, even though the person is speaking, which supports similar findings in Emmorey, Borinstein, and Thompson (2003) for American Codas and illustrates another communicative option for bimodal bilinguals — to speak their signed language. This finding raises the question of what happens when the signed language is the matrix language and the spoken language is the embedded language. Will models such as Myers-Scotton's Matrix Language Frame model (2002) still apply?

In example 19, the reduplicated verb CHIEDE in LIS prompts a spoken repetition of the Italian chiede (asks). Figure 6 shows the participant in this instance.

(19)   chiede, chiede chiede
       CHIEDE CHIEDE CHIEDE

Another LIS influence on spoken utterances is the example of FATTO, the equivalent to ASL FINISH. This sign has multiple meanings in both LIS and ASL, some of which are "already," "done," or "finished" (for further description of the distinct meanings of FINISH in ASL, see Baker-Shenk and Cokely 1980; Fischer and Gough 1999). In context, the sign is often used in asking whether someone has finished a particular action, for example, EAT FINISH? (Have you already eaten?). The corresponding response is often FINISH (Yes, or Yes, I have already eaten). In example 20,

FIGURE 6. *Illustration of (19), the reduplicated LIS verb* CHIEDE *(asks) triggers a repetition in Italian*

the participant on the right (see figure 7, which shows the participants) both speak and sign FATTO (referring to an undetermined topic under discussion). The participant on the left jokingly interrupts and code-blends back, pretending to have heard and understood that the session was finished. The translation of his response would be, "You mean the session is over? We're done?"

(20)   FATTO? FATTO?
       FINISHED? FINISHED?

The meaning and the discourse features of the spoken lexical item 'FATTO' appear to be derived from LIS in this example and would not necessarily be comprehensible to a native monolingual in Italian, suggesting that bimodal bilinguals have the option of "speaking signed language" to one another.

Idiomatic Expressions

Utterances that fell outside the categories of code-blended verbs, nouns, adjectives, and adverbs were very few in number and were idiomatic expressions. In example 21, the expression is code-blended, maintaining grammatically correct Italian and LIS.

(21)   [DATTI] UNA [CALMATA]
       TAKE TRANQUILIZER

Translation: Take a chill pill or calm down.

Further research is necessary to determine whether these simultaneous bimodal utterances indicate that the spoken and the signed utterances are a conceptually cohesive unit. It is also important to question whether or not there are subtle differences in meaning between the signed and

FIGURE 7. *Illustration of (20), code-blended utterance of* FATTO *(finish)*

spoken utterances that, though appearing to be semantically equivalent, may not be. In other words, a bimodal bilingual may be blending because the visual nature of the lexical item offers semantic nuances not available from spoken utterances alone — not only necessarily code-blending on verbs as Emmorey, Borinstein, and Thompson (2003) discussed in their data but also, for example, on nouns. These differences may motivate the bilingual to code-blend, thus adding a fuller meaning to the overall utterance than could be attained through one modality alone.

Real Space

To understand certain features of bimodal discourse, one must first have a basic understanding of the concept of real space. We will use the example of a first-time visitor inquiring about the location of the Linguistics Department on the Gallaudet campus to illustrate a real-space blend. By speaking English and positioning a stapler, a tape dispenser, and a ruler, one can illustrate the location of the department in relation to other campus landmarks. Each object is identified as representing the Linguistics Department, the guardhouse, and the front entrance, respectively. In real space, the stapler, tape dispenser, and ruler remain exactly what they are — a stapler, tape dispenser, and a ruler — but in a real-space blend, they become the Linguistics Department, the guardhouse, and the front entrance to the university. The elements in the blends can now be referred to as 'the Linguistics Department', 'the guardhouse', or 'the front gate'. Additional details could be added by placing a coin by the tape dispenser (the guardhouse) to represent the 'guard' and then have the 'guard' walk over to the 'Linguistics Department' by moving the coin toward the stapler. The 'Linguistic Department blend' will remain activated for as long as one refers to it while speaking (see Liddell [2003] for further explanation of real-space blends). In this study, we will show how real-space blends are useful in explaining why a bimodal bilingual is directing isolated signs toward a particular location or referent while speaking. As described earlier in this article, this meaningful use of space is an important feature of both ASL and LIS.

The following examples are taken from a short narrative that illustrates various points discussed so far (see appendix A for the full story in the original Italian followed by an English translation). It should be noted that the participants in this particular group also switched back and forth quite liberally between Italian and their own particular dialect, adding a dimension of complexity to their language usage unlikely to have come from their deaf parents but instead results from the fact that Codas are hearing. This then becomes a major part of their linguistic identity that they share with the hearing world and not with the Deaf world and merits examination in future research for Codas throughout the world.[15] The participant describes the night a woman called to discuss paperwork related to the sale of a car to the participant's father. The electricity had just gone out moments before the phone call because of a rainstorm. Because it was so dark, the daughter could not see her father signing and was unable to communicate with him. She could not get this point across to the hearing woman on the phone nor could she interpret to her father what the woman was saying to him. In telling the story, the participant had already created a real-space blend in which her 'father' was located on her right and the 'caller' on her left by simply gesturing toward the right every time she mentioned her father and toward the left when referring to the caller. As the participant narrates, she establishes an overall blend of a 'phone call' so all referents during the narrative can be conceptualized under this one main blend. In example 22, the participant narrates how her father was trying to get her attention. Her left hand taps her right shoulder, an action that is understood to mean that the 'hand' belongs to her father. This element is labeled a "partial surrogate blend" because the signer is partially projected onto the blend (Liddell 2003). The insertion of this new element ('the father's hand') does not deactivate the entire 'phone call' blend but, rather, allows for the addition of more details while the overall blend is still activated.

This aspect of ASL has also been described as "partitionable zones" (Dudis 2000). These zones refer to the body subparts that can participate in mappings that create real-space blends. The signer in example 22 maps her 'father's hand' onto the partitionable manual articulator, which creates a visible 'hand' that taps on her shoulder (see figure 8).

(22)   *Mio padre continuava* [CHIAMARE,] *continuava a parlare ...*
       TAP TAP TAP

       My dad kept [CALLING-ME], he kept on talking ...
       TAP TAP TAP

Example 23 shows clear evidence of an established token blend when the participant directs her sign EXPLAIN toward the area on her left that represents the caller. In example 23, the entire spoken utterance is *"spiegare io come"* ("explain I how"). In example 23a, she repeats the sign SPIEGARE (EXPLAIN) while saying *"come"* ("how"). This semantic nonequivalency is buttressed by simultaneous linguistic and conceptual events: the overall activated 'phone call' blend, the sign (SPIEGARE) directed toward the token (the designated area in signing space that corresponds to the referent), and the semantically distinct but complementary spoken utterance *come*. This combination allows the other participants to understand the full, intended information, "How do I (as the 8-year-old) EXPLAIN (to the woman caller)." Figure 9 shows the participant expressing what is shown in example 23 and 23a.

(23)   [*spiegare*] *anche* [*io*]   (23a) [*come*] ?
       SPIEGARE   PRO-*1*   SPIEGARE?

       [explain] also I [how]?
       EXPLAIN PRO-1   EXPLAIN?

The same participant tells another story about a second phone mishap. She takes advantage of the already activated 'phone call' blend and identifies the new caller (a travel agent) by indicating the area off to her left (bolded words in example 24 refer to this area). The continuous activation of the 'phone call' blend requires identifying only the new character who is set up in the same 'caller' area (see figure 10).

(24)   **Lui** *parlava di* brochure *e mio* **padre** *di* depliant
       He was talking about a *brochure* and my **father** about *depliant*

The travel agent is calling to speak to her father about a brochure. The caller uses the word *brochure* but the daughter knows only the word *depliant*. Both words have the same meaning in Italian but have only one

FIGURE 8. *Illustration of (22), surrogate hand (father's hand) tapping daughter's shoulder*

corresponding sign in LIS. The young daughter (7–8 years old) does not realize these two words refer to the same object.

In example 25, the participant is commenting that both the travel agent and her father were talking about the same thing. In contrast to the previous code blends in which the sign and the spoken word (or words) were produced simultaneously, the sign SAME in example 25 was stretched out over the entire spoken utterance (see figure 11), appearing to have more of a co-speech function than a linguistic one (McNeill 2000).

(25)   [*Parlavano della stessa cosa*]
        STESSA   ⎯⎯⎯⎯⎯⟶

        [They were talking about the same thing]
        SAME   ⎯⎯⎯⎯⎯⎯⎯⎯⟶

The prolonged production of the single LIS sign to temporally correspond to an entire spoken utterance suggests the linguistic constraints on the structure of the sign have been "loosened" to some degree. This signed addition to the spoken modality may also add marked evaluative force to the narrative with the purpose of highlighting the main point of the story (that she had not realized both words meant the same thing). Further research into the differences and the boundaries between co-speech gesture and code-blended utterances are necessary to help define the line between the two.

Depicting Verbs

Code-blending (and codeswitching) may also contribute evaluative force to the narration because it deviates from spoken discourse and adds markedness to a particular theme or point. In example 26, the participant uses a LIS depicting verb in her narration; Liddell (2003) defines depict-

FIGURE 9. *Illustration of (23) and (23a), showing the activated 'phone call' blend and the verb* SPIEGARE (EXPLAIN) *moving towards the token blend or caller.*

ing verbs as those that encode "meanings having to do with actions and states" (261). As the participant speaks, she shows a drop of fluid falling (see figure 12):

(26)　　[*Cadeva una goccia giù*]

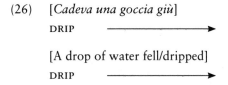

[A drop of water fell/dripped]

DRIP ⎯⎯⎯⎯⎯⎯⎯⎯→

In this example, the participant is creating a "depicting blend" by means of a projection from real space and the event space being discussed. These depicting blends differ conceptually from token blends because the latter have no clear spatial form nor are they placed in a topographical setting (their 'location' in space is not linked to the notion of spatial relationships). Depicting verbs, however, do have both a spatial form and a topographical setting, illustrated by the hand representing both the drop of fluid and the trajectory of the drip.

List Buoys

Another feature of ASL and LIS is the use of list buoys, which involve using the fingers of the nondominant signing hand[16] to serve as conceptual landmarks for enumerating items being discussed. Liddell (2003) labels these elements "buoys" because these signs maintain a physical presence as the discourse continues. Buoys use the signed numbers ONE to FIVE but are differentiated from the corresponding numeral signs because numeral signs are normally produced on the dominant signing hand, generally in front of the shoulder, and with the fingertips oriented upwards. Buoys are produced on the nondominant hand, generally ahead of the chest, and with

FIGURE 10. *Illustration of (24),
indicating token blends to the left and
right in the space ahead of the signer
(left =travel agent, right = father)*

FIGURE 11. *Illustration of (25), showing the duration of the LIS sign same
during the entire spoken utterance*

the fingertips oriented to the side. Example 27 (see also figure 13), taken
from the data, illustrates the concept.[17] The participant is talking about the
different kinds of feelings she experienced as a child and lifts her left hand
into buoy position. She begins listing on her left thumb ("1:"), then her
index ("2:") and last, her middle finger ("3:"). Each time she lists an emotion, she touches the respective finger with her right or dominant hand.

(27)

1: *la angoscia*	2: *l' ansia*	3: *il nervosismo*
anguish	anxiety	nervousness

The other four examples of listing were produced in a similar fashion
and provided evidence to suggest that LIS discourse tools are active during spoken language conversation. In all five cases, the buoys appeared
very briefly, deviating from their extended presence in signed-only discourse. During signing, buoys are often held stationary in signing space
and referred back to over a relatively long stretch of discourse. In cases in
which the buoys are dropped (the left hand is needed to produce signs),

FIGURE I2. *Illustration of (26) code-blended depicting verb* DRIP.

they will often reappear, maintaining the relationship between the particular digit and the conceptual link. However, in this bimodal discourse, the listing buoys serve to emphasize the number of emotions and, because they are not needed for elaboration of those feelings and are not referred back to in later discourse, they are dropped relatively quickly. The location of the hands in these five listing situations was often lower than the higher, more prominent position used for fully signed discourse, and the movements were less enunciated, suggesting that the signed modality is secondary to the spoken output.

SUMMARY

Our data indicate that bimodal bilinguals have their two languages "activated" in naturalistic discourse and exploit the resources of both languages in a variety of ways. Codas prefer to code-blend rather than to codeswitch, a finding that is consistent with that of Emmorey, Borinstein, and Thompson (2003). In both studies, Codas used a larger proportion of code blends for verbs: equal to the proportion used for nouns in this study and surpassing nouns in Emmorey, Borinstein, and Thompson (2003). This finding could possibly be attributed to the different kinds of data analyzed — naturalistic conversation as opposed to elicited narratives based on a Sylvester and Tweety cartoon. The action-packed cartoon may have prompted a higher number of verbs in the recounting than what might naturally appear in a conversation.

Emmorey, Borinstein, and Thompson (2003) also videotaped Codas conversing with one another for fifteen minutes about topics related to Coda experiences. Similar to this Italian study, the participants were asked to discuss deaf-related topics, childhood, and Coda identity to promote

FIGURE 13. *Illustration of (27), showing the use of list buoys during spoken discourse.*

a bilingual frame of mind. It would be interesting to see how the analysis of naturalistic conversation in their study compares with this one. Both studies indicated that the majority of code blends are semantically equivalent and that semantically nonequivalent code blends are relatively rare. In those cases of nonequivalency, locative or spatial information was given manually while morphologically complex verbs were spoken, combining to provide a conceptually complete bimodal utterance. Although these occurrences were relatively rare in both studies, they are intriguing to contemplate. Why are they so infrequent? Is the cognitive load too demanding?

Among the bimodal phenomena that we expected to find (codeswitching, code-blending, and LIS-influenced speech), we also found that the participants used token and surrogate blends, list buoys, and depicting verbs. That these phenomena were present in the data is not at all surprising because similar phenomena have been observed in co-speech gesture among spoken language users (Duncan 2003; Kendon 2004; McNeill 1992). However, the major difference rests in the fact that Codas are not gesturing during code-blended discourse but, rather, are using LIS verbs and pronouns directed toward token and surrogate blends during predominantly spoken discourse. When full utterances were code-blended, LIS grammatical requirements sometimes prevailed and caused grammatical shifts in the spoken utterance, perhaps indicating that the spoken utterance was secondary to the signed one. Often, these spoken utterances were missing prepositions, conjunctions, and copulas, supporting the conclusion in Emmorey, Borinstein, and Thompson (2003) that signed language was actually the base of production in those cases.

Another LIS influence was the reduplication in signed verbs that triggered spoken verb repetition (as in example 19). Some spoken LIS lexical items maintained their LIS meaning and discourse function even though the item was not only spoken but also signed (as in example 20). In some code-blended utterances, a single sign was "stretched" to temporally align with a fully spoken utterance, causing certain phonological changes in the sign. This occurrence may indicate that the signed output is secondary to the spoken output (a co-speech gesture).

A discussion of real space as defined by Liddell (2003) provided a theoretical framework by which to analyze the use of space in code-blended utterances. Data show that bimodal discourse includes the directing of verbs and pronouns toward referents conceptualized in signing space. Because of ever-present real-space blends, both surrogate and token blends were actively used in ways that parallel fully signed discourse, even when the discourse is predominantly spoken. Indispensable to signed language discourse, tokens, surrogates, depicting verbs, and list buoys form part of the bimodal bilinguals' linguistic repertoire and are activated whether signing or speaking. We argue, based on these findings, that the definition of *code-blending* must be expanded to include the presence of systematic and conventionalized real-space blends as are found in fluent deaf signers. Code-blending can also be defined as including utterances that have either Italian or LIS as the base of production (already described in Emmorey, Borinstein, and Thompson 2003) as well as utterances that challenge the base language issue (opposing Myers-Scotton 1993b) and provide evidence that the varieties which interact within codeswitching are non-discrete (Gardner-Chloros 1995).

CONCLUSION

Observations of the group discussions among Italian Codas indicated that the discourse phenomena described therein were unmarked choices for the participants (defined as a "strategy of neutrality" by Myers-Scotton 1993b, 147). Bimodal bilinguals use the features of both their languages in many ways that illustrate their native fluency as well as shared cultural and linguistic background. Being with other Codas, whether in Italy or another country, promotes a bimodal frame of mind, especially when sharing experiences of childhood and family. Conversation among Codas allowed the researchers to see the unique outcomes of using two languages in distinct modalities, and their personal stories provided insights into the complexities of Coda identity.

The initial motivation behind researching outside the United States was to determine whether examples of Coda-talk similar to those found in Bishop and Hicks (2005) and Emmorey, Borinstein, and Thompson (2003) would be duplicated in a country where no CODA organization or "third, Coda identity" was formally established. The findings of this study overlapped substantially with Emmorey, Borinstein, and Thompson (2003), especially with respect to a preference for code-blending, a higher frequency of code-blended verbs as opposed to nouns, and examples of spoken utterances in which signed language was the base language of production. However, equivalent cases of Coda-talk (described in Bishop and Hicks 2005) such as language play (i.e., deliberate mistakes in fingerspelling), description of LIS signs (similar to the example, *My father fork-in-throat,* described earlier), and use of deaf voice were not found in the Italian data. The data did confirm that Italian Codas blend their two languages in a variety of ways similar to those of American Codas; however, conscious, overt language play was minimal (see example 20 for one possible exception). Our findings lead us to hypothesize further (a) that a more developed Coda identity and participation in more formalized Coda gatherings has greatly encouraged the development of Coda-talk in the United States[18] and in other countries that participate in CODA and (b) that Coda-talk is a linguistic outcome of a Coda's deaf-hearing identity.[19] Italy has provided an opportunity to see natural bimodal discourse phenomena that are perhaps more representative of bimodal bilinguals around the world in places where CODA has not yet been established.

This preliminary research has been mainly descriptive in nature and had as its main goal the documentation of different bimodal linguistic phenomena in adult bimodal bilinguals. The study has raised many possibilities for future research. As of this writing, a dissertation on naturalistic discourse among American Codas has been published (Bishop 2006). Of particular interest is the critical question of the differences between code-blending and co-speech gesture in bimodal bilinguals. Results from the Italian data indicate that some cases of bimodal utterances are linguistic and not gestural, as shown pronouns being properly directed in space toward surrogate and token blends.

Adult Codas are an underrepresented group in bilingual studies. To better understand this group's "third identity," researchers need to explore the sociolinguistic functions that code-blending has for this community and the role those functions play in the development of a Coda identity. Specifically, further analysis into how bimodal bilinguals use their communicative options (signing only, speaking only, codeswitching, code-blending, speaking sign language) will expand our concept of bilingualism. How do these linguistic options become conventionalized (e.g., as Coda-talk) in tandem with an emerging Coda identity? Does Coda-talk have its own rules, constraints? Equally important, how are the three groups of bimodal bilingual people — Codas, hearing second-language learners of a signed language, and deaf people who know both a signed and spoken language — different? Does Codas' native fluency set them apart from other bimodal bilinguals?

To date, the field of bilingualism has been largely shaped by studies of spoken languages. The analysis of simultaneous spoken and signed utterances has a great potential to test theoretical models that have been formulated based on a more linear and sequential concept of language mixing.

NOTES

1. CODA is the acronym for the national organization in the United States as well as in many other countries. *Coda* is used to refer to the individual.

2. In the Deaf community the capital D in *Deaf* reflects the cultural and linguistic characteristics particular to Deaf people as opposed to lowercase deaf that refers only to one's audiological status.

3. Davie's (1992) film, *Passport without a Country,* is about the hearing children of deaf parents and the common experiences they share in growing up in the Deaf community amid the hostilities and prejudice of the hearing world. In Petrie's (1985) film, *Love Is Never Silent,* a young woman struggles with her own need for independence and the obligation she feels for her deaf parents. Waldleitner's (1996) film, *Beyond Silence,* shows Lara, a young hearing child, whose two deaf parents depend on her as a link to the hearing world.

4. Jacobs (1992), in a CODA newsletter, discusses the concept of Coda identity as having "parts" — having both deaf and hearing identities.

5. For a more thorough explanation of Coda identity, see Preston (1994) and Bishop and Hicks (2005).

6. In addition, Berent (2004) provides a general discussion on code-mixing and mode-mixing. He proposes a theory-based approach to exploring these linguistic phenomena. The article focuses mostly on deaf bilinguals, with only a few paragraphs devoted to Codas.

7. Responses from several Codas, P. Preston, S. Hicks, D. Prickett, and T. Bull, confirmed that the term *Coda-talk* is used and understood by many Codas who are themselves active in CODA events.

8. This finding is not to imply that these elements are never used in ASL. See Lucas and Valli (1992) for more information on language contact phenomena between English and ASL.

9. Denmark established a similar organization for hearing people with deaf parents in 1979, before the establishment of CODA in 1983 in the United States.

10. Liddell (2003) uses the term *real space* to label "a person's current conceptualization of the immediate environment based on sensory input" (82). The word *blend* in the sense of real-space blend describes the mapping of mental conceptualizations onto physical space and should not be confused with the linguistic phenomenon of code-blends (signing and speaking simultaneously), which are discussed in this paper.

11. It is exactly this kind of parental mispronunciation that is the catalyst for some American Codas to create deliberately mispronounced words when using Coda-talk. Intentional mispronunciations are one way Codas enjoy and honor the aural legacy from their deaf parents or other deaf people in their lives (Bishop and Hicks 2005).

12. Lowercase indicates spoken Italian, and text in small capital letters represents LIS. Translations are provided immediately below each example using the same transcription conventions.

13. The term *single* is a legitimate borrowing from English into spoken Italian, unrelated to the issue at hand.

14. The brackets in this quote represent a single sign. A-N = fingerspelled article, PRO-1 = I or me, PRO = pronoun (he, she) or a point to a location in signing space, and POSS = possessive pronoun.

15. This observation on regional dialect and linguistics variation was made by Ceil Lucas via personal communication May 2006.

16. In signed language research, reference to the dominant hand means the hand consistently used for both fingerspelling and for the majority of the signed output, the other hand serving as support (nondominant). The nondominant hand serves as a support hand for the production of signs. Although fluent signers often fingerspell and sign with both hands, there is a tendency to use one hand more than the other.

17. Although the base language during videotaping was Italian, the occurrences of code blends and code switches allowed the researchers to determine the dominant and nondominant signing hands for each participant.

18. Personal observation of Codas from English-speaking countries such as Ireland, Canada, Australia, and England suggest that Coda-talk is a direct manifestation of a Coda identity and undergoes developmental "spikes" during Coda

gatherings, especially the annual CODA conference. Although CODA conferences have historically been held in the United States, the first international conference took place in 1999 in Coolangata, Australia, directly after the World Federation of the Deaf conference in Brisbane. The next international conference will be in Madrid, Spain, in 2007, also directly after the World Federation of the Deaf conference.

19. Extensive observation of mixed domestic and international Coda gatherings has indicated that Codas from around the world often use an English-based "spoken signed language" as a lingua franca with one another. This phenomenon may be attributed to structural similarities (i.e. no copulas, no inflectional verb morphology) among many different signed languages, which allow the speakers to capitalize on these similarities and to avoid the demands of speaking grammatically correct English when that language is not the primary language.

REFERENCES

Baker, A., and B. van den Bogaerde. In press. Codemixing in signs and words in input to and output from children. In *Sign Bilingualism: Language Development, Interaction, and Maintenance in Sign Language Contact Situations*, ed. C. Plaza-Pust and E. Morales Lopéz. Amsterdam: Benjamins.

Baker-Shenk, C., and D. Cokely. 1980. *American Sign Language: A teacher's resource text on grammar and culture*. Silver Spring, Md.: T.J. Publishers.

Berent, G. P. 2004. Sign language-spoken language bilingualism: Code mixing and mode mixing by ASL-English bilinguals. In *The handbook of bilingualism*, ed. W. C. Ritchie and T. K. Bhatia, 312–35. San Diego: Academic Press.

Bishop, M. 2006. Bimodal bilingualism in hearing, native signers of American Sign Language. Ph.D. diss., Gallaudet University, Washington, D.C.

Bishop, M., and S. Hicks. 2005. Orange eyes: Bimodal bilingualism in hearing adult users of American Sign Language. *Sign Language Studies* 5 (2): 188–230.

Davie, C., prod. and dir. 1992. *Passport without a country*. Motion picture. Princeton, N.J.: Films for Humanities.

Dudis, P. 2000. Tokens as abstract visible blended elements. Paper presented at Conceptual Structures in Discourse and Language 5 conference, May 11–14, University of California, Santa Barbara.

Duncan, S. 2003. Gesture in language: Issues for sign language research. In *Perspectives on classifier constructions in sign languages*, ed. K. Emmorey, 259–68. Mahwah, N.J.: Lawrence Erlbaum.

Emmorey, K. 2002. *Language, cognition, and the brain: Insights from sign language research*. Mahwah, N.J.: Lawrence Erlbaum.

Emmorey, K., H. Borinstein, and R. Thompson. 2003. *Bimodal bilingualism: Code-blending between spoken English and American Sign Language.* San Diego: Salk Institute for Biological Studies and the University of California.

Fischer, S., and B. Gough. 1999. Some unfinished thoughts on FINISH. *Sign Language & Linguistics* 2 (1): 67–77.

Gardner-Chloros, P. 1995. Code-switching in community, regional and national repertoires: The myth of the discreteness of linguistic systems. In *One speaker, two languages: Cross disciplinary perspectives on code switching,* ed. L. Milroy and P. Muysken, 68–89. Cambridge: Cambridge University Press.

Grosjean, F. 1982. *Life with two languages: An introduction to bilingualism.* Cambridge, Mass.: Harvard University Press.

Gumperz, J. 1982. *Discourse strategies.* Cambridge: Cambridge University Press.

Jacobs, S. 1992. Coda Talk column. *CODA Connection* 9 (2): 9.

Kendon, A. 2004. *"Gesture: Visible action as utterance.* Cambridge: Cambridge University Press.

King, K. A. 2000. Language ideologies and heritage language education. *International Journal of Bilingual Education and Bilingualism* 3 (2): 167–84.

Klima, E., and U. Bellugi. 1979. *The signs of language.* Cambridge, Mass.: Harvard University Press.

Labov, W. 1972. *Language in the inner city.* Philadelphia: University of Pennsylvania Press.

Lane, H., R. Hoffmeister, and B. Bahan. 1996. *A Journey into the Deaf-World.* San Diego: Dawn Sign Press.

Liddell, S. 2003. *Grammar, gesture, and meaning in American Sign Language.* Cambridge: Cambridge University Press.

Lucas, C., and C. Valli. 1992. *Language contact in the American deaf community.* San Diego: Academic Press.

Maestas y Moores, J. 1980. Early linguistic environment: Interactions of deaf parents with their infants. *Sign Language Studies* 26: 1–13.

McNeill, D. 1992. *Hand and mind: What gestures reveal about thought.* Chicago: The University of Chicago Press.

———. 2000. *Language and gesture.* Cambridge: Cambridge University Press.

Meadow-Orlans, K., C. J. Erting, and D. P. Spencer. 1987. Interactions of deaf and hearing mothers of deaf and hearing infants. Paper presented at the Tenth World Congress of the World Federation of the Deaf, July 21–24, Helsinki, Finland.

Miller, R. H. 2004. *Deaf hearing boy.* Washington, D.C.: Gallaudet University Press.

Mills, A. E., and J. Coerts. 1990. Functions and forms of bilingual input: Children learning a sign language as one of their first languages. In *Current trends in European sign language research: Proceedings of the Third*

European Congress on Sign Language Research, ed. S. Prillwitz and T. Vollhaber, 151–62. Hamburg: Signum.

Moores, J. M., and D. F. Moores. 1982. Interaction of deaf children with children in the first months of life. *Proceedings of the International Congress on Education of the Deaf*, Vol. 1, ed., 718–21. Heidelberg: Julius Gross.

Myers-Scotton, C. 1993a. Common and uncommon ground: Social and structural factors in code switching. *Language in Society* 22: 475–503.

———. 1993b. *Social motivations for code-switching: Evidence from Africa.* Oxford: Clarendon Press.

———. 1997. *Duelling languages: Grammatical structure in codeswitching.* 2nd ed. Oxford: Clarendon Press.

———. 2002. *Contact linguistics: Bilingual encounters and grammatical outcomes.* Oxford: Oxford University Press.

Muysken, P. 2000. *Bilingual speech.* Cambridge: Cambridge University Press.

Petitto, L., M. Katerelos, B. Levy, K. Gauna, K. Teìtreault, and V. Ferraro. 2001. Bilingual signed and spoken language acquisition from birth: Implications for the mechanisms underlying early bilingual language acquisition. *Journal of Child Language* 28: 453–96.

Petrie, D., prod., and J. Sargeant, dir. 1985. *Love is never silent.* Motion picture. Hallmark and National Broadcasting Company.

Preston, P. 1994. Mother father deaf: *Living between sound and silence.* Cambridge, Mass.: Harvard University Press.

Poplack, S. 1980. Sometimes I start a sentence in English Y TERMINO EN ESPAÑOL: toward a typology of code switching. *Linguistics* 18, 581–618.

Pyers, J., and K. Emmorey. 2005. The eyebrows have it: Evidence for the activation of two grammars in ASL-English bilinguals. Paper presented at Psychonomic Society, November, Toronto, Canada.

———. 2006. The face of bimodal bilingualism. Paper presented at Theoretical Issues in Sign Language Research, December, Florionapolis, Brazil.

Rodriguez, Y. 2001. Toddlerese: Conversations between deaf Puerto Rican parents and hearing toddlers. Ph.D. diss., Lamar University, Beaumont, Texas.

Romaine, S. 1995. *Bilingualism.* 2nd ed. Oxford, United Kingdom: Blackwell.

Schiff, N., and I. Ventry. 1976. Communication problems in hearing children of deaf parents. *Journal of Speech and Hearing Disorders* 41 (3): 348–58.

Van den Bogaerde, B. 2000. Input and Interaction in Deaf Families. In *Sign Language and Linguistics* 3(1): 143–51.

Waldleitner, L., prod., and C. Link, dir. 1996. *Beyond silence.* Buena Vista Home Entertainment.

Winford, D. 2003. *An introduction to contact linguistics.* Malden, Mass. Blackwell.

Zentella, A. C. 1997. *Growing up bilingual.* Malden, Mass.: Blackwell.

Narrative of "The Lights Go Out"

TRANSLATION FROM ITALIAN

They call me. At a certain point, it was raining and the electricity goes out. My father nearby (indicates the area to her right) and the electricity goes out, (picks up the 'ringing phone') and there I am, me, trying to explain to this woman (points to area to her left), (as herself in the narrative) "Excuse me, but the electricity went out." (Points to woman) (she) knew that my father was deaf and was angry anyway (becomes the woman and grumbles). (As herself in the story she responds), "What is wrong with her anyway?"

(Narrates) Because it was, I don't remember what kind of problem, but it was a pretty serious problem and needed to be resolved right away, and I have to hang up and call (surrogate role as herself at 6–7 years old), "Hi, I will call you when the electricity comes back on." (becomes the woman caller and gestures in an upset fashion, "ehhhh").

(Narrates) Obviously the telephone line (indicates phone cord with CL: pinky) had not been affected and I have to explain to her and she (indicates woman caller on her left) didn't understand that my father (indicates area on her right) couldn't talk to us, he couldn't talk to us because (signs DARK/DARKNESS), it was completely dark. . . . (gestures with the right hand in a circular fashion while commenting) . . . it was an emergency . . . etc. (xxxx), and I couldn't see him, and she (points to her left) didn't understand. My father (TAP TAP TAP taps her right shoulder with her left hand) kept on talking because you know that I could hear as he kept talking and I couldn't explain to him (indicates area on right 'father', meaning "I couldn't explain to my father") what the woman (indicates area on her left) was saying and it was also around . . . (unintelligible).

ORIGINAL VERSION IN ITALIAN

Mi chiamano, a certo punto pioveva e va via la luce. Mi padre vicino (indicates space off to right) e va via la luce, (picks up phone) e c'è io . . . spiegare a questa signora (points to area to her left), (as herself in the narrative) "Scusi, è andata via la luce". (Points to woman caller and narrates) sapeva che era sordo mio padre e questa tutta arrabbiata (takes on surrogate role of woman and grumbles, "ma che c'è)?

(Narrates) perchè era, io non mi ricordo che tipo di problema, ma era un problem grosso e che si deve risolvere subito e io devo chiudere e chiamare (surrogate role as herself at 6–7 years old), "ola, ti chiamo quando ritorna la luce" (becomes the surrogate woman and reacts with displeasure by gesturing "ehhhhh!").

(Narrates) Ovviamente, la linea telefonica (indicates phone cord with CL: pinky) non era state interrotta e io devo spiegare, ma non capiva (refers to woman caller by indicating the area to her left), che mio padre (gestures to right) non ci poteva parlare, non poteva parlarci perché (signs BUIO/DARK), c'era il buio totale (gestures with the right hand in a circular fashion while commenting) . . . era una emergenza. eccetera per cui io non lo vedevo e questa (points to left) non capiva. Mio padre (TAP TAP TAP) continuava parlare perché sapete che io sentivo quando mi parlate e io non potevo spiegare (indicates area on right) quello che la signora (indicates left) mi diceva che poi era intorno . . . (unintelligible).

APPENDIX B
Transcription Conventions

How old are you? OLD YOU	For bimodal utterances, the English utterance is written above in lowercase and ASL is written below in small capitals.
[ ]	In bimodal utterances, English words between brackets indicate the word and the ASL sign are temporally aligned. The brackets represent a single sign.
⟶	The arrow indicates that either a signed or spoken utterance is stretched to temporally align with the utterance in the other language
A-N =	fingerspelled article - Fingerspelled words are written in capitals and hyphenated:
#WE =	lexicalized fingerspelled words
PRO-1 =	I/ME Subjects are written from the viewpoint of the person signing
PRO =	pronoun (he, she).

(point) -   Referents are indicated by pointing to a location
                       in signing space

POSS -   Possessive pronouns in ASL are indicated by:

I saw that she was UPSET - During spoken English discourse; code-
switches into ASL are indicated by capitalizing the ASL sign.
                       GP

we just both -   An underlined word indicates a code-blend that
     UNDERSTAND   has been identified as a *growth point* abbrevi-
                       ated as GP over the spoken utterance

Part 3 Variation

NAME Dropping: Location Variation

in Australian Sign Language

Adam Schembri, Trevor Johnston, and Della Goswell

This paper presents the results from the first study in the Sociolinguistic Variation in Australian Sign Language project (Schembri and Johnston 2004). This major project is a replication in the Australian deaf community of the quantitative investigations into variation in American Sign Language (ASL) that were conducted by Lucas, Bayley, and Valli (2001). In this specific study, we consider variation in the location parameter in a class of signs that includes the Australian Sign Language (Auslan) signs THINK, NAME and CLEVER.[1] In their citation form, these signs (like signs in the same class in ASL) are produced in contact with, in proximity to, or at the same height as the signer's forehead or above but often may

The illustrations in this paper were produced by Shaun Fahey. This research was supported by Australian Research Council grant number LP346973 under the Linkage Scheme to the University of Newcastle and the Royal Institute for Deaf and Blind Children. As our chief consultants on the project, Ceil Lucas and Bob Bayley happily shared materials, passed on invaluable advice, and provided inspiration, support and encouragement. Barbara Horvath has also been particularly helpful; a copy of her Filemaker Pro database (created by her daughter Jane Horvath) saved us hours of work in database design, and her hands-on VARBRUL training was much appreciated. Julia Allen (Sydney), Patti Levitzke-Gray (Perth), Kevin Cresdee (Adelaide), Stephanie Linder (Melbourne), and Kim Pickering (Brisbane) acted as our deaf contact people and research assistants. Robert Adam, Breda Carty, Donovan Cresdee, and Brent Phillips provided useful input, and Darlene Thornton assisted with data coding. We are grateful to the management and staff at the Deaf Society of New South Wales, Deaf Education Network, Renwick College, the Thomas Pattison School, the Western Australian Deaf Society, the Royal South Australian Deaf Society, the Victorian Deaf Society, and the Queensland Deaf Society for assistance during data collection. Thanks to Don Kohlman and Pam Spicer for providing accommodation in Perth and Brisbane. Finally, we are especially grateful to the many deaf people across Australia who participated in this study.

be produced at locations lower than the forehead, either on other parts of the signer's body (such as at the cheek) or in the space in front of the signer's chest. Here, we present an analysis of 2,446 tokens of signs from this class that were collected from 205 deaf signers of Auslan in five sites across Australia (Sydney, Melbourne, Brisbane, Perth, and Adelaide). The results indicate that the variation in the use of the location parameter in these signs reflects both linguistic and social factors, as has also been reported for ASL. Despite similarities, however, we find that some of the particular factors at work, and the kinds of influence they have on variation in location, appear to differ in Auslan and ASL. Moreover, our results suggest that lexical frequency also plays a role, a factor not considered in the ASL study.

The paper is organized into four parts. First, we provide a brief overview of sociolinguistic variation in Auslan and review the previous work on location variation in ASL by Lucas, Bayley, and Valli (2001). We then present the methodology used in our study, followed by a description of the results. Last, we discuss the implications of our findings for the understanding of sociolinguistic variation in signed and spoken languages.

AUSTRALIAN SIGN LANGUAGE (AUSLAN)

Auslan is a signed language that is part of the same language family as British Sign Language and New Zealand Sign Language; in fact, these three signed varieties might best be considered dialects of the same language (Johnston 2002a). Auslan seems not to be directly related historically to American Sign Language (McKee and Kennedy 2000). It developed from the varieties of signed language brought to Australia by British deaf immigrants and hearing educators of deaf children from the early nineteenth century onward (Carty 2004; Johnston 1989). Estimates of the number of deaf signers of Auslan vary: some claim that as many as 15,000 deaf Australians (out of a total national population of 20 million people) use Auslan as their primary or preferred language (Hyde and Power 1991) whereas recent research suggests that this number may be closer to 6,500 (Johnston 2004).

Relatively little research has been conducted on Auslan (for a recent overview, see Schembri 2001). Only in 1987 did a linguist produce the first curriculum for Auslan teaching and a sketch grammar of the language (Johnston 1987), with the first doctoral dissertation on the subject following two years later (Johnston 1989). The first volume of Johnston's dissertation provides an overview of the grammatical structure of the language and shows that it shares many of the same general morphosyntactic characteristics as other signed languages such as ASL. The second volume is the first dictionary of Auslan based on linguistic principles, with more than 3,000 entries. A revised second edition of the dictionary has appeared both in CD-ROM and book formats (Johnston 1997, 1998).

Sociolinguistic Variation in Auslan

Johnston's dissertation (Johnston 1989), some of his later research (Johnston and Schembri 1999), subsequent dictionaries of Auslan based on his work (Johnston 1997, 1998; Johnston and Schembri 2003; Bernal and Wilson 2004), and Auslan teaching materials (Branson et al. 1992, 1995) discuss sociolinguistic variation in the language and have documented some of the many examples of regional variation in the Auslan lexicon (e.g., MORNING; see figure 1).

Johnston (1989) proposed that, based on the distribution of lexical variation in core areas of the lexicon such as numbers (especially SIX to TWELVE) and colors (e.g., BLUE, GREEN, BROWN, etc.), Auslan could be divided into two major regional varieties: the "northern" dialect (Queensland and New South Wales) and the "southern" dialect (Victoria, South Australia, Western Australia, and Tasmania). It is possible that these two regional varieties have developed, at least in part, from lexical variation in different varieties of BSL that were used in schools for deaf children in Australia during the nineteenth century, although primary sources documenting signed language use at the time are lacking.

Johnston (2002b) and Schembri (2001) also discuss grammatical variation in signed language that has occurred as a result of language contact with written and spoken English. Recently, Napier (this volume) has begun to explore the results of language contact empirically.

The focus in this paper is on phonological variation. Although other works have discussed or documented sociolinguistic variation in Auslan, they have primarily focused on lexical variation. The research project described in this paper represents the first attempt to empirically investigate an example of phonological variation in Auslan, relating it to both linguistic and social factors.

MORNING (northern dialect)   MORNING (southern dialect)

FIGURE 1. *Regional variants of* MORNING

Phonological Variation in Auslan: The Location Variable

Johnston observed that phonological variation in handshape, location, and orientation in Auslan may be conditioned by the immediate phonological environment:

> Handshape and location and orientation can all undergo significant changes in fluent signing with the immediate phonological environment of a sign influencing, for example, whether handshapes are fully formed or not, or whether they absorb features of previous or following handshapes; whether contact is actually made at locations, simply suggested, not made at all or made at another location altogether, and so on. (Johnston 1989, 33)

Similar claims for ASL were made by Liddell and Johnson (1989). Although Johnston noted that assimilation may occur in three parameters, our study examines variation in only a single parameter — location. More specifically, our investigation of location variation will examine this variable in the class of signs that are produced in contact with, in proximity to, or at the same height as the forehead or above, including the signs THINK, NAME and CLEVER (as illustrated in figure 2). This class of signs includes both signs that primarily act as verbs (e.g., KNOW, NOT-KNOW, REMEMBER, FORGET, UNDERSTAND, WONDER, WORRY, DREAM) and signs that generally function as nouns (e.g., MOTHER, NAME, MIND, SOCCER, GIRL, IDEA, COMMITTEE, DONKEY). It also includes a number of signs that may have an adjectival function (e.g., STUPID, CLEVER, YELLOW, CRAZY, SOPHISTICATED, SILLY, GREEN, BLONDE). Although these signs are produced (in citation form) on, near, or at the same height as the forehead or above, they (as Johnston noted above) may be made at other locations. Their location may vary from the forehead region (i.e., in their citation form) to locations near the eye, on the cheek, at the jaw, or at lower locations in neutral space (as illustrated in figure 3).

This study is only the second study on location variation in this class of signs to have been conducted on a signed language. Our work is a replication of a previous study on location variation in ASL (Lucas, Bayley, and Valli 2001). In the original study, Lucas and her colleagues coded 2,862 examples of signs from the class exemplified by the ASL sign KNOW (all of which were produced in citation form in contact with or in proximity to the forehead or temple region). Those signs were selected from a corpus of conversational and interview data that had been collected from 207 native and near-native deaf signers of ASL in seven sites (Staunton, Virginia; Frederick, Maryland; Boston, Massachusetts; Olathe, Kansas and Kansas City, Missouri; New Orleans, Louisiana; Fremont, California; and Bellingham, Washington) across the United States. The corpus included a mix of men and women, both Caucasian and African-American, from a range of different age groups, language backgrounds, and social classes. The results of that study suggested that location variation is a classic sociolinguistic variable, influenced by the sex, social class, age, ethnicity, and regional origin of the signer as well as by the grammatical function (i.e., noun, verb, adjective, preposition, or interrogative) and immediate phonological environment of the sign (e.g., the location of the preceding sign). We explore those findings in more detail in the discussion below.

The research reported in this paper has two main goals. First, this investigation seeks to improve our understanding of the linguistic and social influences on phonological variation in Auslan. In particular, we attempt to discern whether location variation in the class of Auslan signs exemplified by THINK, NAME, and CLEVER is random or whether the immediate phonological environment is an important influence, as suggested by Johnston (1989). We are also interested in examining what other linguistic and social factors may influence this variation.

Second, the research makes possible a cross-linguistic comparison of location variation in Auslan and ASL. If location variation is indeed systematic in Auslan, then are the same kind of social and linguistic constraints on this variation at work in both languages? The results of this study will enable to us to begin to develop hypotheses about the kinds of

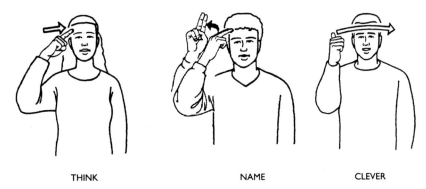

| THINK | NAME | CLEVER |

FIGURE 2. *THINK, NAME and CLEVER*

NAME   FIGURE 3. *Lowered variant of* NAME

factors involved in phonological variation in signed languages and about how these factors compare with those found in spoken languages.

METHODOLOGY

As in the previous work on ASL (Lucas, Bayley, and Valli 2001), we chose to undertake multivariate analysis of the data (i.e., an analysis that considers multiple variables simultaneously) using VARBRUL software, a statistical program developed specifically for sociolinguistic research. Two key principles that guide such research are the principle of quantitative modeling and the principle of multiple causes (Young and Bayley 1996). The first principle refers to the need to carefully quantify both variation in a linguistic form and the relationship between a variant form as well as features of its surrounding linguistic environment and social context. The second principle reflects the assumption that no single linguistic or social factor can fully explain variation in natural language use.

Guided by these principles, Bayley (2002) suggested that the first step in any VARBRUL analysis is to define the variable and the nature of variation. The second step concerns identifying the factors that may influence the variation. Each factor group needs to be motivated by particular hypotheses about its potential effect. We discuss the target signs for our investigation in the next section and outline the social and linguistic factors that are the focus of our study in our discussion of sites, participants, data collection, and coding.

Target Signs

Compiling our data initially involved the coding of ninety target signs, but tokens of eight of these target signs were later removed from the dataset used in this study (as is explained later in the section on coding). The resulting eighty-two target signs were all made in citation form at locations in contact with, in proximity to, or at the same height as the forehead region or above, but they were believed to vary in location. Despite this tendency, the variant forms of these signs (e.g., the two forms of NAME shown in figures 2 and 3) clearly have the same referential meaning as the citation form, and may be considered two ways of saying the same thing. This property makes them an appropriate variable for study using VARBRUL analysis (Bayley 2002).

The target signs in our study differed from those in the ASL study (Lucas, Bayley, and Valli 2001) in two ways. First, we did not include signs that were made in citation form at locations lower than the forehead region. The signs investigated by Lucas and her colleagues included a small number of signs made near the temple region, for example, ASL SEE. Second, we also did not include lexicalized compound signs in which the second component was made at a location lower than the forehead. Target signs in the ASL research included ASL BELIEVE and REMEMBER (in both these signs, the dominant hand moves down from a forehead location to make contact with the subordinate hand). Excluding compared signs resulted in a set of signs in the Auslan data that were more homogeneous in terms of location than the set of signs in the study by Lucas and her colleagues (Lucas, Bayley, and Valli 2001).

Sites

As was mentioned above, many of the common regional variants in the Auslan lexicon have been well documented (Johnston 1998), but little is known about the relationship between phonological variation and region. We believe that regional influences may have an effect on variation in location in Auslan, as has shown to be true of ASL (Lucas, Bayley, and Valli 2001). Previously unrecognized regional influences also appear to be at work in phonological variation in Australian English (e.g., Horvath and Horvath 2002). Thus, to obtain a representative sample of Auslan use across the country, we had to visit a number of different sites. We selected five communities: Adelaide, South Australia; Brisbane, Queensland; Melbourne, Victoria; Sydney, New South Wales; and Perth, Western Australia (see figure 4). More than half of the entire population of Australia lives in these five state capitals, and demographic studies suggest that a similarly large proportion of the Australian deaf community can be found in these cities (Hyde and Power 1991). These five urban areas are also spread across the major regions of the country (Adelaide is in the central part of the south coast of the continent; Perth is on the west coast; while Brisbane, Sydney, and Melbourne cover the northern and southern parts of the relatively densely populated east coast). These cities are also home to the longest established deaf communities, having traditionally been the sites of residential schools for deaf children — all of which were founded in the nineteenth century (Carty 2004). Another reason we chose to collect data in these five urban areas relates to the size of the deaf communities in these cities. We decided that it would be much easier to obtain sufficient numbers of participants from a variety of backgrounds in each city because deaf communities outside these areas of Australia are often particularly small.

Sydney served as a pilot site from June 2003. We collected data in Perth in September 2003, Adelaide in March–April 2004, Melbourne in July–August 2004, and finally Brisbane in October–November 2004.

Participants

A total of 211 deaf people were filmed across the country (although, as table 1 shows, we did not use all of the participants in the final analysis but used only 205, as is explained later). As in previous work on ASL (Lucas, Bayley and Valli, 2001), we used a judgment sample (i.e.,

FIGURE 4. *Map of Australia*

we selected participants to fill preselected social categories) rather than a random sample of the deaf population. Thus, we included deaf signers from a variety of backgrounds, with the stipulation requiring all participants to have been exposed to signed communication in early childhood (more than 95 percent of our participants reported that they had first begun to sign by the age of seven). We selected in each site both deaf people who had deaf parents (i.e., those who had learned to sign in the home) and deaf people who had hearing parents (i.e., those who had learned signed language from their peers at school). Like Lucas, Bayley, and Valli (2001), we recruited neither hearing signers (native or otherwise) nor those deaf people who acquired Auslan later in life, either as a significantly delayed first language or as a second language after the successful acquisition of English. This approach was taken to minimize the possible effects on our data of English influence in the signed language use of hearing native signers and deaf second-language learners (Lucas and Valli 1992) or of late first-language acquisition in deaf late learners of Auslan (for an overview of research on late signers of ASL, see Emmorey 2002).

To ensure that we filmed individuals who were representative of each region, we attempted to focus our recruitment of participants on long-term residents of each city. Slightly more than 90 percent ($n = 194$) of our

TABLE I. *Participants*

Site	Total	Age Younger (<51)	Age Older (≥ 51)	Sex Female	Sex Male	Social class Working Class	Social class Middle Class	Language background Auslan	Language background Other
Adelaide	44	23	21	20	24	38	6	15	29
Brisbane	38	17	21	21	17	30	8	9	29
Melbourne	42	26	16	24	18	28	14	14	28
Sydney	46	31	15	26	20	37	9	23	23
Perth	35	21	14	17	18	28	7	9	26
Total	205	118	87	108	97	161	44	70	135

participants had lived ten years or more in their local deaf communities (i.e., slightly less than 10 percent had moved to the city in which they were filmed in the last ten years), and a little more than 80 percent (*n* = 171) were lifelong residents.

Our sample included similar numbers of men and women, a mix of younger and older age groups, and people from both middle-class and working-class backgrounds. We did not, however, select participants on the basis of ethnicity, a social factor that has been shown to be relevant in ASL (Lucas, Bayley and Valli 2001) and in sociolinguistic variation in spoken languages (Fought 2002). The ethnic composition of the Australian deaf community is unknown, and it is difficult to obtain information about the incidence of deafness in the immigrant population. The general Australian population is approximately 91 percent of European origin, with 7 percent of the population of Asian origin (mainly from Southeast Asia and the Middle East), and another 2 percent of Aboriginal or Torres Straight Islander background. In the 2001 Census, approximately 28 percent of the Australian population was born overseas, and 20 percent used a language other than English in the home. Other than the Anglo-Celtic majority, however, no single ethnic group is predominant either in the general population or in the deaf community. Given this, and the fact that the education of deaf children has never been segregated on the basis of race (unlike the situation in the United States of America) and there are no deaf clubs or associations based on ethnicity in Australia, there does not appear to be much evidence of systematic ethnic variation in Auslan.

In contrast to ethnicity, however, separate education was traditionally provided in Australia on the basis of religion. A school for Catholic deaf children was established in 1875 near Newcastle, north of Sydney. Two other Catholic schools in New South Wales and Victoria opened during the twentieth century (Carty 2004). A variety of Irish Sign Language (ISL) and the Irish manual alphabet were used as the means of instruction in these schools until the 1950s. After leaving school, adult Catholic deaf people continued to use ISL among themselves. Today, however, knowledge of ISL in Australia is now almost entirely confined to those older members of the deaf community who were educated in Catholic schools for the deaf, and almost all of these individuals are bilingual in ISL and Auslan (Johnston 1989). As a result, it is not possible to obtain a balanced sample of Australian deaf people that includes a representative number of ISL users in all age categories across all regions. Although our corpus includes older deaf Australians who were educated in Catholic schools (and in some cases, younger deaf adults whose parents used ISL), we have not included ISL knowledge or use as a social factor in our investigation of location variation in Auslan.

Sex and gender are among the most widely used social categories in sociolinguistic research (Cheshire 2002) and have been shown to play a role in sociolinguistic variation in ASL (Lucas, Bayley, and Valli 2001). As a result, we recruited both men and women for our study, although we were more successful at recruiting female participants in all sites apart from Adelaide. As a result, our corpus overall has a slightly higher number of deaf women than men.

Participants were recruited in four different age groups: (1) ages fifteen to thirty years, (2) ages thirty-one to fifty, (3) ages fifty-one to seventy, and (4) ages seventy-one or older (although, as table 1 shows, we later grouped all participants in two groups of fifty and younger and fifty-one and older for reasons explained later in the paper). Our age categories reflect two possible influences on phonological variation in Auslan. First, age-related variation in language is well documented for both spoken languages (Bailey 2002) and signed languages (e.g., Lucas, Bayley, and Valli 2001; Sutton-Spence and Woll 1990). Often, this age-related variation at any point in time reflects a language change in progress (Labov 1994).

Second, the specific age groupings were intended to reflect changes in language policy in the education of deaf children during the twentieth century (similar changes have occurred in the United States; see Lucas, Bayley, and Valli 2001). Participants in the oldest age group (ages seventy-one years and older) were most likely to have been educated in residential schools for deaf children, often with approaches that emphasized the use of fingerspelling. Auslan was used by school children with one another in the dormitories and on the playground, and some instruction in some schools would also have been by means of signed communication. Like the older group, participants in the fifty-one to seventy years age group would have been educated in centralized schools for deaf children, although many would have experienced the shift to oralism that occurred in a number of schools after World War II. Those in the age category of thirty-one to fifty years would have witnessed major changes in deaf education: the greater use of assistive technology and oralism, the move toward Total Communication and the use of Australasian Signed English, the closure of centralized schools for deaf children, and the spread of mainstreaming. Participants in the youngest age group (fifteen to thirty years) have seen the increasing recognition of Auslan as the language of the Australian deaf community, but most would have been educated in mainstream settings by teachers using Australasian Signed English. Some of the youngest members of this group would have been educated in schools using Auslan as the medium of instruction (at least one school in each of the five sites has introduced bilingual approaches using Auslan and English since the late 1980s).

Because social class is an important factor in many sociolinguistic studies of spoken languages (Ash 2002) and was found to be relevant in the previous ASL study (Lucas, Bayley, and Valli 2001), we recruited individuals from both working-class and middle-class backgrounds. The definitions adopted here defined working-class individuals as those who are employed in unskilled, semiskilled, or skilled manual jobs (e.g., laborer, factory worker, or plumber) or as semiskilled nonmanual workers (e.g., clerk). Middle-class participants are those, possibly with a university education, who work in skilled nonmanual jobs (e.g., Auslan teacher) or in professional or managerial positions (e.g., manager of an interpreting service). Because university education has become generally accessible to deaf people in Australia only after disability discrimination legislation enacted since the 1980s, we could not always rely on tertiary qualifications as a defining part of our social class classification (this factor was a key criterion used in the study by Lucas and her colleagues). Numbers of middle-class participants were considerably smaller than working-class participants in all sites. Of all the sites, the largest number of middle-class individuals was found in Melbourne (many of these participants were graduates from La Trobe University where a degree in education with a focus on signed language teaching has been available for some years now).

Data Collection

The researchers on this project worked closely with one deaf person from each of the five sites who acted as the "contact person" (Lucas, Bayley, and Valli 2001). All contact people were deaf native signers (i.e., deaf adults with deaf parents) who had lived all or most of their lives in the local deaf community. They worked as paid research assistants on the project and were responsible for selecting fluent Auslan signers who had been exposed to signed communication in early childhood and had lived for the last ten years in the same community. In all cases, the contact people participated in one data collection session themselves.

At each site, participants were gathered together in groups, almost always with others of similar age. Altogether, there were seventy groups, each consisting of two to five participants. All but six groups were composed of both women and men. As a result of some participants withdrawing from the study immediately before a filming session was due to begin, one group consisted of men only, and another five groups of women only. On arrival, all participants filled out a short demographic questionnaire, assisted by the deaf contact people and the hearing researchers. Filming sessions consisted of four parts. First, participants were interviewed briefly by the deaf research assistant about their name signs. That interview was followed by thirty to fifty minutes of free conversation among group members, without the hearing researcher (or any hearing people) being present (which was done to minimize possible influences from English on the data, as documented for ASL by Lucas and Valli 1992). As in the American study (Lucas, Bayley, and Valli 2001), most participants already knew one another, so it was not difficult to get a conversation started. In many cases, participants discussed personal experiences (such as recent holidays), shared recollections (such as memories of school), or talked about events in the deaf community (such as birthday parties, weddings, or plans for the Deaflympics in Melbourne). After the free conversation, most participants were invited to stay for an interview conducted by the deaf contact person (due to constraints in time and funding, only 155 people were interviewed out of a total of 211 participants). They were asked about their family, education, work, social life, and patterns of language use in each of these settings. Although the hearing researcher may have been present during the filming, the deaf contact person always interviewed the participants. The interview also included a lexical elicitation task in which the contact people asked each participant to produce their signs for eighty common objects and actions elicited by means of a set of flashcards.

All participants were filmed in comfortable and familiar settings. The signers in Adelaide, Brisbane, Perth, and Melbourne were filmed on the premises of the local state deaf society (i.e., state-based welfare organizations that provide a range of social services for the local deaf community and that have traditionally included a deaf club or hall for social events). Filming sessions in these cities were scheduled during ten-day visits to the site by the researchers. Participants in Sydney were filmed over a longer period in a variety of settings such as at the Royal Institute for Deaf and Blind Children, at the Deaf Society of New South Wales, in the classrooms of the Deaf Education Network, or in the homes of participants themselves. All the deaf people that participated in the project were paid for their time.

Data Coding

The data from 205 of the 211 participants were coded for the purposes of this study. This dataset included data from 199 individuals who reported that their first exposure to signed language occurred before age seven and from six participants who began to sign between the ages of eight and twelve years (the data from these participants were included because they were judged to be fluent Auslan signers by the researchers, contact people, and research assistants). Data from two participants who reported that they first learned to sign after the age of twelve were not included. The data from the remaining four were not coded for a variety of reasons: one signer did not participate very much in the conversation during the filming session (and thus produced no target signs), another wore a cap during filming (preventing us from being able to fully see his use of signs in the target location), and two other signers did not fit our criteria for fluency in Auslan (as judged by the project researchers, two of whom are hearing native signers).

Our goal was to collect ten to fifteen tokens of the variable from each of the 205 participants. We hoped to collect ten tokens from each signer involved in a conversation (n = 205), and five tokens from each participant involved in an interview (n = 149). Thirteen signers, however, did not produce a sufficient number of target signs during the course of the conversation or interview, so we have a smaller number of tokens from these individuals. This lower number of target signs occurred partly because most of our target signs were relatively infrequent and our coding rules were rather strict (as described below, we coded an upper limit of three tokens containing the same lexical item so we could maximize the mix of lexical items investigated in the study). In some cases, then, these parameters made it difficult to collect sufficient examples from those who did not participate very much in the discussion or (for some participants older than the age of seventy years) from those who used a great deal of fingerspelling. Coding began from the beginning of the videotape, once the conversation or interview had begun. We generally coded the first ten target signs (in the conversations) or the first five target signs (in the interviews) that were produced by each participant, unless the signer's posture or some other problem prevented us from seeing the signer properly on the videotape. In this case, we may have ignored target signs that we could not code confidently and, instead, waited until the signer moved into a position in which his or her signing could be seen clearly before continuing coding.

A sign was coded as a citation form (+cf) if it was produced clearly above the eyebrow ridge and as a noncitation form (−cf) if it was produced clearly below the eyebrow ridge. A very small number of signs appeared to be produced on the eyebrow ridge itself and were coded as citation forms.

Many target signs appeared in double-handed form in which the dominant and subordinate hand have the same handshape and location as well as have identical or symmetrical forms of movement. If the dominant hand was at a location above the eyebrow ridge, but the subordinate hand was not, then the sign was coded as a citation form. Double-handed variants of the target signs were coded as noncitation forms only if neither hand was in contact with or in proximity to locations at or above the eyebrow ridge.

To reduce possible lexical effects associated with particular signs, we set a limit on the number of tokens coded with the same lexical item (an upper limit of three tokens with the same lexical item in the conversational data and two in the interview data). These limits were necessary because a small number of target signs occurred much more frequently than the others in our dataset (just ten signs — THINK, KNOW, NOT-KNOW, MOTHER, NAME, REMEMBER, FORGET, UNDERSTAND, WONDER, and WORRY — account for 80 percent of all tokens in the dataset used in this study), and it would have been very easy for the entire study to have been entirely based on data from a handful of very common lexical items.

In this study, we have assumed that the citation form of each target sign was the form from which all other variants are derived. We coded tokens for the possible effects of a range of social and linguistic factors on this underlying form, using a coding scheme based on that used in the ASL study (Lucas, Bayley, and Valli 2001). Linguistic factors included sign frequency, grammatical function, preceding and following phonological environment, and situational variety.

Recent research has suggested that word frequency may have a role in phonological variation and change (Bybee 2002) because frequent lexical items are known to behave differently than less frequent ones. For example, highly frequent lexical items in English are produced with a 20 percent shorter duration than less frequent words in conversation (Jurafsky et al. 2002). Duration is in turn associated with an increased likelihood of the reduction or assimilation of vowel sounds (Thomas 2002). Thus we can conclude that high frequency words undergo greater phonological reduction than low frequency words (Bybee 2002). Because it is possible that high frequency signs are also produced with shorter durations and a greater tendency for reduction and assimilation, we opted to test for the effects of frequent lexical items by coding for high frequency and low frequency lexical items. We coded as high frequency the ten lexical items discussed above that appeared in 80 percent of all the tokens in the dataset used in this study. Interestingly, these items are not only highly frequent in our dataset; most of them are also high frequency signs in the Wellington Corpus of New Zealand Sign Language[2] (McKee and Kennedy 1999). In fact, eight of these ten items appear in the top 200 most frequent lexical items in the New Zealand Sign Language corpus. The remaining eighty lexical items that appeared much less frequently in our dataset were coded as low frequency signs.

For grammatical function, we coded whether tokens were acting as nouns (e.g., NAME, MOTHER), adjectives (e.g., YELLOW, CRAZY), or verbs (e.g., KNOW, THINK). Unlike in the ASL study (Lucas, Bayley, and Valli 2001), there were no grammatical functors (e.g., FOR, WHY) produced at this location in Auslan. We used a number of semantic and morphosyntactic criteria to decide whether a sign was acting as a noun (e.g., nouns generally refer to people, places, or things; act as arguments of a verb; and may be preceded by a determiner), a verb (verbs generally refer to actions or states and act as predicates), or an adjective (adjectives generally describe a property of a noun, may be used attributively, and may be modified by an intensifier such as VERY). In some cases, however, it was not easy to determine the grammatical function of a specific sign. In an utterance such as PRO-I NAME B-E-N, the sign NAME might be acting either as a noun (because the sign glossed here as PRO-I can act as a possessive determiner in Auslan) or as a verb (the sign NAME can sometimes also be used to mean "be called," although other signs such as BE-CALLED or QUOTE are also used for this meaning). In such cases, the coders used their native signer intuitions, sometimes in consultation with the project researchers, to make a decision about the role being played by that sign in that specific context.

For the phonological environment, we coded (a) whether the target sign was preceded or followed immediately by another sign or (b) whether there was a pause before or after it. In coding pauses, we grouped together (a) whether the target sign occurred at the beginning or the end of a turn (in which case the hands moved from or toward their resting position on the signer's lap or an the arm of the chair) or (b) whether the sign was preceded or followed by a discernible hold (i.e., there was a complete stop in the flow of signing). We reasoned that both beginning or resuming motion would involve overcoming the inertia of the hand, for example, and that this change may have similar effects on location variation (i.e., physiological principles of economy of effort would predict that noncitation forms of signs may be more common after a pause or hold).

We also coded the location of the preceding and following sign, noting whether the sign was made at the level of the signer's head or the signer's body (for our purposes, signs that occurred at the level of the signer's neck or below were coded as being made at body level). We coded whether the preceding and following sign appeared to make contact with the body (and if it did, whether it contacted the head or body or whether the dominant hand contacted the subordinate hand). In most cases, contact with the body was clear on the videotape, but in a small number of cases, it had to be inferred from other factors such as the proximity of the hand to the body, the apparent strength of the movement toward and away from the location, and so forth. In the data from Perth, Adelaide, Melbourne, and Brisbane, we also noted whether the target sign was preceded or followed by a sign involving a switch of hand dominance. We found that in approximately 5 percent of all tokens, the sign before or after the target sign was produced with the nondominant hand (e.g., in the phrase PRO-I THINK YOU WRONG, one signer produced the sign PRO-I with the left hand whereas that signer produced the rest of the string with the right hand). We reasoned that because THINK is the first sign in the string being produced on the right hand, the location of the sign PRO-1 on the left hand may have less effect on the location of target sign. Thus, we coded for this aspect of the phonological environment in case it turned out to be relevant for our understanding of location variation.

Unlike the ASL study (Lucas, Bayley and Valli 2001), we did not code for "impeded signing" (i.e., whether the signer's elbows or forearms were resting on a chair or table). Although we filmed all participants away from tables or other surfaces on which they could lean while signing, a small number of signers did sometimes rest their elbows on their legs, and participants in Perth were filmed sitting in chairs with arms that made it possible for participants to lean on their elbows. As far as possible, however, we did not code signs that were produced when signers were resting their arms on a surface because the ASL study indicated signs produced in this way made a noncitation form of target signs much more likely. Because this factor is one that is neither strictly linguistic nor strictly social in nature, we did not want to include it as a possible source of variation in our data.

We also coded for situational variation in which the target sign occurred, noting whether the tokens were collected from conversations or interviews. We reasoned that the more structured nature of the interview might have led to a slightly more formal variety of signing that included a greater use of citation forms.

As described above, we also coded for the following social factors: gender (male or female), age (young, mature, older, and elderly), social class (middle class or working class), region (Adelaide, Brisbane, Melbourne, Perth, or Sydney), and language background (participants with signing deaf parents or with hearing parents).

We conducted an interrater reliability study in which the two coders independently coded the linguistic factors in a subset of the tokens. We compared the coding of the linguistic factors because only these factors were based on observation of the videotaped data. The coding of social factors was based on the participant's responses to the demographic questionnaires; consequently, this information was simply transferred to the coding sheets and involved little decision making by the coders. The two coders achieved an interrater reliability score of 93 percent and were able to resolve all remaining disagreements about coding either by correcting errors on the coding sheets that were attributed to lapses in attention or by reviewing specific examples on the videotapes.

The coding procedure described here initially produced a dataset of 2,667 tokens. After a first analysis of these data, all the tokens of eight signs from the original list of ninety target signs (i.e., TRAIN, QUOTE, TENNIS, NETBALL, TALL, HAIRCUT, KEEN, and CELEBRATE) were removed from the dataset when we later found that native signers appeared to vary in their production of the citation form of these signs (i.e., some signers produced these signs at locations lower than the forehead region). As a result, some 221 tokens (representing 8 percent of the original dataset) were excluded from the analysis presented here, which was conducted on a smaller dataset of 2,446 tokens.

ANALYSIS

We analyzed the data using VARBRUL software to facilitate statistical analysis and cross-linguistic comparison with ASL. The specific software was GoldVarb 2.1, developed by David Rand and David Sankoff at the University of Montréal. VARBRUL enables the simultaneous analysis of multiple factors that influence sociolinguistic variation. As can be seen in the third columns of tables 2 and 3, "the program provides a numerical measure of the strength of each factor's influence, relative to other factors in the same group, on the occurrence of the linguistic variable under investigation" (2001, 46). These numerical values range from 0 to 1.00 and are referred to as VARBRUL "weights." A weight between .50 and 1.00 means that the particular factor "favors" the use of the variant form (i.e., in the case of the location variation discussed here, "favors" means that the noncitation form of the sign is more likely to occur in this context) whereas a weight between 0 and .50 indicates that it "disfavors" the variant (i.e., the noncitation form is less likely to occur).

In addition, VARBRUL also tests the significance of each factor's effect on the use of a variant and the relative strength of the influence of each factor when compared with other factors. The most important factor is referred to as a "first-order constraint." The application of VARBRUL to the study of phonological variation in signed languages is described in more detail in Lucas, Bayley, and Valli (2001), and the use of the software is explained in Young and Bayley (1996), Bayley (2002), and Paolillo (2002).

RESULTS

The results of the VARBRUL analysis showed that location variation in Auslan, as in ASL, is not random but is influenced by a number of linguistic and social factors. Unlike in the ASL data (Lucas, Bayley, and Valli 2001), however, the noncitation forms of these signs (i.e., those produced at locations on or near the body lower than the forehead region) were less common than the citation forms. Citation forms account for approximately 57 percent of the tokens ($n = 1,402$) whereas noncitation forms represent 43 percent ($n = 1,044$).

Linguistic Factors

In terms of the linguistic factors that we analyzed, five proved significant at the .05 level: sign type, preceding location, following location, following sign or pause, and preceding contact. The significant linguistic factors are shown in table 2 with their VARBRUL weights (with the noncitation form, or –cf, as the application value[3]), their input probability (the overall likelihood that signers will choose the noncitation form, expressed as a percentage), and the overall number of tokens with the relevant factor.

An early run of VARBRUL showed that both grammatical function and sign frequency were significant. Verbs appeared to favor the noncitation form whereas adjectives and nouns appeared to disfavor it. High frequency signs (i.e., the ten most frequent lexical items) favored –cf whereas low frequency items disfavored –cf. A closer inspection of the results, however, indicated some unexpected interaction between grammatical function and frequency. It was clear that only a subset of verbs (the high frequency verbs) favored –cf whereas all the remaining verbs, nouns, and adjectives disfavored –cf. A decision was thus made to combine these factor groups to form a new factor group called "sign type" with all lexical items being classified into one of four sign type groups: high frequency verbs, high frequency nouns and adjectives, low frequency verbs, and low frequency nouns and adjectives. The resulting factor group, sign type, proved to be the first-order constraint. We found that frequent verbs favored –cf ($p = .550$) whereas all other sign types strongly disfavored –cf ($p = .311$).

All the remaining significant linguistic factors reflect aspects of the immediate phonological environment. We found that the preceding loca-

TABLE 2. *Linguistic Factors*

Factor Group	Factor	VARBRUL Weight	Percentage of –cf	Overall Number of Tokens with the Relevant Factor (N = 2,446)
Sign type (grammatical function and lexical frequency)	Highly frequent verbs	.550	47	1,951
	Others	.311	26	495
Preceding location	Body	.540	44	1,605
	Head	.377	31	514
Following location	Body	.525	45	1,482
	Head	.445	36	673
Following sign or pause	Pause	.655	56	291
	Sign	.478	41	2,155
Preceding contact	Head or hands	.531	40	620
	No contact	.507	40	651
	Body	.462	42	849
Input	Total	.403	43	2,446

Note: X_2/cell = 1.0227; log likelihood –1534.855; all factor groups significant at $p < .05$.

tion was the strongest of these factors, with preceding signs produced in the body region favoring –cf (p = .540) and those in the head region strongly disfavoring –cf (p = .377). The factor of following location was also important, with similar, although somewhat weaker effects: following signs in the body region slightly favored –cf (p = .525) and those in the head region disfavored –cf (p = .445). Whether the target sign was followed by another sign or a pause was significant: signs followed by other signs disfavored –cf (p = .478) whereas those followed by a pause strongly favored –cf (p = .655). Finally, the preceding sign making contact with the body was also important. Preceding signs that involved contact with the subordinate hand or with the head favored –cf (p = .531) whereas those that made contact with the body disfavored –cf (p = .462). Signs with no contact were the nearly neutral reference point (p = .507).

In summary, the following linguistic factors favored the citation form: (a) high frequency nouns and adjectives; (b) low frequency verbs, nouns, and adjectives; (c) signs that were preceded or followed by signs made in the head region; (d) signs that were preceded by signs making contact with the body; and (e) signs that were followed by another sign rather than by a pause. The following linguistic factors all favored the lowered variants: (a) target signs in the high frequency verb category (i.e., THINK, KNOW, NOT-KNOW, REMEMBER, FORGET, UNDERSTAND, WONDER, and WORRY) and (b) those signs that were preceded or followed by other signs made in the body region, were preceded by a sign making contact with the head or subordinate hand, or were followed by a pause. Finally, the following factors were all shown to be not significant: whether or not (a) the following sign made contact with the body, (b) the target sign was preceded by a pause, and (c) switches in hand dominance occurred before or after a target sign.

Social Factors

Three of the social factors were significant at the .05 level: age, region, and gender. These factors are shown in table 3 with their VARBRUL weights, input probability, and number of tokens.

Age was the second-order constraint overall (ranking just behind sign type), and the strongest of all significant social factors. An early run of VARBRUL showed that people of ages fifty-one–seventy and those of ages seventy-one and older all tended to use fewer examples of –cf whereas those of ages fifteen–thirty and thirty-one–fifty tended to use more, so in later runs, we combined these four groups into two groups ("younger" represents those of ages fifteen–fifty and "older," those of ages fifty-one or older). We found that older signers (i.e., those age fifty-one or older) clearly disfavor –cf (p = .398) whereas younger signers favor –cf (p = .575). The next most important constraint was region. Signers in the smaller cities of Adelaide, Brisbane, and Perth disfavored –cf (p = .456) whereas those in the larger cities of Sydney and Melbourne favored –cf (p = .556). These findings result from combining these five cities into two groups based on patterns found in an earlier run of VARBRUL. Finally, male signers tended to disfavor –cf (p = .464) whereas female signers slightly favored –cf (p = .533).

In summary, older signers, signers in smaller state capitals, and men favored the citation forms of these signs whereas younger signers, participants from larger cities, and women tended to favor the lowered variants. Social class, situational variety (i.e., conversation or interview), and

TABLE 3. *Social Factors*

Factor Group	Factor	VARBRUL Weight	Percentage of –cf	Overall Number of Tokens with the Relevant Factor (N = 2,446)
Age	Younger (< 50 years)	.575	50	1,414
	Older (≥ 51 years)	.398	33	1,032
Region	Sydney and Melbourne	.556	48	1,077
	Adelaide, Brisbane and Perth	.456	38	1,369
Gender	Female	.533	47	1,275
	Male	.464	39	1,171
Input	Total	.403	43	2,446

Notes: X²/cell = 1.0227; log likelihood –1534.855; all factor groups significant at *p* < .05.

language background (i.e., whether signers had deaf signing parents or not) were not significant.

DISCUSSION

Our results show that location variation in the class of Auslan signs exemplified by THINK, NAME and CLEVER is not random, but is simultaneously influenced by a number of linguistic and social factors. In this section, we compare our results with those from the original ASL study, discuss the possible relationship between grammatical function and lexical frequency, and consider the possibility that the lowering of these signs in Auslan represents an example of language change in progress.

Comparison with ASL Results

In terms of linguistic and social factors, our results both resemble and differ from the ASL findings. A comparison of the linguistic factors is shown in table 4. We discuss here only those linguistic factors investigated in both studies (i.e., preceding and following location, contact with the body, and pauses).

Both investigations show that the location of the preceding sign is important, but only in the Auslan results do we also see a significant role for the location of the following sign. In all cases, adjacent signs produced at the neck or below resulted in the greater likelihood of a lowered target sign.

Whether or not an adjacent sign makes contact with the body is also an important factor in both the ASL and Auslan studies, although Lucas, Bayley, and Valli (2001) found it was significant only in the sign following a target sign whereas our data reveal a role only for the sign preceding a target sign. In addition, the types of influence in each language differ. In the ASL results, preceding signs that make no contact with the body favor the noncitation form, and preceding signs that make contact disfavor it. In the Auslan study, following signs that make contact with the head or subordinate hand disfavor the noncitation form, and those that contact the body favor the noncitation form. It is not clear how to account for these differences, although they may be related to methodological differences in the Australian and American studies discussed below.

Finally, the Auslan results also show that whether a sign or a pause follows a target sign is important, with pauses strongly favoring noncitation forms. The fact that results were significant for (a) following location (in which following locations on or near the body rather than the head favored noncitation forms) and (b) following sign or pause may be related. If the hands are moving away from the forehead region either to produce a sign in the body region or to allow the hands to return to a resting position, then this appears to favor the production of noncitation forms. Thus, our hypothesis that a preceding pause may influence the production of noncitation forms was not confirmed.

Overall, the Auslan results indicate relatively more influence from the immediate phonological environment (four significant factor groups) than in ASL (two significant factor groups). Two reasons may explain this difference. First, it is possible that phonological conditioning of location variation is more important in Auslan than in ASL and that the specific details of phonological variation differ from one signed language to the next, as is true of spoken languages. Alternatively, our different findings may reflect different approaches to the investigation of location variation in the two languages. As explained above, the target signs coded in the Auslan study were all produced in citation form at locations in contact with, in proximity to, or at the same height as the signer's forehead or above whereas the target signs in the ASL research also included signs made in citation form at locations slightly lower than the forehead, for example, ASL SEE. In particular, Lucas, Bayley, and Valli (2001) included

TABLE 4. *Linguistic Factors in Auslan and ASL*

Ranking of frequency	Auslan			ASL		
	Factor	Type	VARBRUL Weight	Factor	Type	VARBRUL Weight
1	Sign type (grammatical function and lexical frequency)	High frequency verbs Others	.550 .311	Grammatical function	Prepositions and interrogatives Nouns and verbs Adjectives	.581 .486 .316
2	Preceding location	Body Head	.540 .377	Preceding location	Body Head	.514 .463
3	Following location	Body Head	.525 .445	Following contact	No contact Contact	.525 .466
4	Following sign or pause	Pause Sign	.655 .478	—	—	—
5	Preceding contact	Head or hands No contact Body	.531 .507 .462	—	—	—

lexicalized compounds such as ASL BELIEVE in which the second component of the sign was always produced at a lower location. This choice may
have had an effect on the types of phonological environment that proved
to be significant, particularly those related to the following phonological
environment (i.e., following location and following sign or pause).

Turning to the social factors (shown in table 5), we find that age was
most significant in both the Auslan and ASL results. In both communities, we see younger individuals disfavoring the citation form and older
people favoring it. We also see that regional variation is important, with
Auslan and ASL signers in larger urban communities (e.g., Melbourne,
Victoria, and Boston, Massachusetts) disfavoring the citation form and
those in smaller cities and more rural communities (e.g., Adelaide, South
Australia, and Staunton, Virginia) favoring it.

Gender was also important in both sets of results, but it works differently in the Auslan and ASL data. In ASL, female signers tended to be
conservative and disfavor the noncitation form whereas males favored it.
In Auslan, however, women favored the noncitation form whereas men
disfavored it. The ASL results for gender were explained by Lucas, Bayley, and Valli (2001) as being similar to patterns of variation in spoken
languages where it has been found that men use a higher frequency of
nonstandard forms than women in stable sociolinguistic contexts (Labov
1990). This pattern is referred to as Labovian Principle I and is a fundamental tenet of sociolinguistics (Cheshire 2002). Lucas, Bayley, and Valli
(2001) pointed out that the citation forms of signs in this class are the
variants listed in dictionaries, which are commonly taught in signed language classes and possibly used in more formal situations, and thus the
suggestion that they represent "standard" forms seems well-motivated.

Labovian Principle II states, however, that in most examples of language change, women use a higher frequency of the incoming forms than
men. In the next section, we consider evidence that the lowering of signs
in the class of signs exemplified by THINK, NAME and CLEVER represents
a language change in progress in Auslan. Thus, the fact that women use
more noncitation forms in this instance is not surprising in light of Labovian Principle II. In ASL, however, the fact that men use more noncitation
forms seems to suggest that we have a stable example of sociolinguistic
variation whereas the results from different age groups indicates a possible language change. It may be that change is stigmatized in some way
in the American deaf community (e.g., lowering of this class of signs may

Table 5. Social Factors in Auslan and ASL

Ranking of frequency	Auslan			ASL		
	Factor Group	Factor	VARBRUL Weight	Factor Group	Factor	VARBRUL Weight
1	Age	Younger (<51)	.575	Age	15–25	.602
					26–54	.517
		Older (≥51)	.398		55+	.416
2	Region	Syd. and Melb.	.556	Gender	Male	.544
		Adel., Bris., and Perth	.456		Female	.451
3	Gender	Female	.533	Language background	Hearing parents	.519
		Male	.464		Deaf parents	.444
4	—	—	—	Region	CA, LA, MD, MA, KS/MO	.529
					Washington	.461
					Virginia	.334
5	—	—	—	Ethnicity and social class	Caucasian middle and working class	.555
					African-American middle class	.455
					African-American working class	.314

be considered a "lazy" form of signing), and thus, women tend to avoid the incoming form because it is perceived as nonstandard usage.

Other differences between the ASL and Auslan findings reflect the fact that language background, ethnicity and (to a limited extent) social class proved important in ASL whereas language background and social class were not significant in Auslan (ethnicity was not included in the Auslan study, as explained above). ASL signers with deaf parents (i.e., native signers) favored the citation form whereas signers with hearing parents did not. Caucasian middle- and working-class signers of ASL disfavored the citation form whereas African-American working-class signers strongly favored it. African-American middle-class signers also favored the citation form, but not to the same extent as working-class signers. Thus, native signers and African-American signers of both social classes appear to be more conservative than nonnative signers and Caucasian signers.

These results may reflect sociolinguistic factors unique to the American deaf community. For example, social class differences in ASL location variation and the apparent lack of such differences in Auslan may reflect the history of educational opportunities for deaf people in both countries. Because of the existence of specialized tertiary educational institutions such as Gallaudet University, deaf Americans have had access to university education for a longer period of time than deaf Australians, and this longer-term access for deaf Americans may have allowed more time for a middle-class (and middle-class patterns of language usage) to emerge. Lucas and her colleagues suggested that the results based on ethnicity are not surprising, given other research that suggests that African-American signers tend to use older forms of ASL in general (Lucas, Bayley, and Valli 2001). Native signers, they suggested, also may be more protective in their attitudes toward ASL and, thus, be more inclined to use what are perceived as more standard forms. The Auslan study, in which a relatively larger proportion of participants had deaf parents (seventy individuals compared with forty-five in the ASL study), appears to indicate that this attitude may not be shared by Australian native signers.

Grammatical Function and Lexical Frequency in Signed Languages

As we have seen above, we found that grammatical function was significant in an earlier run, but that it interacted with another significant factor: lexical frequency. Our findings suggest that only a subclass of verbs — the high frequency verbs — significantly favored noncitation forms. There were no differences based on grammatical function alone because other types of verbs, nouns, and adjectives all favored citation forms in the same way.

The ASL study (Lucas, Bayley, and Valli 2001), however, reports clear differences in the likelihood of location variation because of grammatical function, with prepositions (e.g., FOR) and interrogatives (e.g., WHY) clearly favoring –cf and adjectives (e.g., DIZZY) clearly disfavoring it. In their discussion of the relationship between grammatical function and location variation in ASL, Lucas, Bayley, and Valli (2001, 146) acknowledged that "as yet unexplored phonological factors may play a role in the patterning of grammatical constraints" on variation in location. For example, they suggested that the fact that prepositions favor –cf may be related to stress. In spoken languages, prepositions are often unstressed and, thus, are more affected by phonological reduction, so the same may be true of signed languages. Stress, however, is not yet well understood in ASL or other signed languages (although some work has begun; see Wilbur and Schick 1987; Wilbur 1990). As a result, there can be little consensus about how best to code for stress in the kind of naturalistic data used in studies of sociolinguistic variation, and consequently, it has not yet been attempted.

One variable that Lucas, Bayley, and Valli (2001) did not consider is lexical frequency. This omission is not surprising because little information about the frequency characteristics of most signed languages is available, and thus, almost no studies of signed language have taken this factor into account (Morford and Macfarlane 2003). As already mentioned above, Bybee (2002) noted that high frequency words appear to undergo reduction at a greater rate than low frequency words. She also showed that lexical frequency is relevant to our understanding of language variation and change, for example, the deletion of word-final /t/ and /d/ in American English. It may be that some of the conditioning of location variation attributed to grammatical function by Lucas and her colleagues reflects lexical frequency effects. Grammatical function words are much more frequent than many content words, for example. In a small-scale study of the frequency characteristics of ASL reported by Morford and Macfarlane (2003), seven of the ten most frequent lexical items in their minicorpus of 4,111 signs were function signs. The preposition FOR and the interrogative WHY are also frequent in ASL conversations — they appear on Morford and Macfarlane's (2003) list of the top thirty-seven most frequent signs (these thirty-seven signs represent those lexical items that occur more than four times per 1,000 signs in their corpus). As with stress, however, more research is needed into lexical frequency in ASL (and other signed languages) before firm conclusions can be drawn, but the Auslan results presented here suggest that this factor may be important for an understanding of phonological variation in signed languages.

Age, Sign Type, Gender, and Region

As Lucas, Bayley, and Valli (2001) pointed out, the lowering of signs made in the forehead region in ASL appears to be an example of a language change in progress. This claim is based first on the "apparent time hypothesis" (Bailey 2002), which suggests that variation in the linguistic system used by speakers of different ages at a single point in time can indicate a change in progress. Although that hypothesis rests on the assumption that the linguistic usage of a particular age group will not change as this group grows older, this inference has proven reliable in a large number of studies (Chambers 1995). Lucas, Bayley, and Valli's (2001) claim also stems from the fact that the lowering of signs made in the forehead region may reflect a more general pattern in ASL dating back to the nineteenth century. As Frishberg (1975) first observed, ASL signs previously produced in more peripheral areas of the visual field (e.g., HELP) appear to have moved toward more central areas over time.

We would like to draw on the apparent time hypothesis and the fact that the lowering of signs is possibly also a historical process at work in the BSL family of signed languages (e.g., Kyle and Woll [1985] claim that the sign MAYBE in BSL has moved over time from a forehead location to one in neutral space) to suggest that the age variation we have found may also indicate a change in progress in Auslan. When we analyze our results by sign type and age, we find that the percentage of both categories of signs (High Frequency Verbs and Other, including high frequency nouns and adjectives, low frequency nouns and adjectives, and low frequency verbs) in noncitation form is higher for younger than older signers, as clearly shown in figure 5.

In addition, we find that the pattern of diffusion across the five sites also illustrates a typical spread of language change through a community. Research on the pronunciation of vowels in the American English spoken in large northern U.S. cities such as Chicago and Detroit shows that the standard vowel /æ/ is raising and fronting to /ɛ/ so *bat* sounds like *bet*. This change has started in these larger, densely populated urban areas. Because of their importance as cultural centers, the change has spread to other parts of the country, but it has not done so all at once. Research has shown that first, it spread to moderately sized cities; next, to smaller cities; and finally, to rural areas (Wolfram and Schilling-Estes 1998).

Similarly, in our data, we find that when we analyze our results by age and region (see figure 6), we see that both younger and older signers in

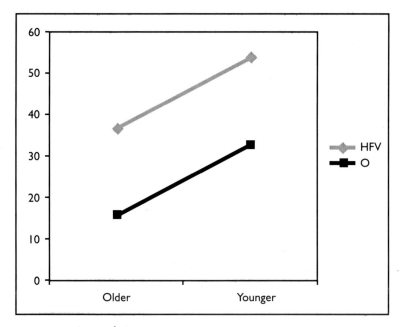

FIGURE 5: *Age and sign type*

the larger urban centers of Sydney and Melbourne use a higher percentage of noncitation forms than younger and older signers in the smaller cities of Adelaide, Brisbane, and Perth.

Last, we find that an analysis of age and gender (see figure 7) shows that younger women use more noncitation forms than older women, younger men use more noncitation forms than older men, and women use more noncitation forms than men in the same age group. As already mentioned, this pattern is an extremely common one in language change.

CONCLUSION

Our results (drawing on the VARBRUL analysis of 2,446 tokens from 205 deaf native and fluent signers in five cities) indicate that location variation in the class of Auslan signs exemplified by THINK, NAME and CLEVER is a textbook example of a sociolinguistic variable influenced by linguistic and social factors, as has also been reported for this class of signs in ASL. These findings also resemble many other examples of phonological variation in spoken languages (Chambers, Trudgill, and Schilling-Estes 2002). Our research strongly suggests that, as has also been proposed for ASL,

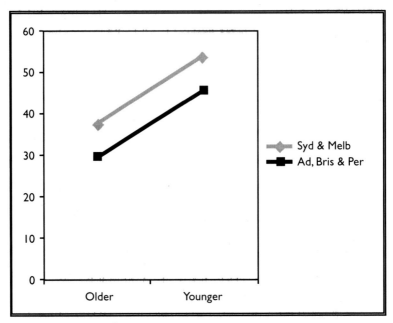

FIGURE 6. *Age and region*

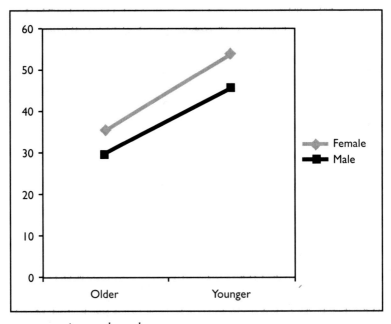

FIGURE 7. *Age and gender*

the lowering of signs made in the forehead region is a language change in progress in Auslan, led by younger signers and those in large urban centers. Unlike the ASL results, we find that this change appears to be led by women, and we do not find evidence that social class influences location variation in Auslan. These results may reflect differences in the social structure, history, and language attitudes in the two deaf communities. Moreover, the linguistic factors indicate a relatively greater role for the immediate phonological environment in the Auslan data than has been reported for ASL, although this finding may reflect methodological differences between the two studies. Finally, our study suggests a role for lexical frequency working in tandem with grammatical function, something not previously investigated in any signed language.

NOTES

1. Videoclips of many of the Auslan signs discussed in this paper may be viewed at the Auslan SignBank Web site (http://www.auslan.org.au), an online version of the Auslan dictionary (Johnston 1997).

2. The Wellington Corpus of New Zealand Sign Language is a transcription of approximately fifty hours of conversational New Zealand Sign Language, a signed language closely related to Auslan. The conversations include a range of topics, discussed by more than eighty deaf signers.

3. In the term *application value*, "the term 'application' refers to the application of a linguistic rule, so the application value means the variant of the variable that is realized by the hypothesized rule. It stands in contrast to the *non-application value*, which may be regarded as the underlying form" (Paolillo 2002, 30).

REFERENCES

Ash, S. 2002. Social class. In *The handbook of language variation and change*, ed. J. K. Chambers, P. Trudgill, and N. Schilling-Estes, 402–22. Oxford: Blackwell.

Bailey, G. 2002. Real and apparent time. In *The handbook of language variation and change*, ed. J. K. Chambers, P. Trudgill, and N. Schilling-Estes, 312–32. Oxford: Blackwell.

Bayley, R. 2002. The quantitative paradigm. In *The handbook of language variation and change*, ed. J. K. Chambers, P. Trudgill and N. Schilling-Estes, 117–41. Oxford: Blackwell.

Bernal, B., and L. Wilson, ed. 2004. *Dictionary of Auslan: English to Auslan (with regional sign variations)*. Melbourne, Victoria: Deaf Children Australia.

Branson, J., B. Bernal, J. Toms, R. Adam, and D. Miller. 1995. *Introduction to Auslan, Level 2: Student workbook*. Melbourne, Victoria: La Trobe University.

Branson, J., G. Peters, J. Bernal, and B. Bernal. 1992. *Introduction to Auslan: Level 1*. Melbourne, Victoria: National Institute for Deaf Studies and Sign Language Research and La Trobe University Language Centre.

Bybee, J. L. 2002. Word frequency and context of use in the lexical diffusion of phonetically conditioned sound change. *Language Variation and Change* 14: 261–90.

Carty, B. M. 2004. Managing their own affairs: The Australian deaf community during the 1920s and 1930s. Ph.D. diss., Centre for Deafness, Griffith University, Brisbane, Queensland.

Chambers, J. K. 1995. *Sociolinguistic theory: Linguistic variation and its social significance*. Oxford: Blackwell.

Chambers, J. K., P. Trudgill, and N. Schilling-Estes. 2002. *The handbook of language variation and change*. Oxford: Blackwell.

Cheshire, J. 2002. Sex and gender in variationist research. In *The handbook of language variation and change*, ed. J. K. Chambers, P. Trudgill, and N. Schilling-Estes, 423–43. Oxford: Blackwell.

Emmorey, K. D. 2002. *Language, cognition, and the brain: Insights from sign language research*. Mahwah, N.J.: Lawrence Erlbaum.

Fought, C. 2002. Ethnicity. In *The handbook of language variation and change*, ed. J. K. Chambers, P. Trudgill and N. Schilling-Estes, 444–72. Oxford: Blackwell.

Frishberg, N. 1975. Arbitrariness and iconicity: Historical change in American Sign Language. *Language* 51: 696–719.

Horvath, B., and R. Horvath. 2002. The geolinguistics of /l/ vocalization in Australia and New Zealand. *Journal of Sociolinguistics* 6(3): 319–46.

Hyde, M., and D. J. Power. 1991. *The use of Australian Sign Language by Deaf people*. Brisbane, Queensland: Centre for Deafness Studies and Research, Griffith University.

Johnston, T. 1987. *A curriculum outline for teaching Australian Sign Language (Auslan) as a second language*. Adelaide, South Australia: TAFE National Centre for Research and Development.

———. 1989. Auslan: The sign language of the Australian deaf community. Ph.D. diss., University of Sydney, Sydney, New South Wales.

———, ed. 1997. *Signs of Australia on CD-ROM: A dictionary of Auslan* CD-ROM, version 1.0 for Windows. North Rocks, New South Wales: North Rocks Press.

————, ed. 1998. *Signs of Australia: A new dictionary of Auslan.* North Rocks, New South Wales: North Rocks Press.

————. 2002a. BSL, Auslan and NZSL: Three signed languages or one? In *Cross-linguistic perspectives in sign language research: Selected papers from TISLR 2000,* ed. A. Baker, B. van den Bogaerde, and O. Crasborn, 47–69. Hamburg: Signum Verlag.

————. 2002b. The representation of English using Auslan: Implications for deaf bilingualism and English literacy. *Australian Journal of Education of the Deaf* 8: 23–37.

————. 2003. W(h)ither the deaf community? Population, genetics, and the future of Auslan. *American Annals of Deaf* 148(5): 358–77.

Johnston, T., and A. Schembri. 1999. On defining lexeme in a sign language. *Sign Language and Linguistics* 2(1): 115–85.

————, eds. 2003. *The survival guide to Auslan: A beginner's pocket dictionary of Australian Sign Language.* Sydney, New South Wales: North Rocks Press.

Jurafsky, D., A. Bell, M. Gregory, and W. D. Raymond. 2001. Probabilistic relations between words: Evidence from reduction in lexical production. In *Frequency and the emergence of linguistic structure,* ed. J. Bybee and P. Hooper, 229–54. Amsterdam: John Benjamins.

Kyle, J., and B. Woll. 1985. *Sign language: The study of deaf people and their language.* Cambridge: Cambridge University Press.

Labov, W. 1990. The intersection of sex and social class in the course of language change. *Language Variation and Change* 2: 205–54.

————. 1994. *Principles of linguistic change: Internal factors.* Oxford: Blackwell.

Liddell, S. K., and R. E. Johnson. 1989. American Sign Language: The phonological base. *Sign Language Studies* 64:195–277.

Lucas, C., and C. Valli. 1992. *Language contact in the American deaf community.* San Diego: Academic Press.

Lucas, C., R. Bayley, and C. Valli. 2001. *Sociolinguistic variation in American Sign Language.* Washington, D.C.: Gallaudet University Press.

McKee, D., and G. Kennedy. 1999. A list of 1,000 frequently-used signs in New Zealand Sign Language. In *New Zealand Sign Language: Distribution, origins, reference,* ed. G. Kennedy, 17–25. Deaf Studies Research Unit Occasional Publication 2. Wellington, New Zealand: Deaf Studies Research Unit, Victoria University.

————. 2000. Lexical comparison of signs from American, Australian, British and New Zealand Sign Languages. In *The signs of language revisited: An anthology to honor Ursula Bellugi and Edward Klima,* ed. K. D. Emmorey and H. Lane, 49–76. Mahwah, N.J.: Lawrence Erlbaum.

Morford, J., and J. MacFarlane. 2003. Frequency characteristics of American Sign Language. *Sign Language Studies* 3(2): 213–25.

Paolillo, J. C. 2002. *Analyzing linguistic variation: Statistical models and methods*. Stanford, Calif.: CSLI Publications.

Schembri, A. 2001. Issues in the analysis of polycomponential verbs in Australian Sign Language (Auslan). Ph.D. diss., University of Sydney, Sydney, New South Wales.

Schembri, A., and T. Johnston. 2004. Sociolinguistic variation in Auslan (Australian Sign Language): A research project in progress. *Deaf Worlds: International Journal of Deaf Studies* 20(1): 78–90.

Sutton-Spence, R., and B. Woll. 1990. Variation and recent change in fingerspelling in British Sign Language. *Language Variation and Change* 2: 313–30.

Thomas, E. R. 2002. Instrumental phonetics. In *The handbook of language variation and change*, ed. J. K. Chambers, P. Trudgill, and N. Schilling-Estes, 168–200. Oxford: Blackwell.

Wilbur, R. B. 1990. An experimental investigation of stressed sign production. *International Journal of Sign Linguistics* 1(1): 41–60.

Wilbur, R. B., and B. S. Schick. 1987. The effects of linguistic stress on ASL signs. *Language and Speech* 30(4): 301–24.

Wolfram, W., and N. Schilling-Estes. 1998. *American English: Dialects and variation*. Oxford: Blackwell.

Young, R., and R. Bayley. 1996. VARBRUL analysis for second language acquisition research. In *Second language acquisition and linguistic variation*, ed. R. Bayley and D. R. Preston, 253–306. Amsterdam: John Benjamins.

Part 4   Discourse Analysis

Establishing and Maintaining Sight Triangles:

Conversations between Deaf Parents

and Hearing Toddlers in Puerto Rico

Susan Mather, Yolanda Rodriguez-Fraticelli,
Jean F. Andrews, and Juanita Rodriguez

An unexplored area of child language research is the study of hearing toddlers of Deaf parents. These children of Deaf adults, or Codas, represent a unique population in which to study parent-child discourse. Although Codas do not share their parents' hearing loss, they inherit their parents' linguistic and cultural heritage (Preston 1994; Singleton and Tittle 2000; Bishop and Hicks 2005). They are raised bilingually, bimodally, and biculturally, using a signed language and a spoken language. Depending on the family background and interests, these children are typically acculturated into both worlds — Deaf and hearing.

This study examined the communication between two hearing toddlers and their Deaf or Coda parents as the toddlers were learning Puerto Rican Sign Language (PRSL) and spoken Spanish at home. When those children eventually go to school, they will learn to read and write Spanish and English (Rodriguez 1993). The toddlers' extended families are composed of many Deaf aunts, uncles, cousins, and grandparents. The toddler Codas in this study also attended various Deaf community functions where they socialized not only with other Deaf adults and Deaf children but also with other hearing adults and children whose parents are Deaf.

Three research questions were asked to assess the communication patterns of the four parents (three are Deaf and one is a hearing Coda) as

This study was funded under U.S. Department of Education grant number H325E980050, Training Doctoral Level Leaders in Deaf Education, Jean F. Andrews, Ph.D., Project Director.

they interacted with their hearing toddlers during activities such as eating, reading a book, and playing with a toy.

1. How does the parent prepare the child before each activity and use a certain object to set up a conversation with the child?
2. How does the parent begin and maintain conversation before, during, and after each type of activity?
3. How does the parent use turn-taking in such conversations?

AN OVERVIEW OF KEY COMMUNICATION FACTORS

The research that has explored various aspects of bilingual and bimodal communication in children has provided a starting point from which to proceed with our investigations. In addition, the investigations into various factors that may affect discourse, including adult communication patterns, cultural influences, gender, and age provide insights and help to frame our work.

The Bilingual and Bimodal Toddler

Toddlers, young children between eighteen months and three years, develop multiple ways of communicating with their parents, particularly if they have Deaf parents. Concerns have been raised that because Deaf parents use signed language instead of spoken native language as a primary mode of communication with hearing children, the hearing children are stymied in language development. On the contrary, hearing children of Deaf parents actually learn two languages. They learn a signed language from their Deaf parents and a spoken language from hearing relatives, peers, and teachers. Furthermore, they learn their languages on similar timetables as other bilingual children who learn two spoken languages. These children are bilingual in sign and English as well as bimodal in that they use the visual-gestural and auditory-vocal channels to acquire language (Griffith 1985; Jones 1976; Petitto 2000; Prinz and Prinz 1979; Schlesinger and Meadow 1972). Such children offer the field of child language tantalizing evidence that goes against historical psycholinguistic theories of the primacy of speech in the acquisition of language — not only traditional ideas that maintain the idea that the learning of signed language interferes with the acquisition of speech (Wilbur 2000) but also myths about the negative impact of bilingualism for children (Baker 2001).

CHILD-LANGUAGE PRAGMATICS

Child-language pragmatics is the study of how children use language in communication. It focuses on conversations beyond the word or sentence levels (Austin 1962; Grice 1975; Searle 1965). This field is concerned with how parents initiate, maintain, and end a conversation with children. It examines communication behaviors such as TURN-TAKING, cooperation, checking for comprehension, changing topics, or clearing up misunderstandings (Crystal 1997). One focus in particular is on how the caregiver-child dyad lays the foundation for language learning by beginning the communication process. Children learn how to communicate their needs, wants and intentions by modeling their parents and engaging in reciprocal interactions. Mather (1993) discusses the importance of eye pragmatics with very young deaf children. She describes that deaf children learn how to use eye gaze for various purposes (e.g., to take the floor in the group activity, to acknowledge the person who is taking the turn, or to recognize who is talking within the group) through active and intentional teaching rather than through use and interaction with adults. Mather (2003) concludes that in deaf educational settings, children cannot acquire language if they do not know how to use the appropriate eye gaze (individual or group) that is necessary for receiving pragmatics either from a peer or from the teacher.

Baby Sign and Baby Talk

Deaf infants and toddlers use pointing, vocalizations, and fingerbabbling to have conversations with their caregivers (Lederberg and Everhart 2000). Shared visual attention requires the use of face-to-face interactions. Caregivers also share affect or emotions to foster attachment and bonding (Mohay 2000; Spencer 2000). As deaf infants become more interested in objects (which occurs between twelve and fifteen months), they engage in what Spencer (2000) calls "triadic visual attention." Spencer reports that these infants "coordinate their visual attention to objects and persons, usually by switching the direction of their gaze from one to another" (2000, 292). Spencer further reports that these triadic visual attention routines are especially important because the infant needs to switch attention between a communication partner and an object to receive communication involving signs, gestures, and speechreading about the object.

But do triadic visual attention routines involve only the gaze behaviors? We think it involves more. Our data suggest that in preparing the child for communication, parents use a set of visual readiness strategies. These strategies include conducting assessments of children's field of vision, waiting for acknowledgment from the child that a communication event will happen, and using visual and tactile attention-getting behaviors (Mather 2003, 1996, 1993).

Vocal and Signed Toddler Talk

When infants move into toddlerhood (from eighteen months to three years), they transition from the prelinguistic stage to the linguistic stage. At ages between one and one and a half years, they acquire their first words. Deaf and hearing (Coda) toddlers acquire a similar signed vocabulary and grammar (Newport and Meier 1985; Petitto 2000). During conversations, these toddlers bring objects to their parents, point, and use vocalizations or sign approximations to name them. They will call out or wave to get attention. Toddlers will learn to say ritual words such as *hi, bye, thank-you* or *please*. To express negative attitudes, they will use the negative, *no*, and shake their heads. These toddlers have an emerging vocabulary of anywhere from 50 to 500 words. They begin to combine words in the two-word and three-word stages as well as develop their morphemic word endings (e.g., Mommy going). They can use language to tease or to reprimand a younger sibling or adult. Toddlers answer simple questions and can say or gesture, "What's that?" to seek a name of an object.

In a study with fifteen deaf and hearing toddlers playing with their hearing mothers in a playroom, Lederberg and Everhart (2000) found that hearing toddlers were most likely to ask questions, make statements, and imitate their mothers. Deaf toddlers were more likely to direct their mothers with nonlinguistic communication such as pointing. Both deaf and hearing toddlers by age three showed increasing conversations with their mothers when mother and child were looking at an object. As the toddlers grew older, from twenty-two months to three years, mothers of hearing and deaf toddlers decreased their communication, allowing their toddlers more control over the topics. Mothers became more responsive to the topics on which the toddlers focused, decreased their use of orders, and shifted to asking more questions for which they did not already know the answers rather than asking questions for which they already knew the answers.

Both infants and toddlers use eye gaze, vocalizations, and gestures with their caregivers, and through those interactions, they acquire a vocabulary. Nouns are more concrete and, thus, easier to learn than verbs, adjectives, and adverbs. Children quickly acquire other word meanings and functions as parents play word games with them (Gleason 1997; Ninio and Bruner 1986). The vocabulary of hearing toddlers has been widely published in the literature (Gleason 1997). Other studies have documented deaf toddlers' vocabularies (Griswold and Commings 1974; Howell 1984).

Mather (1990, 1994) discusses an adult deducing a toddler's interests based on the toddler's eye gaze and modifying her signing space to accommodate a toddler's vision needs. For example, as the toddler looks at an object, the adult moves into the toddler's line of vision and makes a comment about what the toddler is looking at. Also, she discusses how, with toddlers, adults frequently modify citation forms of signed verbs by producing them as locative verbs (formerly known as directional use of normally nondirectional verbs). For example, one would normally use the citation form, SIT-DOWN in front of the torso to ask another person to sit down. But with the toddler, the adult moves his or her hands toward a chair (where the toddler is supposed to sit) and signs SIT-DOWN in a somewhat larger signing frame. Many other signs such as TOUCH, GO, SAME, and YOUR are similarly modified.

Lestina and Lartz (1993) and Mather (1989) find that mothers and teachers produce miniature signs on books or objects to allow toddlers to see their signing while simultaneously looking at book pictures. Rodriguez (2001) also describes toddler signs of hearing toddlers and their Deaf parents.

Adult-Structured Input

Adults have a special way of conversing with their babies and toddlers, using toddlerese. According to Karp (2002), toddlerese refers to a child's primitive language, consisting of short phrases, frequent repetition, and a mirrored level of emotion. This primitive language has been also called "maternal speech," "motherese," "baby talk," and caregiver talk." Mothers use a simplified baby register. They use shorter sentences that refer to the here and the now and focus on talking about shared activities. Mothers' speech is slower than normal, repetitious, high-pitched, and clearly segmented phonologically. Mothers use fewer word endings than they use with adults. The prosody of the sentences is exaggerated and singsong. For instance, a mother may say to an infant, "Baby go bye-bye" and exaggerate the last words, adding musical sounding words.

Deaf mothers, too, use a motherese with their infants. These mothers use positive affect and sign directly in their infants' line of vision (Erting et al. 1990). In addition, deaf mothers sign more slowly, wave their hands, and tap and touch their child's body to get the child's attention (Maestes y Moores 1980). They make sure their signs are seen (Akerman et al. 1990). Mothers will often use toys or objects that are right in front of them to teach the names of items (Harris et al. 1986).

One study contrasted deaf and hearing mothers with their deaf toddlers and found that deaf mothers were more successful in presenting signs in visual contexts. Deaf mothers redirected their children's attention to look to them or at the objects whereas hearing mothers produced significantly fewer signs (Harris 2001).

It has been pointed out that hearing mothers can talk while their hearing child is doing or looking at something. Eye contact is not required. With a deaf toddler, however, the mother must get the child's visual attention before signing (Harris 2001). Deaf mothers use vision and space to ensure that their toddlers see what they are signing. Because toddlers are active, the mother may have to alter the signing space to ensure that the toddler sees her communication (Harris 2001).

Adult Discourse

How does toddler discourse differ from adult discourse? One difference lies in how the Deaf communicator and the hearing communicator prepare their listeners. Deaf adults tend to use eye gaze, waving, tapping, and touching to get the other adult's attention before starting a conversation. In contrast, hearing adults use voice greetings such as "Hey," or "Hey, Bob," before starting a conversation. Although hearing people do not have to be in the same room or in view of one another to carry on a conversation, Deaf people must have eye contact to prepare for, initiate, maintain, and control a conversation. But Deaf adults must do more than simply get eye contact. They must assess the other vision fields of the other people involved and look for a signal in the others to make sure they are paying attention to the conversation rather than staying in a dreaming or relaxed state. The signer has to wait for the listener to give the signer a signal by nodding or acknowledging in some way that the listener is visually ready. After the signer receives the listener's attention, the signer initiates the signing. These steps are referred to as "preinitiation regulators" (Mather 1996).

Understanding adult discourse helps us understand what the child must learn to become a conversational partner. Before examining toddler discourse, however, we must first understand how Puerto Rican culture and language affect the conversations of Deaf adults and toddlers.

PRSL and Puerto Rican Culture

Deaf Puerto Rican adults use a variety of languages such as spoken and written Spanish, PRSL, spoken and written English, and American Sign Language (ASL). The variety of languages used are the result of many factors, including the history of Deaf Education in Puerto Rico — with the influx of Gallaudet-trained teachers in the early nineteenth century who used a form of ASL and then the Spanish nuns in the early twentieth century who dropped signing and, instead, taught oral Spanish only (Rodriguez 1993). Another influence is the close geography and political proximity of the island to the United States as well as the fact that many American teachers have come to the island to work in various programs and to train teachers at the university level, bringing with them ASL.

In addition, the nonverbal communication already present in the Puerto Rican culture may influence Deaf adults' conversations. The suprasegmental aspect of Puerto Rican Spanish is similar to the nonverbal behaviors in the Deaf culture, resulting in a blending of nonverbal communication behaviors. For instance, hearing Puerto Ricans make extensive use of facial expressions, lip movements, and gestures with their spoken Spanish (Nine-Curt 1974).

PRSL has not been studied extensively by linguists. Matos (1988) has compiled a dictionary of both Spanish an English signs used by Deaf adults in the metropolitan area of San Juan. One limitation is that this book mixes Spanish and English signs, which are from two different signed languages. Another limitation is that this book includes only signs collected in urban areas, not in rural areas.

Another published guide, *The Book of Signs* (Departamento de Educación 1981), provides ASL signs with words translated into Spanish. This document is widely used by public schools in Puerto Rico but is not based on the signed language that is used by the Puerto Rican Deaf community.

In fact, there are no published dictionaries on PRSL that are based on linguistic principles. Furthermore, there are no standards for teaching and using PRSL. Teachers of signed language are largely imported from the United States, and they typically teach ASL. But in the cities and rural areas, most Deaf adults use PRSL, which has its own sign vocabularies that differ from ASL (Rodriguez 1993).

The Deaf adults in this study have been influenced by these language mixing factors. But their language has also developed based on the PRSL they learned from other deaf adults on the island. Their use of PRSL and spoken Spanish has influenced their conversations with their Deaf toddlers. Most Deaf adults on the island are active in Deaf organizations and clubs. There, they socialize with other Deaf adults, further developing their use of PRSL. Parents in this study were fluent users of PRSL, as determined through an evaluation by one of the researchers, using her own native abilities in PRSL.

Gender, Age, and Use of Physical Anatomy

In addition to culture, factors such as gender, age, and use of physical anatomy may influence discourse styles. Although no generalization about gender-based behavior applies to all individuals, males and females typically think, communicate, and behave in different ways (Tannen 1990). Tannen asserts that the basic uses of conversation by women are to establish and support intimacy; for men the use is to establish status. For instance, men's conversations tend to be more direct and competitive whereas woman's conversations may seem evasive, cooperative, and overly polite. These styles are a reflection of cultural differences, and one is not necessarily better than the other. Certainly, many behaviors are common to both sexes, and a degree of overlap occurs in the display of other actions traditionally associated with a certain gender.

Gender plays a role in hearing parent–hearing child conversations, too (Edelsky 1981; Hladik and Edwards 1984). Fathers use a simplified register like mothers do, but it has been reported that fathers' conversations are more intense and demanding than mothers' talk. Fathers were also observed using more direct questions and a wider range of vocabulary than mothers (Crystal 1997; Hladik and Edwards 1984).

Age is also a variable in discourse style. When young hearing children talk to older children, siblings, or adults, a power relationship exists. They may use more polite forms such as please and thank-you. Very young children at age four years were observed on the playground to simplify their speech and talk differently to infant siblings than to adults (Gleason 1997).

In conversations, Deaf mothers use physical anatomy to make signs. For example, they make signs on the child's body, including the arms, face, leg, or foot. They also mold the child's hands to make a sign (Maestas y Moores 1980). In addition, mothers make signs directly on storybooks and toys as well as on food dishes and utensils.

Summary of Research

Toddlerese is the special language register that parents use with their children when they are the ages of eighteen-months to three years. If parents are hearing, they use a simplified register, slower speech, a restricted vocabulary, a simple grammar, and repetitious and singsong prosody. Deaf caregivers use a modified sign register, miniature signs, and one-handed signs, all within a restricted sign space. They make signs on the child's body, mold the child's hands to make a sign, or make a sign on the child's toy or book. Parents use visual-tactile readiness strategies such as eye contact, hand waving, and signing in the child's line of vision (Mather 1996).

American Codas develop speech and signed language following the same developmental milestones as bilingual-bicultural children of two spoken languages (Jones 1976). In Puerto Rico, Deaf parents' Puerto Rican culture, use of PRSL (which is a mixture of Spanish signs and American Sign Language), and use of Spanish influences early conversations with their toddlers (Rodriguez 1993). This study explores communication within two Puerto Rican families as Deaf (or Coda) parents communicate with their hearing toddlers.

PARTICIPANTS

Two Puerto Rican Deaf families took part in this study. Each family had a hearing toddler. The parents of one child were Deaf; the parents of the other child included one who was Deaf and one who was a hearing Coda. All names have been changed to protect the identity of the participants.

The Valdez Family

Mr. and Mrs. Jose Valdez, both Deaf, attended oral and mainstreamed classes in Puerto Rico. Mr. Valdez has a high school diploma. He finished an associate's degree in religious studies and anthropology. He has one older Deaf brother, three Deaf cousins, and one Deaf aunt. Mary Valdez was born deaf in a hearing family. She has a bachelor's degree in business. Both Mary and Jose use PRSL, ASL, and spoken Spanish. Both also use speechreading in Spanish. The Valdez family has two hearing daughters: two-year-old Debbie who participated in this study and eight-month-old Mary. Debbie's parents and the researcher have observed her teaching Mary how to sign.

The Torrez Family

Mrs. Teresa Torrez is a hearing woman born to Deaf parents. She has three Deaf aunts and one Deaf uncle from her mother's side. Mrs. Torrez is a first-generation Coda. Her husband, Pedro, was born deaf of hearing parents and has one Deaf aunt, one Deaf uncle, and many Deaf cousins on his maternal side. He studied in a mainstreamed public school using spoken Spanish. Later, he graduated from the University of Puerto Rico with a bachelor's degree in computer science and accounting and currently works for a bank in Puerto Rico. He uses PRSL with his wife, daughter, Deaf relatives, and Deaf friends. He also uses spoken Spanish. Teresa and Pedro's two-year-old hearing daughter is a second generation Coda. The family uses spoken Spanish, PRSL, and ASL.

PROCEDURES: INVOLVING THE DEAF COMMUNITY

Two of the researchers were Deaf and fluent in ASL. All four authors participated in data collection in Puerto Rico and had visited the island on several occasions. One of the researchers (Rodriguez) was Deaf, a native Puerto Rican and fluent user of PRSL, Spanish, English, and ASL. She was one of the founders of the Deaf organization, *Sordos de Puerto Rico*, an advocacy organization for Deaf people. Before videotaping the toddlers, she arranged for two meetings with Deaf adults on the island — one at a Deaf club and the other at a Christmas barbeque party — to give the Deaf community an opportunity to discuss the research. Typically, research with Deaf children and adults does not involve the Deaf community, which often breeds feelings of resentment, oppression, and paternalism. To counteract these negative feelings, the researchers made an effort to build trust and rapport with Deaf families on the island by explaining how the study would benefit both adults and children in Deaf communities. At the first meeting, the researchers discussed informally with Deaf adults how they conduct bathing, eating, reading, and playing routines with their own Deaf and hearing children. After the first meeting, the researchers chose two families with hearing toddlers who used PRSL as the primary language in the home. At the second meeting, the Christmas barbeque, the researchers met the extended family and friends of the two selected families to socialize and further build a comfort level with the families in the study.

Materials

The activities and materials used in the study were chosen thoughtfully and carefully to ensure that they would engage the parents and the toddlers in rich conversations. The researchers also made an attempt to choose activities that were natural and appropriate within a Puerto Rican home. Materials were chosen that were not only age-appropriate, fun, and motivating for the toddlers but also easy for the toddlers' hands to manipulate: Puerto Rican food, picture books, and a toy — all of which matched the toddlers' experiences with daily activities such as dressing, bathing, and eating, and playing.

The two picture books used for this study, *Sleepy Bear*, and *Fuzzy Bear: A Getting Dressed Book*, were both written by Dawn Bently (1998; 1999). In the first book, three main rituals for the nighttime routine are presented, namely, taking a bath, reading a book, and snuggling under the covers. The book also includes three tactile hands-on activities that involve flaps to lift, touch-and-feel elements, and pop-ups. The second book has four main rituals for getting up: (1) getting ready for dressing, (2) putting on clothes, (3) going out for the day, and (4) playing outside. The books encouraged a high level of interaction in that they encouraged discussion of what the bear is doing and hands-on manipulation of the book.

The toy used in the study was Mr. Potato Head. It is a plastic toy with a funny face, which has detachable parts such as ears, eyes, arms, legs, a mouth, a nose, glasses, shoes, a hat, a moustache, and a tongue and teeth. The child was instructed by the parents to attach the small parts correctly onto the larger potato head body. These materials were used in other child language studies and were found to assist in eliciting responses from toddlers.

Family Visits

After the two preliminary warm-up visits, the researchers made three to four additional visits to each family home. During these visits, the researchers attempted to gather data based on natural communication patterns of Deaf adults with their hearing toddler as they ate a meal together, read a book, and played with a toy. Before data collection, the researchers provided warm-up activities in which the parent chose a topic and discussed it. The researchers explained that they would come again several times and observe the families during activities such as mealtime, book reading, and playing.

Each mother and father performed three activities (eating, playing, and reading) with his or her hearing toddler for a total of twelve activities.

The researchers used a Sony digital camcorder to capture the home activities and QuickTime Movies software that allows direct notation of videoclips on the computer screen. Because the goal of the transcription was to analyze the parent-child discourse interactions and language data involving lexical signs, phrases, and sentences, the transcriptions of the signed data include Puerto Rican glosses for the manual signs, information about eye gaze behaviors, and other nonmanual signals used for grammatical and discourse purposes. In addition, the Puerto Rican glosses are accompanied by translated English equivalents for the purpose of analysis. (For the purposes of this paper, only the English translations are provided.)

The researchers visited each family for a total of four days. They spent three to four hours per visit. Not all time was spent videotaping. Parts of the visits involved chatting with family members and playing with the toddlers to create a relaxed environment.

Puerto Rican Cultural Traits

The effect of the Puerto Rican cultural traits upon toddlerese can be summarized as follows: The mother's and father's roles in the family were traditionally Puerto Rican. The mothers and grandmothers prepared the meals. Typical Puerto Rican foods were served, which was reflected in the food signs that were taught to the toddlers (e.g., rice, chicken, soup, and so forth). The extended families (grandmothers, aunts, uncles, cousins) were present at the preliminary meetings and during the home visits. The families taught their toddlers prayers before meals as is the custom in Puerto Rican homes. The parents used facial expressions and lip movements similar to those used in the Puerto Rican culture (Nine-Curt 1974). Some of the Deaf parents used spoken Spanish with the hearing toddlers before signing with them.

RESULTS: JOINT ATTENTION, TURN-TAKING, AND DISCOURSE STRATEGIES

In this section, we discuss our observations of toddlerese or parent-toddler discourse during three activities: eating a meal, reading a book, and playing with a toy. Our observations and analysis focus on the research questions, how does the parent prepare the child before each activity, how does the parent set up the physical space including him- or herself, the child, and the object or book, and how does the parent use turn-taking strategies? In addition, we consider how the parent used eye assessment, summoning strategies, and acknowledgments before, during, and after each activity. Finally, we compare toddlerese with adult discourse and then explain the data within the context of the Puerto Rican cultural traits, gender discourse, age, and use of physical anatomy.

As detailed below, we observed that although certain parents made different sitting arrangements with their child, they consistently established and maintained "sight triangles" that connected the child's field of vision, their parent's signing, and the object being displayed (e.g., book, toy). These triangles enabled all three points to be visible, enabling the child to see the parent's signing and the object being used.

Mealtime Activity

A typical lunch menu for Puerto Rican families is *arroz con habichuelas* (rice with beans). The parent prepared for the mealtime activity by setting up the dishes (e.g., bowls for rice and meat) and arranging the seating. The parents set up a sight triangle so the child's field of vision included her parent's signs and facial expressions as well as the bowl of food. This arrangement made the signing space smaller and more constricted than the signing space typically constructed for adult discourse.

This sight triangle was not static but dynamic, changing in size depending on the parent's communication intentions with the child.

Not all the parents sat in similar sitting arrangements to create a sight triangle. Two of the mothers and one father sat so only one side of the body faced the table and bowl and then placed the toddler on his or her lap, facing toward the bowl (see figure 1). This position allowed the parent to make eye contact, show signs, and display facial expressions. Figure 1 also shows how the mother set up a sight triangle between herself, the child, and the bowl, enabling her to carry on a conversation with the child. The mother in figure 1 engaged in one-handed signing, using peripheral signing, with her face in the center and the signing on either side of the peripheral area.

In contrast to these three parents, one of the fathers sat in a chair away from the child in a way that he was able to engage in two-handed talk and direct, face-to-face signing (see figure 2).

After setting up the sight triangle, the parents used hand waves, taps on the body, smiles, and eye-gazes to get the child's attention before starting their conversations. They also used these visual and tactile behaviors to transition between turns in the conversations. When the parents observed that the child was distracted (i.e., when the child's field of vision was not within the intended sight triangle), the parent assessed the situation and used certain strategies such as a gentle tap-tap and a hand wave to bring the child's field of vision back into the triangle. Following is an excerpt from the transcript of the beginning of one conversation between mother and child. In this excerpt, the mother started to talk with the child by using turn-taking eye gaze between them at a mealtime. In this excerpt, the mother modeled the sign for the food her child was about to eat — RICE.

Mother: (Moves her shoulder to face her daughter)
Child: (Smiles, gazes up at mother)
Mother: (Pauses, gazes down at the child, smiles) RICE. (Points to rice in the bowl)
Child: (Gazes up at mother) EAT.

The mothers also used questions and labeling in the conversations and waited for their child to respond. They frequently asked the children what the name of the food was and then modeled the food signs. All parents taught their child the vocabulary in PRSL for RICE, BEANS, CHICKEN, SOUP, POTATO, MEAT, WATER, and JUICE. They used full sentences, nouns,

FIGURE 1. *Typical seating arrangement during eating activity*

FIGURE 2. *Alternative seating arrangement during eating activity*

and verbs, question words, and locative verbs: WANT EAT, HUNGRY, WHAT SAY NO WANT, NO, WHY, WHAT, SIT OVER-THERE, SIT, COME-OVER HERE, HOT, LIKE, LIKE IT, RICE, BEANS, FINISH, BECOME COLD. See Rodriguez (2001) for pictures of these PRSL signs compared with ASL.

In addition, parents engaged in teaching their toddlers the correct use of the sign. Following is a transcribed excerpt in which one father tried to teach his child new signs related to food at mealtime. In this excerpt, the father tried to teach his child the sign BEANS during mealtime. Within the context of feeding lunch to the toddler, the father engaged the toddler in dialogue about food vocabulary words.

Father: MEAT? (Eyes down)
Child: (Gazes up) MEAT
Father: BEANS

Child: (Attempts the sign) BEANS)
Father: (Corrects the sign) BEANS)
Child: (Makes the correct sign) BEANS
Father: BEANS (Nods his head, yes)
Child: (Smiles at father)

At other times, the parents would point to the bowl during mealtime, move their heads down to the hearing toddler's eye level, then sign around the bowl. In doing so, the parents kept the bowl within the child's sight triangle while the parents taught the child the following signs within the triangle: RICE, BECOME COLD, and LIKE IT.

In another conversation, the hearing toddler showed pragmatic skills by teaching her hearing eight-month-old infant sister some baby signs and making these signs on the infant's body. For example, after the deaf mother modeled the sign SLEEP to the toddler, the child turned toward her infant sister, attempting to teach the baby this sign by making the sign on her body. In addition, she tried to teach the infant SLEEP, BRUSH-TEETH, and BEAR, thus, attempting to become a language teacher to her infant sister. For each of the signs involved, the mother had signed to the toddler using simplified signs. The toddler then modeled the sign for the infant, using simplified signs on the infant's body.

In addition to vocabulary, Deaf parents taught their toddler social skills during the mealtime activity. Following is a transcript excerpt where one parent thanked the child at the table when she covered her mouth with her hand when sneezing.

Child: (Sneezes with her hand covering her mouth)
Mother: SALUD, GRACIAS, THANK YOU. (Smiles at the child)
Child: THANK YOU. (Smiles at mother)

In another conversation among two parents and child, the parents instructed the child not to SPILL FOOD on her blouse, but KEEP IT CLEAN while eating. Her father teased her about table manners by using exaggerated facial expressions. The father signed "MOUTH WITH FOOD A LOT, UGLY, NOT POLITE." The child and the father then laughed together about his teasing.

Book Preparation Activity

All four parents prepared their toddler for the book reading activity by having the child sit on the floor near them. As with the meal activity, the parents created the triangular conversational space. Within that space, the child not only was able to see the parent's eyes, facial expressions, and signs as well as the book but also was able to sign back and be seen by the parent. Parents tended to lean their shoulders into the child's range of vision, thus reducing and constricting the conversational space. Parents also moved their bodies down toward the toddler's eye level. These body movements made their signs smaller. In addition, parents also made signs both on the toddler's body and on pictures in the books.

In one of the observed conversations, one mother included her toddler and eight-month-old daughter as well as one of the researchers in the conversational triangle (see figure 3). This arrangement affected the production of signs and the use of space, allowing the mother to have her hands free to sign because the book was propped up on her knees. She reverted to single-handed signing when she needed to hold a side of the book or turn a page. This arrangement of space around the book allowed the toddler and the infant to see the mother's facial expressions, which are so important to questioning and other grammar features of signing (Valli and Lucas 2000).

In the following excerpt, one father first had his child sit on his lap as he sat on the floor, but the child then moved to sit on the floor beside the father in a conversational triangle. The father asked the child to COME-HERE. He then touched the cover of the story book, which had a fuzzy sock on it. The father pulled up on his own sock and showed his daughter. She spoke in Spanish, saying *"mira"* ("look"), and also signed LOOK with emphasis. He then placed the child again on his lap and positioned the book on his left leg. With his free hand, he signed. His daughter was easily distracted and did not want to pay attention for long (see figure 4).

Father: (Points to socks on cover of book) SOCKS
Father: (Pulls at his own socks, then points to socks in the book) SOCKS (making the sign directly on the book)
Child: (Gazes up at father)
Father: (Taps on child's leg to get her attention, then pulls his socks up and down) SOCKS
Child: SOCKS (using the toddler sign for SOCKS)
Father: (Nods yes) SOCKS(using the regular sign for SOCKS)

Parents set up space for the book reading activity in different ways. As shown above, one father placed his child on his lap, but then she moved to sit on the floor near him. The hearing mother who is a Coda sat with her legs crossed across from her toddler, making sure she was at eye

FIGURE 3. *Arrangement of a conversational triangle during reading activity*

level with her daughter (see figure 5). This seating arrangement freed the mother's hands for signing. Because the mother sat facing the center of the triangular space, she had eye contact with her daughter and directed all her conversations within the direct line of the child's vision. The toddler not only could see her mother's signs but also could look at the book pictures when the mother pointed to them. As the mother pointed to pictures in the book, she reverted to one-handed signs. In addition, she often made signs on the storybook pictures. The toddler sat upright to watch her mother's signs and facial expressions.

The second father used space and seating arrangements in a different manner. At first, he sat with his daughter on the floor. But the girl stood up and walked into the kitchen, and the father followed. At that point, she went back, picked up the book, and joined her father in the kitchen where she showed the father the book. He held the book and lowered his shoulders to the child (see figure 6). The father also created the triangular space with the child and the book. Using her peripheral vision, the toddler could look up and see the father's face and his signing, then look directly in front of herself to see the book. This arrangement allowed the father to hold the book with one hand and use one-handed signs with the other; it also allowed him to sign directly on the pictures in the book. He bent his body toward the child when he signed.

Parents used turn-taking strategies during the book reading activity that were similar to the meal eating activity. The parents got the toddler's attention by hand waving, tapping on a body part, and signing LOOK-AT-ME. One mother pointed to a picture about taking a bath that was in the

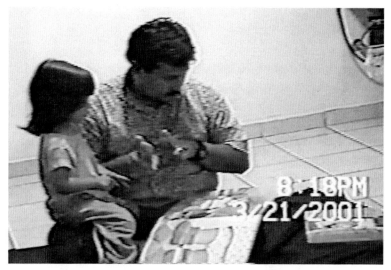

FIGURE 4. *Seating arrangement during reading activity*

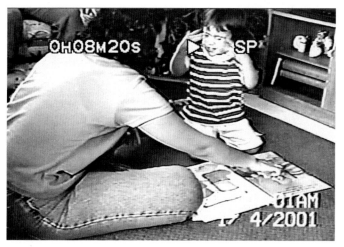

FIGURE 5. *Seating arrangement during reading activity that leaves both hands free for signing*

book, made the sign BATH on her own body, then paused and waited for the toddler to respond. The toddler modeled the sign BATH on her own body. During the conversation, the mother kept eye contact with the child.

In the next transcribed excerpt, one mother used gazes, touching, labeling, and questioning during the book reading activity:

Mother: (Taps child on chest)

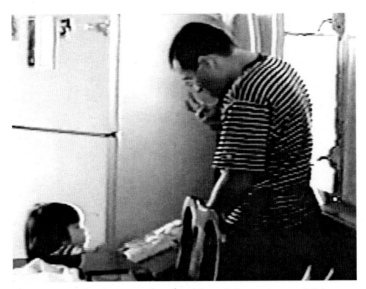

FIGURE 6. *Father lowering his shoulder while signing to child*

Child: (Pulls on book)
Mother: PRETTY (Points to the bear on the book)
Child: (Gazes at the picture of the bear)
Mother: (Points to neck of the bear) WHAT?
Child: (Looks at the book)
Mother: (Taps the child on the leg and neck) WHAT?
Child: (Looks up)
Mother: WHAT?
Child: (Gazes up)
Mother: WATCH-ME. BEAR
Child: (Gazes down at picture of the bear)

During the book reading activity, the mother used the signs BEAR, PRETTY, WHAT, WATCH-ME, SHIRT, BLOUSE, SHOES, SOCKS, GOOD SOCKS, ZIPPER, BUTTON, BUTTON LOST, GOOD, RAIN, RAINCOAT, UMBRELLA, SAME. First, the mother pointed to a picture in the book. Then she made the sign on herself. Next, she encouraged her daughter to model her and make the sign by herself. The mother then gave praise (the high-five hand sign) to the daughter.

In each data sample, parents used summoning behaviors such as signing COME-HERE to initiate the activity, and they ended the book reading activities when their toddlers lost interest. The parents did not push the child into further reading but simply moved on to another activity when the child became distracted.

During the book reading activity, the mothers and fathers tended to use miniature signs on the book. They altered the signing space to show their toddler the link between the book picture and the symbol — the sign. As the parents moved their bodies away from or toward the child, they widened or restricted the triangular space. In addition to using signs alone, parents also used simple sentences. Through the book reading activity, they also taught their toddlers classifiers such as TURN-KNOB, TURN-KEY, and OPEN-DOOR.

One toddler requested that a book be reread to her. The mother followed the child's lead. The child said the Spanish word *via*. During the second reading, the mother pointed to more pictures in the book and waited for the child to respond by giving the sign.

During the book reading activity, one father pointed to the book, made the sign on his body or in the air, and waited for the child to respond by making a sign. The specific signs the father used included SOCKS, FATHER, COME-OVER, SIT-ON-MY-LAP, HAND-ON BOOK, YES, TIME TO GET DRESSED UP, EASY, WATCH-BEAR, YOU WATCH ME, GET READY OKAY, SHOES, PULL UP, and ALL RIGHT. Note the many commands he used during the book reading activity: LOOK AT ME, WATCH BEAR, COME HERE, SIT DOWN, and PULL UP.

Toy Activity

Before their conversations with their toddler about the Mr. Potato Head toy activity, the parents completed five preparatory procedures. First, they took the time to position the toy pieces. Next, they arranged the seating. Third, they created the sight triangle. Fourth, they arranged the space. Fifth, they used a variety of signs, sign phrases, and sentences to get ready for the conversation.

To prepare the child for the activity, the parent gave the Mr. Potato Head toy to the hearing toddler. Each of the mothers sat face to face with the toddler on the floor to place the child in the direct line of vision. The fathers also placed the toy in the center of the sight triangle; however, the fathers, held the toy in their hands and moved the toy up to the child's face. Thus, the fathers changed the size of the sight triangle from a large to a more constricted sign space and back to a large space (see figure 7).

The parent set up the physical space between the child and the toy. One mother placed the Potato Head toy on the floor between the child

FIGURE 7. *By holding the toy in his hands, the father can change the size of the sight triangle*

FIGURE 8. *The mother changes the position of the toy so the child can see the toy and the mother's facial expressions*

and herself. During the activity, the mother changed the position of the toy several times so the child could see both the toy and the mother's facial expressions (see figure 8).

One father used space in a unique way. To keep the eye contact with his daughter, he raised the toy to the child's line of vision. When the girl sat down, the father lowered his arm with the toy to the child's line of vision. Then, while holding the toy in one hand, he signed with his free hand.

The mothers tended to place the toy in front of the child and move the signs down, leaning their shoulders in and making the signs smaller. Nevertheless, all the parents tended to bring the toy up to the child's face. Both sets of parents placed the toy in the child's line of vision before signing a conversation about it.

Mothers and fathers used a variety of turn-taking strategies during the toy activity. Mothers tended to summon or get the attention of the child by tapping or touching anywhere on the body: lower chin, arm, chest, leg, or shoe. The fathers tended to tap the child only on the lower body: the knees, legs, or shoes.

During the toy activity, one mother held the toy to her side and made one-handed signs. When the toddler became distracted, she gently moved the child's chin to a level that allowed them to look at each other. Once she got this attention, the mother began to label parts of the toy: MOUTH, TONGUE, HAIR, EYE, and HAT. She then gave each toy part to the child and instructed her to attach it to the Potato Head toy. When the child made an error (e.g., placing the arm section in the ear), the mother used signs to explain to the child how to correct it. The mother also made signs on the child's body to show signs for body parts and often modeled the signs as well as made them in miniature form so the child could see the signs. To get the child's attention, she tapped the child's hands, knee, leg or shoe. To engage the child in conversations, she frequently asked the questions WHAT? and WHERE? After being asked a question, the child would often respond with a pointing behavior. For example, one mother signed WHERE EYES? and waited for a response; the child pointed to the eyes on the Potato Head toy.

Both mothers modified the citation forms, LOOK-AT-ME, CHANGE, PUT-IN, and TURN-AROUND so they became locative verbs to get attention and give commands. Mothers often pointed to their own body parts to tell the child where to attach the body part on the toy. The mothers modeled more than twenty modified signs, including signs for toy parts, body parts, colors, and praise as well as signs showing negation (NO, NOT), and adjective signs (PRETTY, ANOTHER). In addition, the mothers used question signs (WHERE, WHAT) as well as locatives and directional verbs.

One father used hand waves, shoulder tapping, and the spoken Spanish word *mira* to get his toddler's attention. He also used signs to gently tease the child by signing that he wore earrings, the same as the Potato Head toy. Like the mothers, the fathers used labeling of toy parts, repetition, leg tapping, gazes, smiles, and signed phrases to have a conversation with their daughters, and they always waited a short time for the toddler to respond. In the following excerpt, one father asks his daughter routine questions as one way to engage in conversation with her:

Father: (Taps child on shoes) WHERE ARMS?
Child: (Child gazes up)
Father: (Attaches toy arms to the Potato Head)
Child: (Picks up blue toy shoes)
Father: HAVE SHOES? HAVE SHOES? (Points to his own shoes)
Child: (Gazes up; puts blue shoes on the toy)
Father: WHERE GLASSES? WHERE GLASSES?
Child: (Child picks up glasses)
Father: (Takes toy glasses, nods, and puts them on the toy)
Child: (Gazes up and smiles at father)
Father: (Taps child on leg several times) WHERE MOUTH? WHERE MOUTH?
Child: (Picks up toy mouth)
Father: (Smiles)
Child: (Attaches toy mouth to the Potato Head)
Father: (Taps child) HAIR WHERE? (Points at hair area)
Child: (Gazes up)
Father: HAT WHERE? HAT WHERE?

Parents acknowledged the toddler's replies with head nods, smiles, and praise (high-five sign). They treated the child as a conversational partner, and when the child lost interest, the conversation ended. The parents used questions, commands, and directives as well as gave multiple explanations. When the parent did not get a response from the child, then the parent would pause, smile, repeat the sign to the child, or do all three behaviors. This finding confirms that the parents' conversations had a perlocutionary effect on the toddlers because the toddlers responded with eye gazes, nods, and signs (Austin 1962; Grice 1975; Searle 1965).

We observed gender differences in the toy activities. The fathers' signs were larger and occupied more space within the conversational triangle. Fathers tended to ask more questions and make more commands. The mothers tended to try to pull the information from the child through modeling and pointing.

Other gender issues emerged within the content of the activities. For example, fathers did not choose the book that related to dressing and bathing as the mothers did. The mothers tended to ignore the moustache piece on the Mr. Potato Head whereas the fathers picked up the moustache and played with the child using this piece. One father also picked up an ear piece and put it in his own ear to amuse his daughter.

SUMMARY OF FINDINGS

As we observed, the parents allowed the three activities (eating, reading, playing) to end naturally and did not force the toddlers to repeat the activities. We also noted a common pattern of dialogue between the parents and the toddlers in all three activities. First, the parents indicated that they wanted to engage in a conversation with their child. Second, regardless of their sitting positions, the parent used eye-assessment strategies to establish sight triangles that connected the child's field of vision, their parent's signing, and the object being displayed (e.g., food, book, or toy). Third, the parents also used eye-assessment strategies to maintain the sight triangles. For instance, if the child's line of vision strayed from the sight triangle, the parent regained the child's attention by hand waving, tapping on the child's body, or signing LOOK-AT-ME. Fourth, as long as the child's field of vision was within the sight triangle, the parent waited for the child to respond by making eye contact with the parent to indicate the child's "visual readiness." Once the child was ready, the parent began a conversation by pointing to a food, a book, or an object and modeling the appropriate signed language.

Toddlers often do not have the skills to begin, maintain, and close a conversation. Parents in this study provided them with role modeling by using eye gazes, touching, pauses, repetition, and questioning to engage the child in talk. In addition, before initiating a conversation with the child, the Deaf parent focused on creating and maintaining a sight triangle with their child by bringing and keeping the child's field of vision within the intended sight triangle connecting the signing and the object to be displayed or used.

The conversations of the parents and toddlers can also be described according to Dore's (1974) categories. The parents labeled food items, book pictures, and toy parts. The parents often repeated signs. They answered questions. They requested answers from the toddler. They encouraged the toddler to practice signing. The parents also accepted and acknowledged the child's toddler signs by responding with head nods, a smile, praise signs (high-five) or other signs. In other words, parents taught children how to use eye gaze by setting up the sight triangle to acquire PRSL and to be able to participate in the conversation during a meal, a book reading session, or a toy activity.

RECOMMENDATIONS FOR TRAINING AND RESEARCH

Further research is needed to examine parent-toddler discourse behaviors between Deaf and Coda parents and their deaf and hearing children. Linguistic descriptions of the phonology of toddler signs would be interesting to developmental psycholinguists, applied linguists, and sociolinguists. Such descriptions also would serve a practical use in the training and educating of early childhood specialists for both deaf and Coda children. There is a need for toddler sign dictionaries similar to what Rodriguez (2001) has compiled. Information on visual readiness skills that incorporates eye assessments, body positioning, comprehension assessment, culture, gender, age, and use of physical anatomy traits could be made available to parents. Parent communication guides could be written that incorporate these elements. Many hearing parents may not recognize toddler signs and, consequently, may ignore the responses of their toddler, causing the child to become angry and resentful when his or her needs are not met. Parents and early childhood educators may want to use the activity materials used in this study as useful tools for developing language in toddlers.

In this study, hearing Coda toddlers learned to use sight triangles or direct eye contact for conversations with others, which may pose challenges for them especially when they encounter other cultures in which conversations do not require direct eye-to-eye contact or sight triangles. It is recommended that in those educational settings where direct eye contact is not required, teachers be familiar with the hearing Coda toddlers' reliance on sight triangles for communication to ensure cross-cultural consistency.

REFERENCES

Akerman, J., J. Kyle, B. Woll, and M. Ezra. 1990. Lexical acquisition in sign and speech: Evidence from a longitudinal study of infants in deaf families. In *Sign language research: Theoretical issues,* ed. C. Lucas, 337–45. Washington, D.C.: Gallaudet University Press.

Austin, J. 1962. *How to do things with words*. Cambridge: Harvard University Press.

Baker, C. 2001. *Foundations of bilingual education*. 3rd ed. Clevedon, England: Multilingual Matters.

Bentley, D. 1998. *Fuzzy bear: A getting dressed book*. Raleigh, N.C.: Piggy Toes Press.

Bishop, M., and S. Hicks. 2005. Bimodal bilingualism in hearing adults from deaf families. *Sign Language Studies* 5(2): 188–230.

Crystal, D. 1997. *The Cambridge encyclopedia of language*. 2nd ed. New York: Cambridge University Press.

Departamento de Educación. 1981. *Currículo y metodología de ka enseñanza del niño con problemas auditivos*. Santurce, Puerto Rico: Talleres gráficos.

Dore, P. 1974. A pragmatic description of early language development. *Journal of Psycholinguistic Research* 3: 343–50.

Edelsky, C. 1981. Who's got the floor? *Language and Society* 10: 383–421.

Erting, C., C. Prezioso, H. O'Grady, and O. Hynes. 1990. The interactional context of mother-infant communication. In *From gesture to language in hearing and deaf children*, ed. V. Volterra and C. Erting, 97–106. Berlin: Springer-Verlag.

Gleason, J. 1997. *The development of language*. Needham Heights, Mass.: Viamom.

Grice, H. P. 1975. Logic and conversation. In *Syntax and semantics*. Vol. 3, *Speech acts*, ed. P. Cole and J. L. Morgan, 41–58. New York: Academic Press.

Griffith, P. 1985. Mode-switching and mode-finding in a hearing child of deaf parents. *Sign Language Studies* 18: 195–222.

Griswold, E., and J. Commings. 1974. The expressive vocabulary of preschool deaf children. *American Annals of the Deaf* 119: 16–28.

Harris, M. 2001. It's all a matter of timing sign visibility and sign reference in deaf and hearing mothers of 18-month-old children. *Journal of Deaf Studies and Deaf Education* 6(3): 177–85.

Harris, M., D. Jones, S. Brookes, and J. Grant. 1986. Relations between the non-verbal context of maternal speech and rate of language development. *British Journal of Developmental Psychology* 4: 261–68.

Hladik, E. G., and H. T. Edwards. 1984. A comparative analysis of mother-father speech in the naturalistic home environment. *Journal of Psycholinguistic Research* 13: 321–32.

Howell, R. 1984. Maternal reports of vocabulary development in four-year-old deaf children. *American Annals of the Deaf* 129(6): 459–65.

Jones, M. 1976. A longitudinal investigation into the acquisition of question formation in English and American Sign Language by three hearing children with deaf parents. Ph.D. diss., University of Illinois, Urbana-Champaign.

Karp, H. 2002. *The happiest child on the block.* New York: Random.

Lederberg, A., and V. Everhart. 2000. Conversations between deaf children and their hearing mothers: Pragmatic and dialogic characteristics. *Journal of Deaf Studies and Deaf Education* 5: 303–22.

Lestina, J., and M. Lartz. 1993. Introducing deaf children to literacy: What deaf mothers teach us. Paper presented at the Conference of Educational Administrators Serving the Deaf/Convention of American Instructors of the Deaf conference, June 30, Baltimore, Maryland.

Maestas y Moores, J. 1980. Early linguistic environment: Interactions of deaf parents with their infants. *Sign Language Studies* 26: 1–13.

Mather, S. 1989. *Visually oriented teaching strategies with deaf preschool children.* In *The sociolinguistics of the deaf community,* ed. C. Lucas, 165–87. New York: Academic Press.

———. 1990. Home and classroom communication. In *Research on educational and development aspects of deafness,* ed. D. Moores and K. Meadow-Orlans, 232–54. Washington, D.C.: Gallaudet University Press.

———. 1993. Eye pragmatics. Unpublished manuscript, Gallaudet University, Washington, D.C.

———. 1994. Adult-toddler discourse. In *Post Milan ASL and English Literacy: Issues, Trends, and Research conference proceedings,* ed. B. D. Snider, 283–98. Washington, D.C.: Gallaudet University Press.

———. 1996. Initiation in visually constructed dialogue: Reading books with 3- to 8-year-old-students who are deaf and hard of hearing. In *Sociolinguistics in deaf communities,* ed. C. Lucas, 109–31. Washington, D.C.: Gallaudet University Press.

———. 2003. Is visual readiness a pre-requisite for sign language acquisition? Paper presented at VI Congress Latin American Conference on Bilingual Education of the Deaf, November 20–24, Mexico City, Mexico.

Matos, A. 1988. *Aprende lenguaje de senas en Español-English.* San Juan, Puerto Rico: Editorial Raíces.

Mohay, H. 2000. Language in sight: Mothers' strategies for making language accessible to deaf children. In *Development in context: The deaf child in the family and at school,* ed. P. Spencer, C. Erting, and M. Marschark, 151–66. Mahwah, N.J.: Lawrence Erlbaum.

Nagy, K., D. Bentley, and R. Jablow. 1999. *Sleepy bear.* Raleigh, N.C.: Piggy Toes Press.

Newport, E., and R. Meier. 1985. The acquisition of American Sign Language. In *The crosslinguistic study of language acquisition.* Vol. 1, *The data,* ed. D. Slobin, 881–938. Hillsdale, N.J.: Lawrence Erlbaum.

Ninio, A., and J. Bruner. 1986. The achievement and antecedents of labeling. *Journal of Child Language* 5: 1–14.

Nine-Curt, C. J. 1974. *Non-verbal communication*. Cambridge, Mass.: Evaluation, Dissemination and Assessments Center.

Petitto, L. 2000. The acquisition of natural signed languages: Lessons in the nature of human language and its biological foundation. In *Language acquisition by eye,* ed. C. Chamberlain, J. Morford, and R. Mayberry, 41–50. Mahwah, N.J.: Lawrence Erlbaum.

Preston, P. 1994. *Mother father deaf: Living between sound and silence.* Cambridge, Mass.: Harvard University Press.

Prinz, P., and E. Prinz. 1979. Acquisition of ASL and spoken English by hearing child of a deaf mother and a hearing father: Phase II. Early combinational patterns. *Sign Language Studies* 30: 78–88.

Rodriguez, Y. 1993. *Design for a culture-based curriculum for deaf Puerto Rican students to be implemented in the elementary school of Puerto Rico.* Master's thesis, University of Puerto Rico, San Juan.

Rodriguez, Y. 2001. *Toddlerese: Conversations between hearing parents and their deaf toddlers in Puerto Rico.* Ph.D. diss., Lamar University, Beaumont, Texas.

Schlesinger, H., and K. Meadow. 1972. *Sound and sign: Childhood deafness and mental health.* Berkeley, Calif.: University of Berkley.

Searle, J. 1965. *Speech acts.* Cambridge: Cambridge University Press.

Singleton, J., and M. Tittle. 2000. Deaf parents and their hearing children. *Journal of Deaf Studies and Deaf Education* 5(3): 221–36.

Spencer, P. 2000. Looking without listening: Is audition a prerequisite for normal development of visual attention during infancy? *Journal of Deaf Studies and Deaf Education* 5(4): 291–301.

Tannen, D. 1990. *You just don't understand: Women and men in conversations.* New York: William Morrow.

Valli, C., and C. Lucas. 2000. *Linguistics of American Sign Language: An introduction.* 3rd ed. Washington, D.C.: Gallaudet University Press.

Wilbur, R. 2000. The use of ASL to support the development of English and literacy. *Journal of Deaf Studies and Education* 5(1): 81–104.

Narrative Genre in Québec Sign Language

Marion Blondel, Christopher Miller,
and Anne-Marie Parisot

In a seminal paper, Labov and Waletzky (1967) bring the analysis of narrative structure to bear on vernacular, unplanned narratives of personal experience. Before their paper, these types of narratives had received less attention than the planned, literary narratives that were traditionally the object of such analyses. Alongside the thematic and temporal structure of narratives, Labov and Waletzky propose that a second, evaluative function of structure is related to the two principal functions that narratives fulfill. A first and obvious function is referential, which is simply the function of referring to or reporting a sequence of events that transpired (or are claimed to have transpired) in the past; this function thus gives rise to the thematic and temporal structures referred to above. However, a text that contains merely a reported sequence of events fails to fulfill a second essential function of narrative: it must have a point. In other words, the narrator must in some way show how the reported events are relevant to the experience of the audience or, put differently, must show the value of the information being communicated. The degree to which a narrator succeeds in communicating this second function, the evaluative function, is central to the effectiveness of a narrative.

To our knowledge, analyses of sign language narratives have not yet addressed this aspect of narrative structure. The present paper is thus

This article is a synthesis and expansion of three papers (Blondel and Miller 1998; Miller 1998; Lajeunesse and Parisot 1998) delivered at the sixth Theoretical Issues in Sign Language Research conference (TISLR 6) at Gallaudet University. Earlier versions of this synthesis have been presented by the second author to audiences at the Universities of Tours and Toulouse-Le Mirail in France in 1999; in Lausanne, Switzerland, the same year; the University of Manitoba in Winnipeg, Canada, in 2002; and at Charles University in Prague, Czech Republic, in 2003.

conceived as a preliminary exploration of the ways the evaluative function can be realized in two kinds of narratives in one sign language. We hope that the findings we report here will serve as a basis for comparison in subsequent research both on other sign languages and on the variety of narrative types that may be encountered in sign languages.

The LSQ88 corpus (Dubuisson 1988) contains a number of narratives of personal experience, of which perhaps the most interesting, both for its intrinsic content and in linguistic terms, is one that occurs at the very end of the last recording in the series of conversations in Quebec Sign Language (henceforth LSQ, for the French name *Langue des signes québécoise*) that make up the corpus. At the end of this video, the facilitator of the conversation remarks that she is tired and has a long bus trip in the morning to a summer festival where she has a job teaching children sign language. At this point, she starts describing the situation to her interlocutors, explaining how and why she was hired to teach signs to the children; in other words, she begins recounting a narrative of personal experience. What is most interesting about this story and what sets it apart (besides its length) from other such narratives in our corpus, is the fact that in the middle of the story, she launches into the fable of the Tortoise and the Hare or, more precisely, her adaptation of this traditional fable into LSQ.

The fact that the fable of the Tortoise and the Hare, a formal performance narrative, is embedded in a spontaneous narrative of personal experience, is relatively unusual in itself. More interesting yet is the fact that the narrator does not suspend the narrative of personal experience, retell the fable in a single block, and then return to the original matrix narrative. Instead, she retells the story of the Tortoise and the Hare as an illustration of *how* she told the story to the children, within the context of the main story. The overall impression one gets is that she weaves the two stories in and out of each other like the strands in a rug.

In this paper, we will compare the ways the narrator encodes evaluation in her two narratives. To do so, we will first need to describe the overall structure of each of the two narratives. Despite the temporal overlap between the two stories, each can be analyzed on its own terms. By doing so, we will be better able to show the striking structural differences between the two, which in part underlie important differences in the form that evaluation takes in each.

The first section of this paper gives an overview of the model of narrative analysis developed in Labov and Waletzky (1967) and Labov (1972,

1997) and concentrates on the evaluative function as well as the forms that it has been observed to take. The second section of the paper is devoted to a structural analysis of each of the stories — first to the Children story, then to the retelling of the Tortoise and the Hare, highlighting similarities and contrasts between the two. The subsequent two sections build on these analyses to describe the form evaluation takes in the two narratives. The final section is devoted to a twofold discussion of the findings in the preceding sections. On the one hand, we compare our observations on the form of evaluation in the Children story with observations made on the basis of spoken language narratives of personal experience; on the other hand, we contrast these observations with the form taken by evaluation in the Tortoise and the Hare, explaining that form as a consequence of the formal, preplanned poetic structure of the fable.

NARRATIVE STRUCTURE

The research published in Labov and Waletzky (1967) and Labov (1972, 1997) has given rise to an approach to narrative analysis that emphasizes the importance of (spontaneous) narratives of personal experience as a genre distinct from more formal, planned types but a genre in which those formal types can ultimately be argued to have their roots. Although this research gives an important place to the evaluative function and to the related notion of reportability of an incident, evaluation and reportability are ultimately dependent on the referential function of narrative, which forms the basic framework on which they are built.

The General Structure of Narratives

The referential function of narrative involves the basic necessity of reporting a series of at least two temporally ordered, related events. A basic narrative must therefore contain at least two temporally ordered clauses whose order reflects the temporal sequence of events. Although one can find devices such as flashbacks to an earlier event or syntactic embedding that reverses the order of clauses referring to a sequence of events, Labov argues that these devices are exceptions to the rule of temporal sequencing.

A sequence of clauses reporting a sequence of events is the simplest form a narrative can take, and it is indeed the one essential element for any narrative, successful or otherwise. However, more fully formed narratives may include up to a total of six temporally ordered sections:

1. The **Abstract** briefly summarizes the story before the story itself is recounted.
2. The **Orientation** sets the scene for the narrative. It introduces the (main) protagonists, the location, and the time when the events to be reported took place.
3. The **Complicating Action** section is made up of the clauses that recount the events essential to the unfolding of the story, namely, those that include the most reportable or newsworthy information.
4. **Evaluation** was seen in Labov and Waletzky (1967) as a section intervening between the Complicating Action and Resolution. Labov (1972) shows that it is not necessarily a separate, self-contained section that is ordered with respect to the others but, in fact, one that can permeate the structure of the narrative in all areas. This characteristic is arguably a result of the fact that it fills a function that is complementary to that of the other components whose function is referential — that is, simply to report information about the nature of the events, the protagonists, and their setting in space and time.
5. The **Resolution** reports the result of the complicating action, in other words, the consequences for the narrator, other protagonists, or both.
6. The **Coda** summarizes the narrative and brings it to a close, returning the narrator and audience to the present time in which the narrative began.

Structural Realizations of Evaluation

The evaluative function of a narrative can be realized in a number of different forms. The most basic dichotomy is between external and internal (or embedded) evaluation. External evaluation is simply the insertion of evaluative statements that suspend the actual narration itself. When evaluation is actually framed as part of the sequence of events in the narrative, it is considered to be internal, or embedded. As such, it may take the form of a statement or thought attributed either to the narrator at the time of the story or to another character in the narrative. At a deeper level of embedding, evaluation can be framed as an action performed by someone in the story. We will see in this paper that each of these degrees of embedding of evaluation is present at some point in the narrative we analyze here.

According to Labov (1972), the linguistic devices used to carry out evaluation can be analyzed in terms of how much complexity they add or do not add to the basic syntax of the narrative. Labov observes that typical narrative clauses are quite simple in their structure and can be described (for English) by means of a template made up of eight potential elements in sequence. These are (1) conjunctions, (2) simple subjects, (3) the auxiliary or quasimodals (*begin, keep, want,* etc.), (4) preterit verbs, (5) complements (direct and indirect objects), (6) manner or instrumental adverbials, (7) locative adverbials, and (8) temporal adverbials and comitative clauses.[1] Labov observes that deviations from this syntactic template add marked evaluative force to the narration. He classifies such deviations into four categories: intensifiers, comparators, correlatives, and explicatives.

The first category, intensifiers, does not add complexity to the basic narrative syntax whereas the other categories do. Intensifiers include the use of gesture, the addition of expressive phonology, the addition of quantifiers, and the use of repetition. Given a linear sequence of events, intensifiers select one of these events and highlight it, giving it greater prominence than the others.

The second category, comparators, involves the addition of complexity to the basic syntactic template. Comparators take a sequence of events that occurred and compare these events with an event that might have occurred but did not actually occur in the narrative as a means of highlighting and showing the interest or relevance of the absence of that state of affairs. One simple comparator is the use of negation. Saying that something did not happen (although it might have happened) compares that state of affairs with what actually did happen and points out why what did happen is worth reporting. Another type of comparator is the use of imperatives. Imperatives describe an action or event that has not occurred at the time of narration but, more important, imply that something else (important to how the story turns out) could happen if the imperative is not complied with. Questions are classed as comparators for similar reasons. Asking a question implies that an answer is expected; in other words, there is an underlying challenge. If no answer is given, then there is a potential for negative consequences, which are compared to what actually happens in the story. Finally, according to Labov, comparative structures (including superlatives) are a form of comparator, since they set off what occurred against another potential state of affairs.

Correlatives, Labov's third category, are syntactically complex because they take two events that occurred and combine them in a single clause rather than express them in linear sequence. They include participle constructions in English; they are evaluative because they suspend the action, highlighting its importance against the background of other co-occurring events in the narrative.

The fourth and final category, explicatives, adds syntactic complexity by adding explanations of an event, either in the form of causal subordinate clauses introduced by conjunctions such as *because* or *(for-) to* or qualifications introduced by *although* among other such conjunctions. Explicatives are evaluative to the extent that they explain why a state of affairs in the story is of interest — in other words, worth reporting.

In later sections of this paper, we will point out various how evaluation is realized in the two connected LSQ narratives in ways similar to what Labov reports for English. At the same time, we will see certain differences that we can explain by the structural peculiarities of LSQ as a sign language. Comparing the two stories, we will see that evaluation is realized at a different level of structure in the Tortoise and Hare fable, a fact we believe is due to the formal, nonspontaneous structure of this story.

THE STRUCTURE OF THE TWO STORIES

The two co-occurring stories we analyze present interesting differences in structure.[2] As a spontaneous narrative of personal experience, the matrix story in which the narrator tells about her experience of teaching LSQ to hearing children contains the basic elements proposed by Labov. However, the story is told in a rather complex manner: the narrator divides it into two contrasting time periods and, furthermore, embeds the fable of the Tortoise and the Hare into the story as a way of illustrating how she taught the children signs. The fable of the Tortoise and the Hare is actually told as part of the Children story, as a way of illustrating how the narrator taught the children some signs in LSQ and how she managed to get them interested in learning about signs and deafness. At another level though, it is clear that the Tortoise and Hare story is *not* about the narrator's personal experience. It is clearly a rehearsed performance of the traditional fable: its structure and content are distinct enough from that of the matrix narrative that it can be extracted from the former and analyzed on its own merits. For this reason, we present the two stories' structure independently in the following two sections.

The Children Story

The story about teaching the children signs occurs at the end of a two-hour evening recording session, the last of five in which the LSQ88 video corpus was recorded. After the scheduled topics of the interview are exhausted, the facilitator checks the time and says that she is tired: she has to get up early in the morning for a long bus trip to a suburb across the river from Montreal where she is working at a summer day camp for children. At this point, she starts to explain that she (with a colleague) has been hired to teach the children at the camp some signs in LSQ. Having had a session that day with the hearing children, she begins to recount the story of what happened when she was teaching them signs, emphasizing all along the positive interaction she had with the children.

Analyzing the story in terms of the components proposed by Labov reveals the following overall structure, with levels of embedding indicated by successive indentation and numbering.

1. FIRST CHILDREN STORY
    1.1. orientation (lines 1–12)
    1.2. abstract (lines 13–22)
    1.3. complicating action (lines 23–37)
    INTERRUPTION BY INTERLOCUTOR AND REPLIES (lines 38–39)
2. SECOND CHILDREN STORY
    2.1. (secondary) orientation (line 40)
    2.2. abstract (lines 41–46)
    2.3. complicating action (teaching signs, including the Tortoise and Hare story) (lines 47–242)
        2.3.1. TORTOISE AND HARE STORY part 1 (lines 58–139)
        2.3.2. SECOND CHILDREN STORY: "medal" episode (lines 140–174)
            2.3.2.1. abstract (line 140)
            2.3.2.2. complicating action (lines 141–165)
            2.3.2.3. resolution (lines 166–174)

It can be seen from the above schema that this story (which lasts for approximately seven minutes, twenty-one seconds) has a fairly complex structure. The narrator not only embeds the fable of the Tortoise and the Hare in this story but also begins by talking about her experiences with one group of children on a previous day before she develops the story of what happened with the most recent group of children. Most interestingly, the orientation for the first segment of the Children story is by and large reused for the second segment. In this orientation, she introduces herself, an LSQ interpreter, the deaf friend who is working with her, and the children as protagonists in the story. At the beginning of the video excerpt, the narrator has already mentioned the existence of the children, the interpreter, and the friend she worked with at the festival, but she has not yet situated them in a narrative space.

The first time the person later to be identified as the interpreter is associated with a spatial locus (to the narrator's right), this is done with the directional verb HIRE-r (see illustration 1a). The children are then set up in an arc in front of the narrator (illustration 1b). This general region in which the children are situated is then taken up in several following signs: POINT-ctr, CHILDREN HEARING AREA-IN-FRONT, and so on.

Although most of the protagonists are introduced in the orientation itself, she waits until the complicating action has begun before introducing her friend. When she describes how she interacts with him before the children, demonstrating greetings in LSQ, she introduces him with his name sign "S" on her right. This sign is accompanied by eye gaze and is followed by a POINT-r sign (see illustration 2).

a) HIRE-r   b) SHOW-arc

ILLUSTRATION 1

This, together with the other means described in the preceding paragraphs, populates her signing space as shown in illustration 3. The lines
with arrows indicate the spatial axes along which the narrator shows
interaction between characters in the story.

The only element of orientation that is in fact unique to the first segment of the Children story is embedded in the abstract section (line 15,
time code 146184) in which the narrator mentions that the children were
between three and five years old.

She continues to use the spatial map she has set up when she starts
telling a story about a more recent group of children, now ranging in age
from six to nine, after an interruption from one of her two interlocutors.
Because of the interruption, the story about the earlier, younger group
of children is never finished, but is recycled, with the older group taking
the place of the younger children. For this reason, she does not need to
provide a full-fledged orientation section. Since all the basic elements are
the same, the orientation is inherited from the first segment of the story,
and the only new orienting information that she adds is that the newer
group is between six and nine years old (line 40, time code 147076). For
this segment of the narrative, she provides a new abstract that, as we will
later see, doubles as evaluation, in which she emphasizes how well this
group interacts with her.

The second and main segment of the narrative is especially complex,
since it is divided into several nearly autonomous episodes. The two principal episodes (sections 2.3 and 2.4 in the outline of the narrative's structure) deal respectively with teaching the children some simple LSQ signs
(TORTOISE WIN, HARE LOSE), and introducing the idea of deafness and
Deaf people into their world. The most complex section — the core of
the narrative — is section 2.3, the "teaching signs" episode. This section

a) 'S'   b) POINT-r

ILLUSTRATION 2.

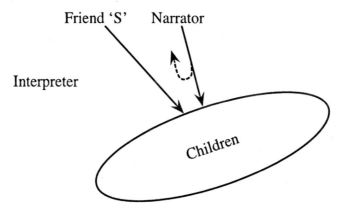

ILLUSTRATION 3. *Character spatial map for the children story*

is the one in which the narrator illustrates how she taught the children signs and how she managed to awaken their interest in LSQ by telling them the story of the Tortoise and the Hare. She recounts how she told the story to the children, interspersing the fable itself with comments about the interpreter and how she, in the guise of both the Tortoise and the Hare, "emerged" from the fable to interact with the audience. The most extensive of these metanarrative breaks occurs in the "medal" episode (section 2.3.2 of the outline presented above), a narrative in itself, where she (as the Tortoise) brings one of the children into the action. The child is given the role of a judge who gives the Tortoise a medal. After the extensive section on teaching the children signs via the Tortoise and Hare story, the narrator segues into a much shorter section (section 2.4 of the outline) in which she introduces the idea of deafness and Deaf people to the (fascinated) children. This short section is then followed by a resolution section

(section 2.5 of the outline) in which the children become primary actors, asking questions and demonstrating their knowledge of fingerspelling. The two-line coda recaps the narrative by repeating that these children are from six to nine years old, followed by the comment that they were "super."

As we will show in the section titled "Evaluation in the Children Story," and as can be seen in the bolded portions of the transcription, the narrator uses evaluative mechanisms, both external and embedded, throughout the narrative, whether in the matrix or during the portions where she recounts the Tortoise and Hare fable. Whether they occur in the matrix story or are interspersed with the fable, these evaluations (individually or as part of a pattern) all underline the narrator's success in communicating with the children and involving them in the workshop.

Although the narrator intersperses the fable of the Tortoise and the Hare with evaluative comments belonging to the Children story as part of the process of showing how she recounted the fable, the fable itself has a distinct narrative structure and set of evaluative mechanisms, to which we now turn.

The Fable of the Tortoise and the Hare

Unlike the story about teaching signs to the hearing children, which narrates recent personal experiences, the story of the Tortoise and the Hare is a retelling of a traditional fable handed down through the millennia. The narrator merely recounts how she had already told the story to the children when she last saw them; the version of the fable that she performs has already been planned out and rehearsed as the traditional story it is. Because the fable is presented as a performance narrative, one might expect it to show some structural features that are different from the Children story, and this is indeed the case.

In general terms, the fable can be analyzed into sections along the same lines as the Children story. The story begins with an orientation section in which the Tortoise and Hare characters appear. The orientation is immediately followed by a complicating action section that includes all interaction between the two characters, starting with their first introductions, and followed by the Hare's mockery of the Tortoise, the Tortoise's challenge to a race, and the race itself, right up to the point where the Tortoise wins the race and turns the tables on the Hare. The narrator adds a final resolution section in which the two protagonists become friends and walk off together, arm in arm.

The structural complexity of the fable does not end here, however. Closer observation of the fable reveals that it contains several layered structural patterns that set it apart from the Children narrative. When these patterns are taken together with the thematic content, we are able to discern a structure reminiscent of some kinds of poetic verse. Two kinds of patterns are important here. At one level of analysis, the fable is organized into a hierarchy of lines and stanzas correlated with thematic content, similar to what is proposed by Bahan and Supalla (1995). At a second level intimately connected with the first, we find that the use of a "spatial map," as described by Mather and Winston (1996), is central to how the narrator sets up the basic framework on which she builds the verse structure of the fable.

Bahan and Supalla (1995) base their scheme for narrative analysis on the alternation of thematic content and eye-gaze shift. In their system, a line corresponds to an idea unit, a stanza corresponds to a unit with uniform topic content, a strophe is characterized by a thematic similarity in a broader sense, and a section groups together several strophes. The core of their analysis is that eye-gaze shift outlines boundaries, together with pausing, head nods, and eye blinks. These nonmanual behaviors contribute overall to the subdivision of the whole narrative into coherent structural units. Although we do not examine the nonmanual behaviors described by Bahan and Supalla, we indeed find that a variety of other means are used by the narrator to build the overall poetic structure of the fable. We will show that the fable's verse structure relies heavily on repetition and symmetries, both in space and in time. Interestingly enough, although the narrator, whose first reading language is French, can be assumed to be familiar with the traditional version of the fable by Jean de la Fontaine, the poetic macrostructure she builds in the LSQ version is unrelated to that in la Fontaine's French adaptation of the fable.

The symmetries and repetition we analyze below are built up on a "spatial map" similar to what Mather and Winston (1996) describe, in other words, a framework that associates different elements with different regions in space as a means of organizing the referential and thematic structure of discourse. In an ASL narrative that they examine, they show that two distinct regions of space function to provide a framework for different events in the unfolding of the story and to structure the narrative at a rhythmic level. In the fable of the Tortoise and the Hare, we find that space is used to superimpose a poetic structure on the narrative, not only at the level of rhythmic structure as described by Mather and

Winston but also at a metaphorical level in which the moral of the story is developed. The spatial map that situates the characters in the Tortoise and the Hare story is illustrated in illustration 4.

In this map, the narrator alternates between the roles of the Tortoise and the Hare: in interactions between the two, the Tortoise is located on the left side of the narrator's space, and the Hare is located on the right. Their relative locations are symbolized by the two smaller ovals; the fact that both loci (or surrogates) are essentially overlaid on the physical location of the narrator is symbolized by the larger oval that encloses the other two. Apart from the mutual axis of interaction, a diagonal line angling outward and slightly to the narrator's left traces the general direction of the race course in the story. This line is an axis of action along which the race section of the narrative takes place.

At one level of analysis, the spatial map serves to establish and distinguish the referents in the story. However, the narrator exploits the spatial map at another level, tying it in with rhythmic structure and other dimensions of space to draw a portrait of the two protagonists. When we compare the structure of the dialogue between the two protagonists with the way rhythmic and spatial structure are manipulated, two underlying organizing principles surface at all levels. These principles are parallelism, or symmetry, on the one hand, and contrast on the other, and they play complementary roles in constructing meaning during the course of the narrative. When they are analyzed in terms of the way rhythm, space, and dialogue are structured in the fable, the function of the contrasts and symmetries becomes clearer: they construct the character portraits of the Tortoise and the Hare by setting up contrasts between them at each level of structure. Beyond the purely structural function of providing a poetic framework around which she constructs the story, the narrator exploits these contrasts for metaphorical purposes and uses them in such a way that the moral of the story, rather than being explicitly stated, is built into the structure of the narrative itself. We will return to this use of contrast in section considering evaluation in the Tortoise and the Hare.

OVERLAPPING LEVELS OF STRUCTURE

Unsurprisingly, a first glance at the Tortoise and Hare story shows that the dialogue and interaction between the two characters plays an important role in the organization of the story's overall structure. We notice a series of alternations involving constructed action and constructed dialogue, conversational turns (who addresses whom and about what) and

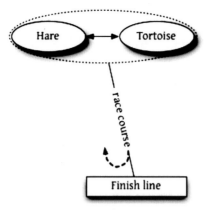

ILLUSTRATION 4. *Character spatial map for the Tortoise and Hare story*

proposition types (questions, statements). On the basis of these alternations, we have subdivided the fable into segments and subsegments that share numerous characteristics with poetic verse structure.

Figure 1 compares action and dialogue alternations within the main thematic sections in the story. In the first section, the narrator enacts the meeting between the Tortoise and the Hare (which corresponds to the orientation plus the beginning of the complicating action). The Hare then makes fun of the Tortoise for being slow, and the Tortoise challenges the Hare to a race. The Tortoise proposes a route for the race, and the Hare agrees to the challenge. In the second section, we see how each character runs the race and how the Tortoise wins. In the third section (dialogue-centered again), they take stock of the situation. Following an interlude where the narrator returns to the Children story, she brings the fable to a close with a dialogue and action-based section in which the Tortoise and the Hare make up and leave the scene together.

Proceeding from the generally defined sections above, we can refine the division by taking into account the thematic content and the context of utterance (who addresses whom). For instance, as shown in figure 2, the thematic content of the first section is as follows: the characters introduce themselves, the Hare makes fun of the Tortoise; the Tortoise protests, then proposes a race, then maps out the route for the Hare; then both agree on the route. Three of these five subsections are introduced by the narrator addressing the two interlocutors to whom she recounts the stories, and all contain a speaker-addressee alternation in which one character addresses the other, then the other replies.

Section	Alternation	Content	Time codes
1	Dialogue	Abstract through agreement on race course	147463–148542
2	Action	The race and Tortoise's victory	149079–149562
3	Dialogue	Tortoise claims victory, upbraids Hare	149578–150132
	Interlude: episode from the children narrative		
4	Dialogue + action	Tortoise and Hare reconcile	150560–151092

FIGURE 1. *Major sections: constructed dialogue compared with constructed action*

a. Introductions

N → ch	PT-1 TORTOISE
N → ch	(Tortoise persona: slow, low to ground) PAWS-PLOD-ALONG++
N → Ch	PT-high-rt = Hare (Hare persona) HARE CL-V̈–"leaping around in the air"
N → Ch	(right hand) Hare-LOOK-AT-lf = Tortoise (left hand) Cl-V̈–lf = Tortoise————
H → T	[$_{H>T}$ WHO?]
T → H	[$_{T>H}$ PTI-1 TORTOISE PT-1 PT-2 WHO PT-2?]
H → T	[$_{H>T}$ PT-1 HARE PT-1, HELLO]
T → H	[$_{T>H}$ HELLO]
(… T → H)	[$_T$ PAWS-TOGETHER begin-PAWS-PLOD-ALONG]

b. The Hare mocks the Tortoise

N → Ch H → T	PT-Hare [$_H$ PT-Tortoise SLOW PAWS-PLOD-ALONG SLOW! "cover mouth, slap knee laughing"
H → T	PT-1 CL-1 "shoot off into the distance like a rocket"
T → H	[$_T$ WHOA NOT FUNNY 2-SAY-TO/C/-1
(…T → H)	[$_T$ NOT FUNNY 2-SAY-TO-1 TORTOISE-PAWS

c. The Tortoise's challenge

N(as T) → Ch	[$_{T-CHILDREN}$ "ONE-SECOND" HAVE-IDEA EYE PT-children (wink eye)

T → H	[_T HEY-Hare WANT CHALLENGE RACE TO-GOAL LINE TOUCH WANT PT-2?
H → T	[_H YES!
T → H	[_T READY PT-2?
H → T	[_H YES! PT-1 READY

d. Describing the route of the race

T → H	[_T 1-TELL-2 PT-1--
N → Ch	UH-UH/5/ "WHOA"
T → H	[_T 1-TELL-2 PT-1 IDEA MUST PT-2:
(... T → H)	[_T TOUCH TREES-going-by-along-route 2 KM ... FINISH
(... T → H)	[_T THEN: TOUCH LAKE MUST TOUCH PT-2 DIVE SWIM++ TO-GOAL FINISH
(... T → H)	[_T THEN: WINDING-ROAD SEE-in front CL-SS 'posts' LINE TOUCH

e. Agreeing on the route

(...T → H)	[_T OK PT-2?
H → T	[_H OK (2h)
T → H	[_T TELL-1 WHAT/1/ PT/A/-2
N → Ch	START TELL-STORY "HOLD-ON"
N → interloc.	CORRECT
T → H	[_{T-H} 1-TELL-2 END CORRECT?
H → T	[_{H-T} PERFECT
H → T	[_{H-CHILDREN} TRUE PT-arc-children?
Ch → H	[_{CHILDREN} SAY-YES-2h-alternating

FIGURE 2. *Thematic content and context of utterance (N → Ch = Narrator addresses children; H → T = Hare speaks to Tortoise; T → H = Tortoise speaks to Hare; T → Ch = Tortoise speaks to children; H → Ch = Hare speaks to children)*

This secondary subdivision based on the presence of speaker-addressee alternations can be refined by taking into account alternations between questions and answers in the dialogue between the Tortoise and the Hare, as shown in figure 3.

We see from the above illustrations that alternations between speaker and addressee combine with alternations in the content of the constructed

a. Introductions

Q	[$_{H>T}$ WHO?]
A	[$_{T>H}$ PTI-I TORTOISE PT-I
Q	PT-2 WHO PT-2?]
A	[$_{H>T}$ PT-I HARE PT-I
S	HELLO]
A	[$_{T>H}$ HELLO]

b. The Hare mocks the Tortoise

S	PT-Hare [$_H$ PT-Tortoise SLOW PAWS-PLOD-ALONG SLOW! (laughs at Tortoise)
(… S)	PT-I Cl-1 "shoot off into the distance like a rocket"
A	[$_T$ WHOA NOT FUNNY 2-SAY-TO/C/-1
(… A)	[$_T$ NOT FUNNY 2-SAY-TO-I TORTOISE-PAWS

c. The Tortoise's challenge

S	[$_{T-CHILDREN}$ "ONE-SECOND" HAVE-IDEA EYE PT-children (wink eye)
Q	[$_T$ HEY-Hare WANT CHALLENGE RACE TO-GOAL LINE TOUCH WANT PT-2?
A	[$_H$ YES!
Q	[$_T$ READY PT-2?
A	[$_H$ YES! PT-I READY

d. Describing the route of the race

S	[$_T$ 1-TELL-2 PT-I--
(… S)	[$_T$ 1-TELL-2 PT-I IDEA MUST PT-2:
(… S)	[$_T$ TOUCH TREES-going-by-along-route 2 KM … FINISH
(… S)	[$_T$ THEN: TOUCH LAKE MUST TOUCH PT-2 DIVE SWIM++ TO-GOAL FINISH
(… S)	[$_T$ THEN: WINDING-ROAD SEE-in front Cl-ss 'posts' LINE TOUCH

e. Agreeing on the route

Q	[$_T$ OK PT-2?
A	[$_H$ OK (2h)
Q	[$_T$ TELL-I WHAT/I/ PT/A/-2

A	CORRECT
Q	$[_{T-H}$ 1-TELL-2 END CORRECT?
A	$[_{H-T}$ PERFECT
(Q-A alternation outside the fable proper:)	
(Q)	$[_{H\text{-}CHILDREN}$ TRUE PT-arc-children?
(A)	$[_{CHILDREN}$ SAY-YES-2h-alternating

FIGURE 3. *Question, answer, statement (S = statement; Q = question; A = answer or response)*

dialogue to establish a clear line structure within thematically coherent episodes that correspond to stanzas at a structural level. As we show in the next section, this structure is reinforced by the way the narrator uses space.

SPATIAL MACROSTRUCTURE

It is well known that sign languages exploit space for establishing and tracking referents in discourse: one overview of this function can be found in Emmorey and Reilly (1995). Beyond these basic morphosyntactic functions, which are probably common to all genres of sign language texts, the way signs and nonmanual behaviors make use of space may play a specific role in structuring poetic narrative. This possibility is pointed out in Winston's (1995) study of the role of spatial mapping in discourse structure. She shows how the repeated use of spatial loci contributes to the cohesion of the overall structure of the discourse and how spatial mapping in general sets up discourse frames in which comparisons are made.

A similar and in fact more complex pattern shows up in the structure of the fable. When we examine the fable, we observe that it is built around three types of spatial macrostructure. First is a constant right-left division used when the Tortoise and the Hare engage in dialogue or otherwise interact with each other. The Tortoise is on the left side, from the narrator's point of view, and the Hare is on the right side, as shown in illustration 4. Thus the narrator shifts her body each time the protagonist changes. Figure 4 shows that these body shifts emphasize the boundaries established in figures 2 and 3.

a. Introductions

→	[_{H>T} WHO?]
←	[_{T>H} PT-1 TORTOISE PT-1 PT-2 WHO PT-2?]
→	[_{H>T} PT-1 HARE PT-1 HELLO]
←	[_{T>H} HELLO]

b. The Hare mocks the Tortoise

→	PT-Hare [_H PT-Tortoise SLOW PAWS-PLOD-ALONG SLOW! (laughs at Tortoise)
→	PT-1 Cl-1 "shoot off into the distance like a rocket"
←	[_T WHOA NOT FUNNY 2-SAY-TO/C/-1
←	[_T NOT FUNNY 2-SAY-TO-1 TORTOISE-PAWS

c. The Tortoise's challenge

←	[_{T-CHILDREN} "ONE-SECOND" HAVE-IDEA EYE PT-children (wink eye)
←	[_T HEY-Hare WANT CHALLENGE RACE TO-GOAL LINE TOUCH WANT PT-2?
→	[_H YES!
←	[_T READY PT-2?
←	[_H YES! PT-1 READY

d. Describing the route of the race

←	[_T 1-TELL-2 PT-1--
←	[_T 1-TELL-2 PT-1 IDEA MUST PT-2:
←	[_T TOUCH TREES-going-by-along-route 2 KM ... FINISH
←	[_T THEN: TOUCH LAKE MUST TOUCH PT-2 DIVE SWIM++ TO-GOAL FINISH
←	[_T THEN: WINDING-ROAD SEE-in front Cl-SS 'posts' LINE TOUCH

e. Agreeing on the route

←	[_T OK PT-2?
→	[_H OK (2h)
←	[_T TELL-1 WHAT/1/ PT/A/-2
→	CORRECT
←	[_{T-H} 1-TELL-2 END CORRECT?
→	[_{H-T} PERFECT

FIGURE 4. *Body shift (*← *= to narrator's left side, facing right;* → *= to narrator's right side, facing left)*

Apart from the mechanism of body shift, the narrator manipulates space by constructing an "action space" along a depth axis that extends forward and slightly to her left from the front of her body. Along this axis, the Tortoise maps out the race course with a step-by-step description of the route, drawing lines with geometric contours for the finishing posts, the finish line, the road, and trees along the road. A third mechanism she uses is eye gaze: while the Tortoise describes the route, he has his gaze fixed on a distant point at the end of this depth axis. This use of eye gaze can be seen clearly in the series of illustrations appearing in illustration 5.

The action of the race itself is constructed on this depth axis, and the Tortoise, when plodding along the path, keeps his eyes fixed on the end of the axis while the Hare runs downs the route, looking off to the side (see illustration 6).

Superimposed on the uses of space involving body shift and the depth axis is a height axis along which the narrator sets up a high-low distinction between her two characters. The Tortoise is depicted as a typical Tortoise, low in height and close to the ground while the Hare is depicted as an anthropomorphized, vertical, cartoon-style character such as Bugs Bunny or Roger Rabbit (illustration 7).

Thus, the narrator directs her eye-gaze upward and to her right when she plays the role of the Tortoise and downward and to her left when she plays the role of the Hare (illustration 8).

The observations we have made with respect to conversational alternations and their relation to the narrator's use of space are paralleled at the level of rhythmic structure. We consider this structure in the next section.

RHYTHMIC STRUCTURE

Observing the overall rhythmic structure of the fable, we notice striking differences from what we see in the narrative of personal experience. Rhythms in the fable involve marked contrasts in speed between accelerated and slowed-down versions of signs. These contrasts are exploited to

| TOUCH | TREES | WINDING-ROAD | SEE | LINE |

ILLUSTRATION 5.

(Tortoise)   (Hare)

ILLUSTRATION 6.

build rhythmic patterns that we do not observe in the rest of the narrative. These patterns are used as a way of contrasting the characters of the Tortoise and the Hare; however, in the matrix narrative, we do not see any similar use of rhythmic contrast.

When the narrator refers to or takes on the role of the Hare, the signs take on an accelerated, rapid rhythm, whether the Hare is acting or speaking. When she refers to or takes on the role of the Tortoise, the rhythm of her signs becomes slow and measured. In fact, if we examine this contrast more closely, it is difficult for us to describe the signs associated with the Hare in terms of any specific rhythmic pattern whereas the rhythmic pattern of signs associated with the Tortoise is clearly distinguished, whether that pattern affects a sequence of signs or only one. In figure 5, we illustrate this contrast by comparing the way the movements of each protagonist are depicted in the action sequences. We see that the Hare is depicted as jumping up and down or running at full speed whereas the Tortoise is shown as plodding slowly along (in the introduction and during the race); these patterns are reversed at the end of the race.

Rhythm is based on variations in the speed and strength of some kind of temporally regular physical behavior when measured across adjacent intervals of time. Rhythmic phenomena include, among other things, the

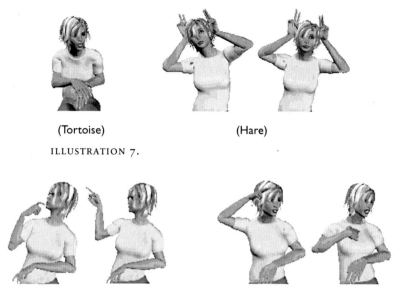

(Tortoise)   (Hare)

ILLUSTRATION 7.

[T>H ... WHO PT–2]   [H >T ... HARE PT–I ...]

ILLUSTRATION 8.

sounds of music; the relative stress and length of syllables in language; and the arm, leg, and body movements of dance. In sign language, Miller (1998) distinguishes bimoraic long syllables from monomoraic short syllables (referred to elsewhere as repeated "oscillating," "local," or "secondary" movements) in LSQ to account for the phrasal distribution of repeated or nonrepeated variants of short-movement signs. From a phonetic point of view, long movements generally correlate with "path movements" of the gross articulators (upper arm or forearm) and short syllables with "local movements" of the small articulators (the fingers, wrist, or rotating forearm). We have found this distinction between isolable individual short and long movements helpful in establishing rhythmic contrasts in poetic structure (Blondel and Miller 2000). We continue to make use of this distinction here; however, we will refer to the duration of each movement in video frames rather than couch the description in terms of syllable structure.

To define the boundaries of movements, we take the plausible position that the beginning of a new movement corresponds to a change in direction or orientation of an articulator. We observe that in a stretch of signing, some movements are phonologically salient in comparison with others. It seems natural to use the term *stressed* to refer to these movements, though

Rancourt (1998) points out that this term is ambiguous and that it is difficult to determine precise parameters for describing stress. In our case, the movements we perceive as prominent are often — though not always — directed downward. In addition, the impression of salience is reinforced if a movement is accelerated, is followed by a hold, or is accompanied by a forward movement of the head, body, or both.

In figure 5, we compare signs describing the movements of the two protagonists in segments that are already established on the basis of their thematic content. We divide movements into their component cycles, measured in frames of approximately one-thirtieth of a second in length: when there is a preparatory or transitional movement, we include it in the movement structure of the sign; similarly, we take into account holds following the end of a sign's movement. For signs with short, repeated movements (including oscillating movements), we distinguish each half cycle of the oscillation or, when appropriate, each direction of the overall short movement. Movements we perceive as salient are indicated in bold.

When we look at the movements of the Tortoise character in parts a–d of figure 5, the overall impression is one of slowness. This impression comes about in part because of the many holds, the length of the movements themselves (eight frames on average, within a range of five to twelve frames), and the fact that both hands are involved. In contrast (except for his imitation of the Tortoise's slowness), the Hare's movements are much faster (typically, two to three frames, that is, barely a third of the duration of the Tortoise's) with multiple repetitions, and no holds. Moreover, the Hare and the Tortoise contrast in other dimensions of movement: the Tortoise's movements are always in the same direction whereas the Hare's movements are scattered seemingly randomly in the signing space. In addition, for the Tortoise, the movement of the hands is coordinated with body movements whereas we do not find this kind of coordination in the case of the Hare. From a perceptual viewpoint, the way the Tortoise moves appears as a regular pattern while the way the Hare moves lacks this regularity (see illustration 9).

In parts e and f of figure 5, the rhythm of the Tortoise's plodding changes. The holds disappear, and in part e, both hands overlap, moving continuously in alternation. Thus, the duration between two stressed syllables is shortened and the rhythm is accelerated; nevertheless, the location of the hands is still constant, and the movement of the body is still synchronized with the movement of the hands. These contrasts in rhythm

a. Tortoise and Hare characters appear

PT-1 TORTOISE

(Tortoise persona: slow, low to ground) PAWS-PLOD-ALONG++
(right hand)   ...↑9 *m*↓7h16
(left hand)   ...↑21 *m*↓8h16

PT-high-rt = Hare (Hare persona) HARE (flighty, self-absorbed)
(head: ←6 →6)
↓ *3* ↑2 ↓2 ↑2 ↓2 ↑2 ↓2 ↑2 ↓2 ↑3 ↓3h4 Cl-V̈–"leaping around in the air"

(right hand) Hare-LOOK-AT-lf = Tortoise
... 6 *m*3h17

---

b. Tortoise and Hare exchange introductions

[_H>T_ WHO?]
... 5 *m4* ... 3 *m3*

[_T>H_ PTI-1 TORTOISE PT-1
... 8 *m10* ... 9 *m6 m12*h6

PT-2 WHO   PT-2?]
m10 *m6* ... 3 m3   *m8*h10

[_H>T_ PT-I   HARE PT-I,   HELLO]
      m5   ... 6 *m5*   *m3*h16   ... 5 *m8*h5
[_T>H_ PT-I -
          HELLO]
        ... 6 h6 *m5*h10

[_T_ PAWS-TOGETHER begin-PAWS-PLOD-ALONG]
   ... 16 h11   ... 11 *m7*h24

---

c. Hare mocks Tortoise

PT-Hare [_H_ PT-Tortoise SLOW PAWS-PLOD-ALONG SLOW! "cover mouth, slap knee laughing"
     m5   *m12* ... 5h4 ... 7 *m7*h21 ... 9h9 *m4*   ... 7h9 ... 8 *m8*

PT-1   Cl-1 "shoot off into the distance like a rocket"
   m9 ... 20 o3 o3 o3 o4 o2 o2 o1

---

d. The race starts

      [_T_ PLOD-SLOWLY-2h-alternating WIPE-FOREHEAD
(Rh) ... 11 *m8*h18————————... 11 *m8* ... 16 *m12*
(Lh)   ... 16 *m6*h12

PT-Hare Cl-V̈–"leaping around in the air"
m4 ... 6 ↑3 ↓3 ↑3 ↓2

[$_H$ Cl-HH-ears "cartoon Hare expressions: rolling eyes, sticks out tongue, sneering"

... 9h9 m9   (head → center:) m9 (body wiggles left-right:) m4 m3 m3

Cl-V̆–"leap forward" CL-55-'run at high speed'
m9   m5 m4 m3 m3 m3 m3

Cl-V̆–"leap forward" THEN Cl-V̆–"speed down winding path"
m10   m8   ... 3 o4 o4 o3 o3 h8

---

e. Tortoise perseveres while Hare sleeps

PT-1 [$_T$ PLOD-SLOWLY-2h-alternating
(RH:) ... 6 *m9* (LH:) ... 8 *m8*

[$_T$ PLOD-SLOWLY-2h-alternating
(RH:) *m3* (LH:) ... 10 *m7* (RH:) ... 8 *m8*

---

f. Tortoise finishes race

[$_T$ PLOD-QUICKLY-2h-alternating+++
(RH:) ... 4 *m5* ... 7 *m5* ... 5 *m8*
(LH:) ... 5 *m6* ... 8 *m5*   ... 8 *m5*

Cl-11-'finish line poles approach gradually'
... 8 *m6 m8* h7 *m6* h5 *m5*

Cl-HH-'finish line tape approaches gradually'
... 9 *m5* h2 *m7* h5 *m6* h3

[$_T$ Cl-HH-'finish line tape' 'breaks through finish line tape'
m35   *m37*

---

g. Tortoise wins, Hare loses

[$_T$ ("yelling") "arms in the air, jumping up and down"   Cl-V̆–"leaping around in the air"

(body mvt.) ...4 *m4* ...3 *m2* ...3 *m3* ...2 *m2* ↑2↓2↑2↓2↑2↓2↑2↓2↑2↓2↑2↓2

NATURAL Cl-V̆ "leaping around in the air"
↑4 ↓3 ↑3 ↓3 ↑3 ↓3

PT-Hare [$_H$ "shoulders sag in despair"
... 15 *m8*h10+

FIGURE 5. *Tortoise's and Hare's movement rhythms compared (... = transitional, preparatory movement; m = lexical movement; h = final hold; o = half-cycle of oscillating short movement; ↑ = upward movement; ↓ = downward movement)*

reinforce the other kinds of contrasts and alternations we have discussed and strengthen our arguments for a poetic structure in the fable.

The overall poetic structure of the story that emerges from our observations is shown in figure 6. In thematic terms, the stanzas are — with few exceptions — organized into pairs that reflect each other progressively

Tortoise plodding

Hare jumping

ILLUSTRATION 9.

across a central midline of symmetry. This symmetry shows up somewhat less clearly in the rhythmic and spatial structure of the stanzas. It is striking nonetheless how this mirror structure recalls that of a children's poem in French Sign Language analyzed in Blondel and Miller (2001). This similarity reinforces in our minds the formal nature of the fable when compared with the Children story.

So far, we have shown how contrasts at various levels are exploited by the narrator to form a macropoetic structure. At another level of analysis, contrasts are used to draw a metaphorical picture of each character that is exploited for purposes of evaluation. We deal with this aspect of the fable's structure in a later section on evaluation in the fable of the Tortoise and the Hare.

EVALUATION IN THE CHILDREN STORY

Earlier, we summarized the types of evaluative devices discussed by Labov, including external evaluation (i.e., comments inserted by the narrator) and the various types of internal evaluation that are embedded in the narrative itself. Examining the Children story, we are struck by

A Stanza 1 Tortoise & Hare characters appear
B Stanza 2 Tortoise & Hare exchange introductions
C Stanza 3 Hare mocks Tortoise
D Stanza 4 Tortoise challenges Hare
D′ Stanza 5 Tortoise maps out the race
D″ Stanza 6 Agreement on the route
E Stanza 7 The race starts
F Stanza 8 Hare takes a nap
FF Stanza 9 Tortoise perseveres while Hare sleeps
EE Stanza 10 Tortoise finishes race
DD Stanza 11 Tortoise wins, Hare loses
CC Stanza 12 Tortoise reminds Hare of mockery
CC′ Stanza 13 Hare concedes, Tortoise wants prize
BB Stanza 14 Tortoise & Hare reconcile
AA Stanza 15 Exhausted Hare trails behind Tortoise

FIGURE 6. *Overall poetic structure of the Tortoise and Hare story*

how well Labov's typology fits the devices used here. Little in the way of modification appears to be necessary other than taking into account the different physical form of the signal in a sign language narrative. In the paragraphs that follow, we (a) illustrate the different types of evaluation used by the narrator to make her story interesting and (b) discuss, where appropriate, relevant differences that appear to be to the result of modality.

External Evaluation

Although most of the evaluation in the story is embedded, we do find a few examples of external comments in the narrator's own voice. One of them, INTERESTING, is in fact repeated at several points through the narrative at lines 72, 95, and 106; in a couple of cases, the narrator suspends the action at crucial points to insert this comment. At lines 101 and 105, although describing her rendition of the fable, she comments that she was "miming" and "inventing" elements of the story, thus asserting her skill at making the story interesting to the children. A final type of external evaluation we observe is the narrator's relatively frequent use of qualifiers such as CUTE, INTELLIGENT, BEAUTIFUL, COMICAL, and SUPER to describe how wonderful the children were; similarly, she makes an interesting use of gesture following CHILDREN in line 37, dropping her hands loosely onto her knees as if at a loss for words to express her feelings.

Internal Evaluation

The most abundant types of evaluation used in the narrative fall under the various types of internal evaluation described in Labov's work. We recall from the earlier discussion that Labov (1972) distinguishes two types of internal evaluation: those that add complexity to the basic syntactic template for the narrative clause and those that do not. We will deal with those that complexify the syntax (including comparators, correlatives, and explicatives) in a later section. In the sections immediately below, we describe how those realizations of internal evaluation that do not complexify the syntax are expressed in LSQ.

INTENSIFIERS

Evaluation that does not affect narrative syntax includes a variety of means that serve to intensify one element in the clause, heightening its salience against the background of the rest of the clause. These intensifiers include expressive phonology, repetition of an element, addition of quantifiers, and use of reinforcing gesture.

EXPRESSIVE PHONOLOGY

Clearly, the realization of expressive phonology in a sign language will take a different form from what we find in spoken languages. Keeping this fact in mind, we find that this kind of evaluation is used at several points by the narrator. Two kinds of mechanisms are used: one is the use of expressive nonmanuals; the other is the addition of emphasis (acceleration or tension) to the movement of the signs themselves. We find both used, but in contrasting manners, in the signs in illustration 10. In the first sign, RAISE-HANDS (2h-alt), the narrator takes on the role of the children raising their hands and intensifies the sign by pluralizing it with the addition of a second hand and alternating movement. She also accelerates the movement of her hands and adds appropriate facial expressions to show the children's excitement and eagerness. In the second sign, the signer accelerates the separating movement of the two hands from a slow beginning to a rapid, sharp end with long final hold. She coordinates this movement with a movement of her body toward the right and eye gaze that sweeps from left to right. The whole sign is accompanied by a facial expression of delighted astonishment. Both of these examples are found at more than one point in the narrative; many other signs are similarly intensified by changes to their movement structure and by the addition of expressive nonmanuals.

Repetition of an element

Repetition of an element is an effective means of emphasizing it, and we find numerous examples of repetition being used in the narrative. Introducing a distinction between two different kinds of repetition will be useful here, a distinction that Labov does not himself discuss. The repetitions that Labov discusses are local in nature, intensifying an element within a local span of text and, at the same time, suspending the action. A second kind of repetition is nonlocal, occurring over larger spans of text. Tannen (1989) discusses this type of repetition which, besides highlighting the repeated element, contributes to the overall structure of the text and enables involvement from the audience, a set of characteristics that fit in well with the basic function of evaluation in the Labovian framework.

The narrator uses local repetition at several points, suspending the action to highlight something she wishes to emphasize as significant. Interestingly, she uses local repetition in two ways. The simplest of the two is wholesale or nearly exact repetition of an element, sometimes with added information accompanying the repetition (see figure 7).

In lines 19 and 20, we see the sign MIME repeated, the second time with the additional information FIFTEEN MINUTE. The additional information is in turn repeated in line 22 with topic marking, introducing subsequent information. Later in the story, during the episode involving the child and the medal, repetition is used to emphasize the importance of two events: the child's excitement at volunteering (figure 8) and the child's bewilderment when the "medal" falls off the narrator's hand (the "tortoise's paw") (figure 9).

A second way of repeating elements involves repetition of a single idea by using synonymous elements. This kind of repetition heightens the vividness of the emphasis by varying the particular signs used to express the

RAISE-HANDS (2h-alt)   Cl.44 'big line in front of me'

ILLUSTRATION 10.

same idea. A striking example of this type of repetition is reproduced in figure 10: the signer repeats the same idea four times in succession, finding three different ways of saying that the children were not using their ears.

We find a similar and particularly effective use of repetition by synonymy slightly later when the narrator again finds three different ways in a row to say that the children were looking at her (or her friend) in total fascination (see illustration 11).

The device of nonlocal repetition plays an important role in structuring the story, punctuating the narrative action again and again with a specific evaluative "theme." It could be argued, for example, that the repetition in illustration 11 is nonlocal since the signer does not repeat the three variations one right after the other but, instead, punctuates the text with them, introducing each of them, refrain-like, after a distinct step in the action sequence. We also find two kinds of nonlocal repetition that play a basic role in structuring the narrative through its evaluation component. The first consists of a series of comments about the presence or absence of the interpreter; the second involves the repetition near the end of the story of statements first introduced near the beginning, forming a sort of narrative and evaluative parenthesis that highlights the important points of the story and brings it to a close.

An important evaluative leitmotif involves the role of the interpreter at the day camp. Though not a main protagonist in the story (not one sequential narrative clause refers to her), she does play a central role in the narrative's evaluative component. She is the person the narrator-LSQ teacher depends on to interpret her LSQ signs into French for the children's benefit. For this reason, the narrator constantly refers to the presence of the interpreter, who interprets from LSQ into French as the narrator signs to the children. A couple of examples are given in figure 11.

Interestingly, when the narrator recounts how she taught the children signs, it becomes important for her to emphasize that the interpreter was

18.	146248	IDEA MAKE-UP
19.	146258	PT-1 MIME++
20.	146276	THEN FIFTEEN-- FUNNY FIFTEEN MINUTE MIME
21.	146304	ENERGY! WOW! OVERFLOWING! "HOLD-OFF"
22.	146338	FIFTEEN MINUTE: 1-TEACH-children #LSQ PT-1

FIGURE 7. *Local repetition using nearly exact repetition of an element*

no longer interpreting. She emphasizes this fact by repeating (with one variation) that the interpreter (and French) had been "sidelined" (see figure 12).

It bears mentioning that the variations on the children not using their ears discussed above and shown in figure 10 occur in between the first and second variations on the absence of the interpreter and of "words." In this context, they can be seen themselves as an elaboration on the absence of French interpretation, so important to the point of the story at this stage.

The second type of nonlocal repetition involves the reoccurrence at, or near the end of the story, of statements first made near the beginning. In figure 13, we see the repetition of two predicates that indicate the children's involvement. This repetition serves structurally to bring a close to the main episode about teaching the children signs, at the same time reiterating the evaluative point of the story. Finally, figure 14 shows the repetition at the very end of the narrative of the children's age range, which underlines how well the narrator established a rapport with them.

Addition of quantifiers. According to Labov, "quantifiers are the most common means of intensifying a clause" (1972, 379). Common quantifiers he cites are adverbial *all* and numerals. In this narrative, quantification seems to be expressed by morphological modifications of signs. Pluralization by doubling of hands with alternating movement can be seen in figure 13 in the sign "RAISE-HANDS" (2h-alt)+++ (lines 48 and 212) and in BRING-IN(2h-alt)+++ (lines 50 and 213). Quantifying classifiers are used in several verbs in the narrative; a good example is Cl-44(2h)!-'big/huge line in front of me' (lines 51 and 216; "big" in line 51; "huge" in line 216). One sign in particular, when modifying a preceding sign, takes on the semantics of a quantifier: WOW. This quantifying property of the sign WOW can be seen at line 21 (ENERGY! WOW! OVERFLOWING! "HOLD-OFF"), at line 51 (Cl-44(2h)!-'big line in front of me'

142.   150160 PT-children: [_CHILD "RAISE-HAND" (excited)

143.   150168 PT-children CHILD [_CHILD "RAISE-HAND" (excited)

FIGURE 8. *Local repetition to emphasize the importance of an event*

158.   150343 PT-child UNDERSTAND PT-child (headshake)
         [_CHILD "looks down at ground, then up at narrator"

159.   150355 UNDERSTAND PT-child (headshake)

FIGURE 9. *Local repetition to emphasize the importance of an event*

WOW), and at line 181 ([_H Cl-HH-ears "cartoonish expressions, rolling eyes" TIRED WOW).

REINFORCING GESTURE

Along with the strategies discussed in the preceding three subsections, Labov cites reinforcing manual gesture as one way that an element in the clause can be intensified. This is indeed a fundamental characteristic of spoken discourse, as shown in the extensive descriptions and analyses reported in McNeill (1992) and numerous other publications on the relation between gesture and spoken discourse. The meanings communicated in the flow of speech are constantly reinforced by conceptually related gestures that relate to the content of the speech in a variety of different ways described by McNeill — though the proportions and types of gesture vary from culture to culture — in large part because this secondary expressive channel, not used as part of the linguistic signal (interpreting the word *linguistic* in a narrow sense) is available to be used in this reinforcing role.

What kind of equivalent reinforcing gesture might have in a sign language raises some complex and interesting issues that go beyond the scope of this paper. The basic problem is this: since most gesture accompanying speech is manual, and since the main linguistic signal in sign languages is articulated in the manual channel, it seems unlikely that manual gestures would play the same kind of role since those that are part of the signing stream would not combine simultaneously with the signs of the language with the same ease as manual gestures do with spoken words. When we consider the types of gestures that "reinforce" spoken discourse, two kinds seem particularly salient: iconic gestures that visually illustrate or enact some aspect(s) of the events being described, and metaphorical

235.	1520305	tell-story
236.	152310	[ch (look up at narrator fascinated) children-Cl-FF-look-at-1
237.	152316	finish:[$_{narr-ch}$ "s" person/bb/-rt pt-rt born hearing/4/like pt-2-arc hearing/4/] pt-1
238.	152352	[$_{ch}$(look up at narrator fascinated) children-LOOK-AT/55/-1
239.	152360	pt-1 [$_{NARR-C}$SICK AGE^THREE MUMPS
240.	152386	[$_{ch}$(look up at narrator fascinated) children-look-at-1

CL-FF-look-at-1   LOOK-AT /55/-1   LOOK-AT-1
ILLUSTRATION 11.

202.	151341	HAVE-neg EARS(-2h) COVER-EARS
203.	151353	[$_{CH}$ "stick fingers in ears"
204.	151364	CUTE
205.	151367	[$_{CH}$ "stick fingers in ears"

FIGURE 10. *Local repetition that heightens emphasis by varying the signs used to express the same idea*

gestures that, among other means, often use some variety of handling classifier to represent ideas being communicated as manipulable objects with a size, shape and even location in the visible gesture space. In sign languages, the first of these have their fairly direct formal and semantic equivalent in what have commonly been called "classifier predicates," also labeled as "depicting verbs" (cf. Liddell 2003) among other terms, as well as in various lexical verbs of action. The second type does not seem to have a similarly direct sign language equivalent though: the function of representing ideas as "entities" during discourse seems instead to be shared by manual and nonmanual strategies for "locating" ideas in different areas in space, simultaneous with the actual signs being made. However, these strategies are very different in nature from the gestures

71.	148111	INTERPRETER PT-rt Cl-S 'hold microphone'
96.	149003	THEN SIGN WITH INTERPRETER Cl-S-'hold microphone'
150.	150250	PT-rt-interpreter Cl-S-'hold-microphone'

FIGURE 11. *Nonlocally repeated references to the interpreter as an evaluative leitmotif*

that co-occur with speech. Some of these gestures have been lexicalized in sign languages, losing their metaphorical discourse-related function and taking on much more precise lexical denotations, such as the "pinching" /F/ handshape that shows up in (ASL) PREACH or (LSQ) COURSE, or the double /5/ handshape gesture in WHAT in these two languages.

While the above discussion is necessarily brief, it illustrates the difficulty of finding any near equivalent of reinforcing gesture in a sign language. It turns out that in the approximately seven minutes and twenty-one seconds of our corpus, the only example that comes anywhere close to the kind of reinforcing gesture cited by Labov is "AT-A-LOSS-FOR-WORDS" in line 37, which co-occurs with the second half of the mouthed word "enfant" (which begins on the sign CHILDREN). However, this gesture, made by the two hands falling onto the signer's knees at the end of the sign CHILDREN, does not in fact co-occur with a sign, but rather with (part of) a mouthed word. The closest thing to a subsidiary channel for meaning-bearing units in sign languages is in fact the oral channel in which both mouthed words from an oral language ("word-pictures") and sign language-specific lexical or morphological mouth shapes and movements are formed. As a working hypothesis for future research, we will tentatively propose that such word-pictures and mouth shapes or movements might perhaps be used in a similar way, as evaluative reinforcements of the meanings communicated by the signs of the manual channel. For this hypothesis to be confirmed, it would need to be demonstrated that these oral components are not lexically required and that where they are used, they do in fact serve to highlight the accompanying sign in some relevant way when compared to the same sign or signs used on their own. As a first hint that this may be the case, we note that the sign CHILDREN does not lexically require the added word-picture "enfant" in LSQ. The first time it appears in the text, when the children are introduced as participants in the narrative and located in the signing space in line 4, no mouthing is used. However, when the mouthing appears with the sign in line 37, this happens at the end of a series of external evaluative clauses that

196.	151246	THEN HAVE-neg INTERPRETER SWEEP-ASIDE-interpreter PT-I
206.	151284	HAVE-neg WORD SWEEP-ASIDE-interpreter
208.	151457	NOW: HAVE-neg INTERPRETER SWEEP-ASIDE-interpreter

FIGURE 12. *Repetition to emphasize that the interpreter was no longer interpreting*

bring to a close the first episode of complicating action in the Children story: (line 35:) EXCITED! (line 36:) WOW^FAST! (line 37:) CHILDREN/'en-' "AT-A-LOSS-FOR-WORDS"/ '-fant'. Each of these clauses shows, in its own way, how impressed the narrator is with the children, and line 37 seems to sum the others up by mentioning the children directly in both sign and mouthing, accompanied by an upward turning of the signer's gaze that shows how much she adored and admired them. An English equivalent would be "What incredible kids!"

COMPLEXIFICATION OF BASIC NARRATIVE SYNTAX

When we examine the basic syntax of narrative clauses in the two LSQ stories, an overall template appears that differs in some respects from Labov's template for English. This template, like Labov's, contains eight slots, but their contents are slightly different because of differences between LSQ syntactic structure and that of English. Consistent with Labov, the intent is not to model grammatical relations as a series of positional slots, but to draw attention to the appearance of elements that add complexity to the form of the basic narrative clause; we do not claim to describe more than the structure of a basic narrative clause on this basis.[3] The basic slots in our template are as follows:

- Temporal reference point adverbs: THEN, BEFORE, NOW, YESTERDAY
- Simple subjects: accented pronouns, names, det+N /N+det.
- Quantified temporal expressions (e.g., FIFTEEN-MINUTE, ONE-WEEK-PAST, CONTINUALLY, YEARLY, NEVER, *même* + TIME (where même is the French word meaning 'same' mouthed simultaneously with the sign) and possibly quasimodals (one example: START)
- "Familiar" or "identifiable" direct objects, in the sense of Lambrecht (1994)
- Preterit verbs or role shift predicates (The majority of narrative clauses consist only of a verb, whether or not its subject and object are encoded in its form.)

First occurrence

47.	147273	(to children) WHO WANT?
48.	147279	(children) "RAISE-HANDS("excited")"(2h-alt)+++!
49.	147292	JOIN
50.	147297	BRING-IN(2h-alt)+++!
51.	147305	Cl-44(2h)!-'big line in front of me' WOW

Repetition near end

211.	151530	THEN: [$_{\text{NARR-CH}}$ WHO WANT JOIN-IN HERE STAGE
212.	151554	[$_{\text{CH}}$ "RAISE-HANDS("excited")"(2h-alt)+++!
213.	151568	BRING-IN(2h-alt)+++!
214.	151576	Cl-44(2h)-- NOW Cl-44(2h)!-'huge line in front of me' KID
215.	152003	YESTERDAY (neg. headshake), TWO
216.	152018	NOW Cl-44(2h)!-'huge line in front of me'

FIGURE 13. *Nonlocal repetition involving repetition of two predicates that indicate the children's involvement*

First occurrence (second orientation)

40.	147076	NOW: AGE+++	NINE, APPROXIMATE
		SIX ———————	=

Second occurrence, in coda

251.	152517	NOW AGE SIX-lf ELEVEN-rt—(negative headshake)
		NINE

FIGURE 14. *Nonlocal repetition of children's age range to emphasize how well the narrator established rapport with them*

- Direct and indirect objects (default slot), adjective or noun predicates without an overt verb
- Manner adverbs (EYES-WIDE-OPEN)
- Temporal adverbs and phrases (FINISH, SINCE TWO-WEEKS, ALWAYS, BEFORE) and comitative clauses (one occurrence)

One complicating element in this schema is the behavior of weak, unaccented pronominals (POINT-X, POINT-ARC-X). As observed in Miller (2004), these can appear in several positions: directly after the verb (and before a complement), directly after the verb phrase, or at the end of the sentence.[4] Pronominals in these positions are nearly always subjects and, consistent with the cross-linguistic findings of Lambrecht (1994), are, in general, topical, that is to say, active in the current discourse context. Despite the mobility they show in general, they appear most often in absolute final position in the narratives under study. Nonetheless, one example of a weak pronominal appearing between a verb and its temporal complement appears in the second transcribed clause in figure 15, (THEN PT-1 ~~ASL~~ GO-TO-ctr PT-1 SINCE TWO-WEEK) which illustrates how several examples of basic narrative clauses fit into this template.

The eight slots in the template in figure 15 schematize the boundaries and possible contents of the basic narrative clause. Discussing the forms taken by evaluation that result in narrative syntax whose structure goes beyond these basic slots, Labov highlights three important types: Comparatives, Correlatives, and Explicatives. Each of these contributes in its own ways to complexification of the basic syntax of the clause, as we will see in the following sections.

Comparatives

The basic function of a simple narrative clause is to report a discrete event that actually occurred during the story being told (or is alleged to have had occurred; for example, the famous race between the Tortoise and the Hare probably never really took place). Labov points out that negatives, which deny that an occurrence or state of affairs took place, seem surprising in this context. One reason is because their function is to point out something that might have taken place at a given point in the story, but did not. Seen in this light, negatives are a means of comparing a possible state of affairs off the narrative time line with what actually occurred in an effort to underline the significance of what did happen. Other ways of comparing potential situations with those in the story time line are nonpresent tenses such as future, auxiliaries and quasimodals, imperatives and questions and, furthermore, comparative and superlative constructions themselves. Each of these elements sets off a potential situation against what actually occurred, which highlights the significance of what did occur.

Negatives, as explained above, contrast a possible state of affairs with what actually happened. In the Children story, negatives play two kinds of evaluative roles. When the narrator repeatedly says that no interpreter was present while she was teaching the children signs, she is emphasizing the fact that she no longer needs that intermediary to communicate with the children: she has succeeded in establishing a direct relationship with them. A second function of negation, which we see in figures 16 and 17,

1	2	3	4	5	6	7	8
Temp RefPt	Simple Subject	Quantified TempExpr	Fam/ID DirObj/	PreteritV/ RoleShift	Direct/ Indirect Object	Manner	TempAdv/ Phrase
THEN	PT-I			rt-HIRE-1	THEATRE-VIS. DEAF		SINCE TWO-WEEK
THEN		FIFTEEN MINUTE		$_{\text{ASL}}$GO-TO-ctr PT-1 MIME			
WITH 5-arc	PT-I	FIFTEEN MINUTE		I-TEACH-children "HELLO"	#LSQ PT-I PT-3		
				1-SAY-TO-children			
BEFORE	PT-I			TELL-STORY/*fable* PT-I			BEFORE PT-3 HARE
		START		TELL-STORY			
THEN			GLASSES	PUT-ON-GLASSES [$_{\text{Tortoise}}$ PLOD			
THEN	PT-I			SIGN			WITH INTERPRETER

FIGURE 15. *Syntax of various narrative clauses in the two stories.*

| 153. | 150285 | CAN'T "hands palms up" (indistinguishable spoken French) |

FIGURE 16. *Negation that suspends the action by highlighting an obstacle, which is then overcome*

| 158. | 150343 | PT-child UNDERSTAND PT-child (**headshake**) |

FIGURE 17. *Negation that suspends the action by highlighting an obstacle, which is then overcome*

suspends the action by highlighting an obstacle, which is then overcome in the following action.

Nonpresent tense markers in LSQ consist basically of time adverbs that refer to specific periods of time relative to the (unmarked) tense. In narrative discourse, the unmarked tense is the past, and other time periods are marked by explicit time adverbs, such as BEFORE in figure 18. The adverb in this example serves to interrupt the narrative sequence at the point where the narrator first recounts how she teaches the children signs, setting the stage for a flashback to how she recounted the fable of the Tortoise and the Hare. This flashback highlights the reason she chose to teach these particular four signs and shows vividly why learning these signs was interesting for the children.

Unlike English, LSQ does not have auxiliary verbs as such and, instead, makes use of quantified temporal expressions. In the same slot, we also find quasimodals such as START. The examples in figure 19 both introduce an evaluative comment that passes a judgment on the children's abilities over a span of time compared with the immediate past time of the narrative, in effect showing why their interest in learning signs is significant.

Questions posed by a protagonist, as Labov says, set up a situation in which the other protagonist is challenged to choose between possible courses of action. The action taken in response is thus contrasted with actions not taken, which could have determined a different outcome to the story. In figures 20 and 21, a protagonist in the story asks the children a question. Hypothetically, they could have been uninterested enough not to respond, but in both cases, they are shown to have responded with enthusiasm, cooperating with the narrator's goals.

Explicit comparatives seem less common than others discussed above, but we indeed find two (see figures 22 and 23). The first is an evalua-

57. 147443	fable
	BEFORE PT-1 TELL-STORY PT-1 HARE...

FIGURE 18. *Explicit time adverb marking a time period relative to the unmarked tense (in this case, the past)*

43. 147210	(brow raise) now smooth! always
44. 147235	tomorrow+++: make-progress(puffed cheeks)!

FIGURE 19. *Evaluative comment that passes a judgment on the the children's abilities over a span of time compared with the immediate past time of the narrative*

tive comment on the children's progress, setting the stage for the significance of the narrative to follow. The second compares how the children perform the LSQ signs they just learned with how the narrator and her friend perform them: that the children, according to the narrator, make them the same way shows that the gap between them and the narrator has been bridged and that she has been successful in bringing them into her world.

Correlatives

Correlatives are means of suspending the narrative sequence to highlight it against something else that is happening at the same time. A particularly interesting example of this suspension, shown in illustration 11, happens when the narrator repeatedly says that the children kept looking at her in fascination while she talked to them about being born, or becoming, deaf. Repeating that they were continually watching her emphasizes how involved they had become in her story.

Explicatives

Explicatives often add some of the greatest complexity to the basic narrative clause structure, often doing so by adding subordinate clauses to the simple narrative clause. Many explicatives appear to punctuate the fable, explaining how the narrator was inventing and miming details of the story as she went along. The examples in figures 24 and 25 show two such explicatives. The first explains the significance of the narrator's being asked to participate in the day camp while the second serves, in a somewhat more subtle way, to underline the smooth manner in which the interpreter eased the narrator's communication with the children.

47. 147273	(to children) WHO WANT?
48. 147279	(children) "RAISE-HANDS("excited")"(2h-alt)+++!

FIGURE 20. *The narrator describes the children's reaction after being asked a question the narrator in the Children story*

92. 148550	[_{H-CHILDREN} TRUE PT-arc-children?
93. 148558	[_{CHILDREN} SAY-YES-2h-alternating

FIGURE 21. *The narrator describes the children's reaction after being asked a question by a protagonist in the fable*

EVALUATION IN THE TORTOISE AND THE HARE

The traditional fable of the Tortoise and the Hare illustrates a moral point dressed up in the form of a story about a race between the two animals. The various oral and written versions of Aesop's fable, such as the adaptation into rhyming verse by the French author la Fontaine, use natural characteristics of the Tortoise and Hare characters to metaphorically embody human traits. The bursts of speed of the Hare interspersed with stops to eat and rest stand for human traits of impetuousness and lack of foresight. The fact that the Tortoise eventually arrives at his destination despite his almost painfully slow gait represents the human traits of patience and perseverance. This metaphorical use of the animals' natural traits is a heightened form of evaluation since it takes their actions in the story and generalizes them to human personality traits: the actions in themselves transcend the simple narrative sequence, whether or not the moral of the story is explicitly stated at the end. In the LSQ version, however, metaphorical evaluation is taken one step further and is encoded directly in the spatial and rhythmic structure of the story. It turns out that although the narrative uses many of the conventional evaluative mechanisms already seen in the Children story, its more formal, poetic structure is exploited to superimpose another layer of evaluation that metaphorically embodies moral traits in each of the characters.

Conventional Mechanisms Used in the Tortoise and the Hare

Many of the evaluative mechanisms discussed earlier in the paper are found again in the LSQ version of the Tortoise and the Hare; it is informative to review these briefly before discussing the mechanisms that set the

| 41. 147173 | RECENT ONE-WEEK-PAST "not really" CONTACT |
| 42. 147193 | (brow raise) NOW SMOOTH! ALWAYS |

FIGURE 22. *An explicit comparative*

| 221. 152104 | SAME-AS! children-SAME-AS! |

FIGURE 23. *An explicit comparative*

fable apart from the Children story. Intensifiers are used at several points in the story: for example, when the narrator depicts the Hare's actions and speech, she uses exaggerated facial expressions and head-body movements that intensify the negative depiction of his character. During stanza 2 (B in figure 6), the Introductions section (see figure 3, part a), the narrator makes effective use of repetition: the Tortoise and the Hare repeat each other's words in a duet, setting up an (albeit temporary) atmosphere of harmony between the two. Quantification is exploited in the depiction of the Tortoise's plodding and the Hare's leaping all over the place. Under comparatives, we find questions and negatives. The most significant question comes when the Tortoise asks the Hare whether he wants to race, thus showing his willingness to assert his own confidence in his self-worth. An overt use of negation for evaluation shows up when the narrator emphasizes the Tortoise's persistence in line 115: NEVER STOP. We see a very interesting use of correlatives in stanzas 10 and 11 (EE and DD in figure 6), where the Tortoise finishes and wins the race. Here, the narrator slows down the action in time and then suspends it by signing a sequence of incremental aspect forms showing the poles and tape gradually approaching, then at the moment when the Tortoise breaks the tape, she signs that at the "same time," the Hare wakes up.

Although succinct, this survey makes it clear that the fable does use a range of evaluative devices similar to the Children story. We turn in the next section to the way the narrator uses metaphorical devices that reinforce the more conventional ones reviewed here.

Structure and Metaphor in the Fable

Earlier in the paper, we saw how the narrator exploits space, both for referential purposes and by the use of alternations between the left and right sides of space, to reinforce a contrast between the Tortoise and the Hare in the poetic structure of the fable. When she draws the portrait

6. 145477	3lf-ASK-1 #THÉÂTRE-VISUEL-DES-SOURDS POSS-1
7. 145493	PT3-lf WHY 3lf-ASK-1?: BECAUSE DEAF NEW!

FIGURE 24. *An explicative*

96. 149003	'bbbbbbbbbbbbbbbb'
	then sign with interpreter Cl-5- 'hold microphone'

FIGURE 25. *A second explicative*

of each animal's character, she not only contrasts the Hare's impetuous speed with the exaggerated slowness of the Tortoise but also draws a metaphorical portrait of their characters by exploiting the vertical and horizontal axes in space.

When the Hare is depicted (up until his undoing), he is always mapped out on vertical rather than horizontal space. This depiction contrasts with the depiction of the Tortoise, who is mapped out on horizontal space, along the axis of the race. The Tortoise is depicted as low in height, close to the ground, with his gaze nearly always fixed on a distant goal before him while the Hare's attention is always fixed to his immediate surroundings. We see this contrast in illustrations 5 and 7, shown earlier. The vertical depiction of the Hare is unusual and taken to almost cartoonish extremes but, at another level, is an embodiment of the metaphor GOOD IS UP. We see then that at least on a superficial level, the Hare is faster, bigger, and therefore better than the Tortoise. However, the Tortoise's lower stature is compensated for by his character's horizontal mapping. With his constant gaze on a destination he will eventually reach, we see that, intellectually, he is able to extend himself into the future. His character portrait is an embodiment of the metaphor the FUTURE IS AHEAD, so widely exploited in the form of the time line in sign languages. That this metaphor is integral to his character portrait is confirmed in stanza 5 (D' in figure 6) where the Tortoise gives the Hare a lengthy description of the route of the race. On the other hand, the Hare is incapable of such intellectual profundity: in stanza 6 (D" in figure 6), he is incapable of any but the most brief answers to the Tortoise's fully formed questions.

Now we understand that the Hare is in fact superficial, arrogant, and self-centered: he is better only in his own mind, which is confirmed when he brings himself down morally by mocking the Tortoise. In other words, he is fixed in the here and now whereas the Tortoise has the (superior) ability to plan in space and in time. We could say that the depth axis that we described previously illustrates the Tortoise's intellectual profundity, and finally shows that he, in fact, is superior.

These metaphorical character portraits are drawn at the beginning of the fable. They are not permanent, though: the narrator "plays" with the space-based portraits she has drawn to encode the moral of the story directly in the way she maps the two characters onto the vertical dimension. When the Hare has covered enough ground to put the Tortoise behind him, he tires and decides to take a nap against a tree. This act is his undoing. In his self-assuredness, he himself undoes two of his seeming advantages: he withdraws from the vertical dimension and is now no higher than the Tortoise; even more, he not only is no longer faster than the Tortoise: he is now motionless! He never recovers from this mistake. When the Tortoise happens by and discovers him sleeping, the Tortoise is able to inherit some of the Hare's speed. We see this acceleration clearly in parts e and f of figure 5. Finally, when the Tortoise wins the race, the speed of his movements not only accelerates dramatically to what was originally the Hare's speed (part g of figure 5) but also the narrator uses exactly the same predicate for the Tortoise as she originally did for the Hare: now it is the Tortoise who is leaping up and down in the air! At the same moment, the Hare wakes up. We see him beginning to stretch his arms up in the air as he yawns, but he is cut short as he sees the Tortoise ahead of him. In the dramatic dénouement, the Hare, in a movement as slow and drawn out as the Tortoise's original plodding, deflates. Both lightning speed and the vertical dimension, which once seemed his, are now the Tortoise's. The turning of the tables can be seen clearly in illustration 12.

The narrator does not need to explicitly state the moral of the fable; the way she has manipulated space and rhythm for metaphorical purposes allows her to build it right into the structure of the fable. The fable's moral, being the overarching element of its evaluation component, is thus encoded into the fable in a manner that contrasts dramatically with the more conventional means that are also used throughout the story.

SUMMARY

The LSQ narrative analyzed here is particularly interesting, being made up of a story about teaching children signs interwoven with the fable of the Tortoise and the Hare. At one level, the fable is used evaluatively, to

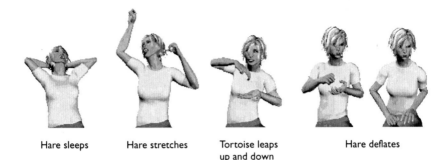

| Hare sleeps | Hare stretches | Tortoise leaps up and down | Hare deflates |

ILLUSTRATION 12.

illustrate the interest of the main story, namely, teaching hearing children signs. However, when analyzed on its own terms, it reveals a rich poetic structure based on alternations that exploit patterns in space, rhythm, action, and interaction between the two characters. Each narrative makes use of a range of devices for evaluating or demonstrating the interest of the story that — taking into account differences in form between the spoken and signed modalities — are equivalent to those described for spoken languages by Labov. However, although the fable exploits a comparable range of conventional evaluative devices, the narrator exploits the spatial and rhythmic possibilities of signing to build metaphorical character portraits of the Tortoise and the Hare. She manipulates these portraits during the narrative to encode the moral of the fable: the Hare, at first characterized by speed and verticality, loses these traits to the Tortoise whereas the Tortoise, at first depicted as slow and earthbound, becomes the speedy one and moves up into the positive vertical dimension.

NOTES

1. Because of differences in syntactic structure between English and LSQ, this template will need to be modified to a certain extent for our purposes, but overall, the similarities outweigh the differences.

2. The entire narrative is transcribed in appendix A of this paper.

3. These positional slots were arrived at through analysis of the narrative clauses in the narrative described here. Results are consistent with observations, based on other data, made in Miller (2004).

4. They frequently may appear simultaneous with a sentence or phrase, but this fact is not relevant for our purposes.

REFERENCES

Bahan, B., and S. Supalla. 1995. Line segmentation and narrative structure: A study of eyegaze behavior in American Sign Language. In *Language, gesture and space*, ed. K. Emmorey and J. Reilly, 171–91. Hillsdale, N.J.: Lawrence Erlbaum.

Blondel, M., and C. Miller. 1998. Spatial superstructure, rhythm and metaphor in a performance narrative: The Tortoise and the Hare. Paper presented at the Sixth Conference on Theoretical Issues in Sign Language Research (TISLR 6), Nov. 14, Gallaudet University, Washington, D.C.

———. 2000. Rhythmic structures in French Sign Language (LSF) nursery rhymes. *Sign Language & Linguistics* 3 (1): 59–77.

———. 2001. Movement and rhythm in nursery rhymes in LSF. *Sign Language Studies* 2 (1): 24–61.

Dubuisson, C. 1988. Corpus LSQ 88. Videotape corpus, Université du Québec à Montréal.

Emmorey, K., and J. S. Reilly. 1995. Theoretical issues relating language, gesture, and space: An overview. In *Language, gesture and space*, ed. K. Emmorey and J. Reilly, 1–16. Hillsdale, N.J.: Lawrence Erlbaum.

Engberg-Pedersen, E. 1995. Point of view expressed through shifters. In *Language, gesture and space*, ed. K. Emmorey and J. Reilly, 133–54. Hillsdale, N.J.: Lawrence Erlbaum.

Labov, W. 1972. The transformation of experience in narrative syntax. In *Language in the inner city*, 354–99. Philadelphia: University of Pennsylvania Press.

———. 1997. Some further steps in narrative analysis. *Journal of Narrative and Life History* 7-14: 395–415.

Labov, W., and J. Waletzky. 1967. Narrative analysis: Oral versions of personal experience. In *Essays on the verbal and visual arts,* ed. J. Helm, 12–44. Seattle: University of Washington Press.

Lajeunesse, L., and A. M. Parisot. 1998. TORTOISE WIN, RABBIT LOSE, CHILDREN "INCREDIBLE": Narrative structure and evaluation in the retelling of personal experience. Paper presented at the Sixth Conference on Theoretical Issues in Sign Language Research (TISLR 6), Nov. 14, Gallaudet University, Washington, D.C.

Lambrecht, K. 1994. *Information structure and sentence form. Topic, focus and the mental representations of discourse referents.* Cambridge: Cambridge University Press.

Mather, S., and E. A. Winston. 1996. Spatial mapping in an ASL narrative. Paper presented at the Fifth Conference on Theoretical Issues in Sign Language Research (TISLR 5), Sept. 21, Montreal. Manuscript sponsored by Gallaudet University, Washington D.C., and Educational Linguistics Research Center, Takoma Park, Md.

Miller, C. 1998. Constructing and maintaining reference and topic in spatial grammar. Paper presented at the Sixth Conference on Theoretical Issues in Sign Language Research (TISLR 6), Nov. 14, Gallaudet University, Washington, D.C.

———. 2004. The bases of LSQ syntax: Constituency, order, and information structure. Paper presented at the Sixth High Desert Linguistics Society Conference, November 4–6, University of New Mexico, Albuquerque N.M.

Rancourt, R. 1998. A typology of emphatic stress in LSQ. Paper presented at the Sixth Conference on Theoretical Issues in Sign Language Research (TISLR 6), Nov. 14, Gallaudet University, Washington, D.C.

Tannen, D. 1989. *Talking voices: Repetition, dialogue, and imagery in conversational discourse.* Vol. 6, *Studies in interactional sociolinguistics. 6,* General ed. J. Gumperz. New York: Cambridge University Press.

Winston, E. A. 1995. Spatial mapping in comparative discourse frames. In *Language, gesture and space,* ed. K. Emmorey and J. Reilly, 87–114. Hillsdale, N.J.: Lawrence Erlbaum.

APPENDIX A
Transcription of the Narratives

The two narratives are transcribed by numbered line, each line corresponding in our analysis to an independent proposition or idea unit. Each line's contents is preceded by the embedded time code at which the line begins, abbreviated from h:mm:ss:s/10 format. The lines are grouped by narrative constituents for ease of comparison with the text of the article. Evaluative clauses are bolded. The sections of the transcribed narrative that belong to the fable of the Tortoise and the Hare have been shaded to set them off from the Children story proper, which has no shading.

The gloss transcription adopted in most respects follows conventions common in the sign language literature. We have, however, adopted several conventions that merit explanation:

CONVENTIONS AND EXPLANATIONS

?	To save space, we use a question mark to indicate that the preceding clause is a question (yes/no or wh-).
:	To save space, we mark constituents with brow raise with a following colon ' : '. Rhetorical questions are thus followed by ' ?: '.

NEW!	Emphatic signs are marked with an exclamation mark.
HEARING/4/	When variants of a sign with the same meaning exist, the variant in question is distinguished by the symbol for its handshape between slashes.
$_{asl}$go-to	Loan signs are tagged with a subscript naming the language of origin.
"GESTURE"	Gestures are transcribed as glosses between double quotes. For gestures glossed with more than one word, the words are joined with hyphens, as in normal sign glosses.
"action"	Constructed actions are transcribed in lower case between double quotes.
Cl-F-'medal'	Lower case explanations in single quotes following a gloss add information not directly recoverable from the sign's lexical meaning.
(children)	Lower case text between parentheses provides notes explaining information otherwise not available from glosses.
GLOSS--	A double dash after a gloss indicates a false start.
[$_{T\text{-}CH}$	Left square brackets introduce a constructed action or dialogue frame; the subject (and addressee if necessary) are indicated in subscript upper case. If the context requires, the end of the frame is indicated with a right square bracket. The following abbreviations are used: T = Tortoise, H = Hare, NARR = narrator, CH = children, "S" = person with the name sign "S".
CEGEP- PROFESSIONAL- COLLEGE	Underlined letters in a gloss indicate initialized signs, which use the manual alphabet handshape(s) corresponding to the underlined letter(s) of the relevant word in the written language.
"S"	A name sign using the intitial letter S

The narrator makes heavy use of simultaneity in this text, whether mouthing French words together with signs or producing different signs on her right (strong) and left (weak) hands at the same time. To save space, we have tried in most cases to avoid indicating this information, but in several cases the simultaneity is indispensable to the syntax: in such

cases we have noted it. Principal conventions we use to notate simultaneity are given below.

même TIME	Mouthing simultaneous with, but distinct from, a sign is noted in lower case above the sign's gloss. Italics indicate French words.
en- *fant* CHILDREN "AT-A-LOSS-FOR-WORDS"	A spoken word simultaneous with more than one sign or gesture is noted to show how each part of the word aligns with each sign or gesture.
PT-1———— HELLO	When the hands simultaneously make distinct signs, the right hand is noted on the top line and the left hand below. If a sign on one hand is held so that it is simultaneous with one on the other hand, the hold's duration is shown by a mid-height extender line.

TRANSCRIPTION OF CHILDREN STORY

FIRST CHILDREN STORY

- **orientation**

1. 145351   rt-HIRE-I THEATRE VISUAL DEAF
2. 145375   MY+ WORK
3. 145389   rt-HIRE-I
4. 145401   FOR SHOW-arc-front-ctr = 'children' CHILDREN HEARING/4//5/-arc-children!
5. 145435   PT-3-lf ORGANIZE FESTIVAL SUMMER COUNTRYSIDE PT-3-lf
6. 145477   3-lf-ASK-I #THÉÂTRE-VISUEL-DES-SOURDS POSS-I
7. 145493   PT-3-lf WHY 3-lf-ASK-I?: BECAUSE DEAF NEW!
8. 145522   LOVE/LIKE CONTINUALLY YEARLY INVITE FASHION VARIOUS, DANCE JAZZ, DIFFERENT+
9. 145573   DEAF NEW!, RIGHT+
10. 146000   PT-3-lf HOW DEAF ACQUAINTED-WITH?: BECAUSE CEGEP-PROFESSIONAL-COLLEGE SELF-3 MAN HEARING/8/ CEGEP-PROFESSIONAL-COLLEGE WITH WOMAN C.L. ... CONTACT
11. 146095   SEARCH PT-I 3-CALL-UPON-I
12. 146116   GOOD CONTACT-all-around NICE

- ABSTRACT

13.	146134	THEN PT-I $_{ASL}$ GO-TO-ctr PT-I SINCE TWO-WEEK!
14.	146164	PT-1 $_{ASL}$ GO-TO-ctr I-SHOW-arc-children+
15.	146184	AGE+++ 3-lf 5-rt——— CUTE!
16.	146226	HEARING/4/ 5-arc-children
17.	146232	THEN PT1 SHOW$_N$ FOR-children
18.	146248	IDEA MAKE-UP
19.	146258	PT-1 MIME++
20.	146276	THEN FIFTEEN-- FUNNY FIFTEEN MINUTE MIME
21.	146304	ENERGY! WOW! OVERFLOWING! "HOLD-OFF"
22.	146338	FIFTEEN MINUTE: I-TEACH-children #LSQ PT-I

- complicating action

23.	146368	HAVE-IDEA PT-I I-"HELLO"-ctr I-"DOING-FINE?"-ctr I-SHOW-children
24.	146404	'S.'-lft PT-r r-SAY/C/-I r-"HELLO"-1h
25.	146415	PT-1 I-"HELLO"-r
26.	146430	rt-"DOING-FINE?"-1
27.	146438	PT-I "DOING-FINE"-rt
28.	146454	I-SHOW-ctr I-DIALOGUE-rt
29.	146468	WITH 5-arc-front PT-1 "HELLO" PT-children
30.	146495	(right hand not used) (left hand:) children-"HELLO"-1
31.	146505	I-"DOING-FINE?"-children

32. 146512 (right hand not used)
           (left hand:) children-"DOING-FINE"-1
33. 146527 EXCELLENT GOOD CAPABLE! PT-2-children
34. 146548 OK OTHER SIGN
35. 146565 EXCITED!
36. 146574 WOW^FAST!
37. 146590 en-   *fant*
           CHILDREN   "AT-A-LOSS-FOR-WORDS"

INTERRUPTION BY INTERLOCUTOR

38. 147008 #EX PT-2? (yields floor)
39. 147025 INTERESTING (yields floor)

SECOND CHILDREN STORY

• (secondary) orientation

40. 147076 NOW: AGE+++   NINE   APPROXIMATE
             SIX ——— =

• abstract

41. 147149 INTELLIGENT SIGN-FLUENTLY
42. 147173 RECENT ONE-WEEK-PAST "not really" CONTACT
43. 147193 (brow raise) NOW SMOOTH! ALWAYS

44. 147210 TOMORROW+++: MAKE-PROGRESS(puffed cheeks)!
45. 147235 SINCE 1-ASL GO-TO-ctr PT-1 SIGN("ill at ease") NO/1/(2h)
46. 147266 NOW: WOW

• complicating action

47. 147273 (to children) WHO WANT?
48. 147279 (children) "RAISE-HANDS("excited")"(2h-alt)+++!
49. 147292 JOIN
50. 147297 BRING-IN(2h-alt)+++!
51. 147305 Cl-44(2h)!-'big line in front of me' wow
52. 147331 PT-1 SIGN
53. 147348 1-SAY-TO-children BEFORE PT-children
54. 147365 TORTOISE WIN, HARE LOSE
55. 147419 PT-1 APPLAUD+++
56. 147437 GOOD PT-children
57. 147443 *fable*

BEFORE PT-1 TELL-STORY PT-1 HARE

TORTOISE AND HARE STORY

• *orientation*

58. 147463 PT-1 TORTOISE
59. 147468 (tortoise persona: slow, low to ground) PAWS-PLOD-ALONG++

60. 147492   PT-high-rt = hare (hare persona) HARE(flighty, self-absorbed) Cl-V̈-"leaping around in the air"

• *complicating action*

61. 147513   (right hand) hare-LOOK-AT-lf = tortoise
              (left hand) Cl-V̈-lf = tortoise﹖

62. 147522   [$_{H-T}$ WHO?]

63. 147528   [$_{T-H}$ PT1-1 TORTOISE PT-1

64. 147546   PT-2 WHO PT-2?]

65. 147559   [$_{H-T}$ PT-1 HARE PT-1, HELLO]

66. 147580   [$_{T-H}$ PT-1————
                       HELLO]

67. 148000   [$_T$ PAWS-TOGETHER begin-PAWS-PLOD-ALONG]

68. 148012   PT-hare [$_H$ PT-tortoise SLOW PAWS-PLOD-ALONG SLOW! "cover mouth, slap knee laughing"

69. 148051   [$_H$ PT-1 cl-1 "shoot off into the distance like a rocket"]

70. 148070   [$_T$ WHOA NOT FUNNY 2-SAY-TO/C/-1

71. 148111   babababababa
              INTERPRETER PT-rt Cl-S "hold microphone"

72. 148135   (head nodding) INTERESTING

73. 148157   [$_T$ NOT FUNNY 2-SAY-TO-1 TORTOISE-PAWS

74. 148170 [$_{T-CH}$ "ONE-SECOND" HAVE-IDEA EYE PT-children (wink eye)
TORTOISE-PAW

75. 148186 [$_T$ HEY-hare WANT CHALLENGE RACE TO-GOAL LINE TOUCH WANT PT-2 (head nodding)?
76. 148250 [$_H$ YES!
77. 148260 [$_T$ READY PT-2?
78. 148270 [$_H$ YES! PT-1 READY
79. 148304 [$_T$ 1-TELL-2 PT-1--
80. 148323 UH-UH/ʃ/ "WHOA"
81. 148330 [$_T$ 1-TELL-2 PT-1 IDEA MUST PT-2:
82. 148351 [$_T$ TOUCH TREES-going-by-along-route 2 KM ... FINISH
83. 148284 [$_T$ THEN: TOUCH LAKE MUST TOUCH PT-2 DIVE SWIM++ TO-GOAL FINISH
chemin
84. 148433 [$_T$ THEN: WINDING-ROAD SEE-in-front CL-SS 'posts' LINE TOUCH
85. 148478 [$_T$ OK PT-2?
86. 148487 [$_H$ OK (2h)
87. 148495 [$_T$ TELL-1 WHAT/1/ PT/A/-2
88. 148507 START TELL-STORY "HOLD-ON"
89. 148521 [$_{(NARR-INTERLOCUTOR)}$ CORRECT
90. 148529 [$_{T-H}$ 1-TELL-2 END CORRECT?
91. 148542 [$_{H-T}$ PERFECT

92.	148550	[H-CH TRUE PT-arc-children?
93.	148558	[CH SAY-YES-2h-alternating
94.	148570	AGREE PT-arc-children PT-1
95.	148597	INTERESTING
96.	149003	'bbbbbbbbbbbbbb'
		THEN SIGN WITH INTERPRETER CL-5-'hold microphone'
97.	149029	POSSESSIVE-rt-'interpreter' "THAT'S-ALL" AUTOMATIC (rubs nose)
98.	149051	THEN PT-1: [T RAISE-PAW PLOD-inchoative
99.	149069	ALWAYS-SAME SLOW PT-1
100.	149079	[T PLOD-SLOWLY-2h-alternating WIPE-FOREHEAD
101.	149119	MIME
102.	149125	PT-hare CL-V̈-'leaping around in the air'
103.	149135	[H CL-HH-ears "cartoon hare facial expressions: rolling eyes, sticks out tongue, sneering"
104.	149159	CL-V̈-"leap forward" CL-55-'run at high speed'
105.	149173	INVENT-2h-alt++
106.	149188	INTERESTING
107.	149197	Cl-V̈-'leap forward' Cl-V̈-'speed down winding path'
108.	149214	[H TIRED BINOCULARS-LOOK-rt-backwards
109.	149230	[H HAVE-neg TORTOISE
110.	149238	[H "FORGET-ABOUT" CHALLENGE

111.	149252	[$_H$ cl-1 1-'stretch out legs in front'
112.	149260	GLASSES PUT-ON-GLASSES
113.	149266	[$_H$ "lean back, cross hands behind head" TREE "take it easy"
114.	149290	PT-1 [$_T$ PLOD-SLOWLY-2h-alternating
115.	149303	NEVER STOP
116.	149312	GOAL WANT++ WIN++
117.	149334	PT-1 EYE PT-arc-children
118.	149345	[$_T$ PLOD-SLOWLY-2h-alternating
119.	149360	THEN [$_{T\text{-}CH}$ WHERE HARE WHERE?
120.	149382	PT-children [$_{CH}$ (excited) PT-behind-narrator
121.	149392	PT-1 [$_{T\text{-}CH}$ PT-rt-hare "SHHH" PT-hare HARE SLEEP
122.	149418	[$_T$ PLOD-QUICKLY-2h-alternating+++
123.	149442	cl-11-'finish line poles approach gradually'
124.	149456	cl-HH-'finish line tape approaches gradually'
125.	149470	[$_T$ cl-HH-'finish line tape' "breaks through finish line tape"
126.	149492	même
		TIME [$_H$ STRETCH-2h "yawning"
127.	149522	cl-1-'arrive in front of hare's vision'
128.	149529	[$_T$ ("yelling") "arms in the air, jumping up and down" cl-V̈-"leaping around in the air"
129.	149550	NATURAL Cl-V-"leaping around in the air"
130.	149562	PT-hare [$_H$ "shoulders sag in despair"

- *resolution (part 1)*

131. 149578   [T-H WIN PT-1
132. 149596   [T-H BEFORE 2-SAY/C/-1 [I-H-T SLOW! "laugh" "COVER-MOUTH"
133. 150022   [T-H 2-MOCK-1
134. 150027   [T-H NOW PT-1 FAST MORE-THAN PT-2
135. 150045   [T-H PT-2 SLOW PT-2
136. 150060   PT-hare [T-H "pensive" EXCUSE-ME TRUE
137. 150098   [T-H PT-1: 2-GIVE-PRESENT-1 WHAT?
138. 150112   [T-H WANT PT-1 PAWS-side-by-side "pensive"
139. 150132   [T-H PT-2--

SECOND CHILDREN STORY: *"medal" episode*

- *abstract*

140. 150139   HAVE-IDEA

- *complicating action*

141. 150144   [T-CH JUDGE WHERE? WHO?
142. 150160   PT-children: [CHILD "RAISE HAND" (excited)
143. 150168   PT-children CHILD [CHILD "RAISE HAND" (excited)
144. 150182   CL-S-BRING-FORWARD-1
145. 150197   [T-CHILD 2-GIVE-PRESENT-1 PAWS-side-by-side
146. 150210   [CHILD "hesitant, confused"

147. 150214   MIND^FROZEN

148. 150222   PT-1 1-SAY-TO-child MEDAL

149. 150237   PT-child [CHILD "decisive"] READY

150. 150250   PT-rt-interpreter Cl-S-'hold-microphone'

151. 150259   PT-child INVENT [CHILD Cl-F-'medal'-GIVE-rt(narrator))

152. 150278   PT-1 PAWS-side-by-side

153. 150285   CAN'T "hands palms up" (indistinguishable spoken French) INVENT
      PT-1 PAWS-side-by-side

154. 150314   (right-)PAW
      Cl-F-'medal'-put-on-paw

155. 150318   PAWS-side-by-side "suddenly bends forward"

156. 150322   pow
      Cl-F-'medal'-flies-down-off-paw

157. 150330   PAWS-side-by-side "bent forward"

158. 150343   PT-child UNDERSTAND PT-child (headshake) [CHILD "looks down at
      ground, then up at narrator"

159. 150355   UNDERSTAND PT-child (headshake)

160. 150362   PT-1 WALK PICK-UP/G/-medal 1-GIVE/G/-child

161. 150393   [CHILD HOLD-medal "confused"

162. 150403   [NARR-CHILD 2-GIVE-1 2-PUT-AROUND-NECK-1

163. 150418   [CHILD PUT-AROUND-NECK-1(-up-rt)

164. 150438   SELF-child

165. 150443   PT-1 Cl-F-'medal'-on-chest

resolution

166. 150448 [NARR-CHILD THANK-YOU
167. 150457 [NARR KISS-ON-CHEEKS
168. 150469 [NARR-CHILD NICE PT-2
169. 150484 [NARR-CHILD THANK-YOU BYE-BYE
170. 150495 [CHILD-NARR BYE-BYE "smiling, looking back at narrator" Cl-v(-" walks back to group"
171. 150510 [NARR-CHILD Cl-c-'medal' PT-1 WIN PT-1
172. 150522 [CHILD-NARR WIN PT-2
173. 150534 [NARR-CHILD WIN PT-1
174. 150547 Cl-v↓(-" walks back to group"

TORTOISE AND HARE STORY: REPRISE

• *resolution (part 2)*

175. 150560 THEN PT-1 [T-H 2-DUAL -1 TRUE--
176. 150585 [T-H PT-2 NICE PT-2
177. 151004 [H-T 2-DUAL-1 FRIEND (nodding)
178. 151020 [T-H SHAKE-HANDS-WITH-hare (smiling)
179. 151031 [H-T GIVE-ARM-TO-tortoise (smiling) ——
180. 151040 [H PAW-PLOD-SLOWLY
        (... GIVE-LEFT-ARM) —
181. 151051 [H Cl-HH-ears "cartoonish expressions, rolling eyes" TIRED WOW
        (... GIVE-LEFT-ARM) ——————

182. 151060 [H 'looking at tortoise, tongue lolling' TONGUE-LOLLING WOW
(... GIVE-LEFT-ARM)

183. 151078 Cl-1-(tortoise)'moves forward past hare'
Cl-1-(hare)

184. 151088 (right hand/arm not used)
GIVE-LEFT-ARM

185. 151092 [H 'looking at tortoise, tongue lolling' Cl-1-(tortoise) 'moves forward past hare'
Cl-1-(hare)

• *coda*

186. 151101 CLUMSY PT-1

187. 151115 FINALLY PT-1

188. 151132 PT-children APPLAUD

SECOND CHILDREN STORY: *"teaching signs" episode*

• *complicating action*

189. 151146 THEN PT-1 [NARR-CH WANT 1-TEACH-2 SIGN WANT? (head bounce: 'and then')

190. 151162 [NARR-CH (demonstrates sign) TORTOISE

191. 151182 PT-children [CH (looking up at narrator) TORTOISE

192. 151195 THEN PT-rt-friend-("S") ["S"-CH (demonstrates sign) HARE

193. 151211 "S"-TEACH-children FINISH

194. 151217 THEN PT-1: [$_{NARR-CH}$ (demonstrates sign) WIN
195. 151231 PT-"S" [$_{"S"-CH}$ (demonstrates sign) LOSE
196. 151246 THEN HAVE-neg INTERPRETER SWEEP-ASIDE-interpreter PT-1
197. 151258 PT-children [$_{CH}$ "with concentration" HARE-- (children's attempt:) "HARE"
198. 151284 HAVE-neg WORD SWEEP-ASIDE-interpreter
199. 151295 PT-1 [$_{NARR-CH}$ (demonstrates sign) HARE
200. 151300 children-COPY-1 WORD-pl FOUR WORD-pl, FINISH:
201. 151322 THEN children-LOOK-AT-1-2h! EYES-WIDE-OPEN
202. 151341 HAVE-neg EARS(-2h) COVER-EARS
203. 151353 [$_{CH}$ "stick fingers in ears"
204. 151364 CUTE
205. 151367 [$_{CH}$ "stick fingers in ears"
206. 151373 [$_{NARR-CH}$ (head nod: "ok, now...")
207. 151380 PT-1 [$_{NARR-CH}$ (demonstrates signs) TORTOISE WIN, HARE LOSE
208. 151457 NOW: HAVE-neg INTERPRETER SWEEP-ASIDE-interpreter
209. 151476 PT/5/-arc-children PT-children [$_{CH}$ "deep concentration" (copy signs) HARE
LOSE, TORTOISE WIN
210. 151523 [$_{NARR-CH}$ CORRECT
211. 151530 THEN: [$_{NARR-CH}$ WHO WANT JOIN-IN HERE STAGE
212. 151554 [$_{CH}$ "RAISE-HANDS("excited")"(2h-alt)+++!
213. 151568 BRING-IN(2h-alt)+++!
214. 151576 cl-44(2h)-- NOW cl-44(2h)!-'huge line in front of me' KID
215. 152003 YESTERDAY (neg. headshake), TWO
216. 152018 NOW cl-44(2h)!-'huge line in front of me'

217. 152032   PT-1 cl-V̈-"sitting in a circle"
218. 152046   "s" ["s"-CH "CONDUCT-ORCHESTRA" (narrator laughs) "PUT-HANDS-DOWN-ON-TABLE" (head nod: "ok, now …")
219. 152084   ["s"-CH (demonstrates sign) TORTOISE
220. 152096   [CH (copy sign) TORTOISE
221. 152104   SAME-AS! children-SAME-AS!
222. 152115   [CH (copy signs) TORTOISE WIN
223. 152140   [CH (copy sign awkwardly) "WIN"] VARIOUS
224. 152156   [CH (copy signs) HARE LOSE
225. 152177   PT-1 APPLAUD! (excited)
226. 152188   APPLAUD
227. 152195   BEAUTIFUL! PT-1
228. 152209   cl-55-wiggle-'children go back to their places'
229. 152216   [CH (excited) EXCITED] cl-V̈V-'sit-down' FINISH

SECOND CHILDREN STORY: "life story" episode

• *complicating action*

230. 152236   [NARR-H NOW PT-1 STORY LIFE POSS/B/-1
231. 152255   [NARR-H PT-1 BORN DEAF
232. 152267   [NARR-H PT-1 FAMILY HEARING/4/ SURPRISED
233. 152279   [NARR-H DEAF NATURAL
234. 152296   [NARR-H KNOW^NEG MAYBE SELF-arc-children
235. 152305   TELL-STORY

236. 152310 [_CH (look up at narrator fascinated) children-CL-FF-look-at-1

237. 152316 FINISH: [_NARR-CH "S" PERSON/BB/-rt PT-rt BORN HEARING/4/ LIKE PT-2-arc HEARING/4/] PT-1

238. 152352 [_CH (look up at narrator fascinated) children-LOOK-AT/55/-1

239. 152360 PT-1 [_NARR-CH SICK AGE^THREE MUMPS

240. 152386 [_CH (look up at narrator fascinated) children-LOOK-AT-1

241. 152398 SURPRISED

242. 152404 1-INFORM-children++ UNTIL-END FINISH:

- *resolution*

243. 152418 THEN children-ASK-QUESTION-1-2h-alternating+++

244. 152442 (a child:) [_CH (confident) PT-1 ACQUAINTED-WITH SIGN A^B^C

245. 152467 [_NARR-CH COME-HERE

246. 152473 PT-3 [_CH (signs awkwardly to self) "A^C^B"

247. 152492 COMICAL

248. 152501 SHOW-EXAMPLE

249. 152507 SIGN-FLUENTLY-2h-alternating++

- *coda*

250. 152517 NOW AGE SIX-lf ELEVEN-rt-- (negative headshake) NINE

251. 152553 "SUPER"

He and I: The Depersonalization of Self

in an American Sign Language Narrative

Bryan K. Eldredge

The purpose of this paper[1] is to demonstrate connections between theories in linguistic anthropology and actual instances of discourse in the DEAF-WORLD.[2] I focus on the attempts of a Deaf person to illuminate and recreate connections between himself and the DEAF-WORLD, connections that he sees as favorable. The data at the heart of this paper are contextually situated discourse in the form of a lecture in which the lecturer presents some information about himself that threatens to call into question his claim to a culturally Deaf identity and the to the DEAF-WORLD itself. These connections between and among Deaf individuals are at the heart of Deaf studies because, in a very real sense, they *are* the DEAF-WORLD. The study of these relationships raises questions important to us all, including What does it mean to be Deaf?, Who is Deaf? and, crucially for this study, *When* is a person Deaf?

THE SELF

In his article "Pronouns, Persons, and the Semiotic Self," Milton Singer (1989) argues for an anti-Cartesian conception of the self based in the semiotic work of C. S. Peirce, a conception that is "neither bounded nor unified, without introspection, extroverted rather than introverted, with

I thank my classmates and particularly my instructor, Laura Graham, from the Ethnography of Communication class at the University of Iowa for helpful comments and research suggestions. In addition, I thank Laura Graham, Julie Eldredge, and Doug Stringham for comments on earlier drafts of this paper. Correspondence concerning this article should be addressed to Bryan K. Eldredge, Department of Foreign Languages — 167, Utah Valley State College, 800 West 1200 South, Orem, UT 84058-5999. Phone calls may be placed to (801) 222-8529 v/vp, and electronic mail may be sent to eldredbr@uvsc.edu.

an existential rather than a reflexive self-consciousness" (Singer 1989, 255). Singer traces this line of thought to ancient Greece:

> Peirce's anti-Cartesian doctrine that knowledge of the self depends on external observation rather than on private introspection and on indubitable intuitions of a thinking substance has much in common with the "spontaneous objectivity" of classical Greek. (1989, 264)

The Cartesian conception of the self is bounded by introspection. In contrast, Peirce's anti-Cartesian semiotic self has an extended social identity (Singer, 1989, 281).

This fluid, socially constructed conception of the self has been drawn on quite broadly in linguistic anthropology, particularly in discourse-centered approaches (e.g., Crapanzano 1996; Graham 1994, 1995; Hill and Irvine 1992; Silverstein and Urban 1996; Urban 1989) that recognize that "social interaction is the primordial means through which the business of the social world is transacted, the identities of its participants are affirmed or denied, and its cultures are transmitted, renewed, and modified" (Goodwin and Heritage 1990, 283). Graham (1994) notes,

> By situating the locus of identity and continuity of the self in processes of semiotic communication rather than within the human organism, Peirce's anti-Cartesian formulation of the self embraces the potential for creative, emergent, and multiple self identities. (724)

This dialectic approach assumes a "continuous, emergent process of self-constitution through the mediation of the other, itself continuously emergent" (Crapanzano 1996, 112). The impetus for this emergence, according to Erik Erikson, is interaction with the "Other." Erikson argues it is through this social contact that a person's original sense of being is heightened until the original "I" "gradually face[s] another counterplayer, namely, my Self—almost an Inner Other" (Erikson quoted in Singer 1989, 268). This framework is particularly useful because it attends to (a) the relationships between discursive forms and functions as they are used in "social communication" and (b) the ways those relationships are used toward "certain ends of communication" beyond the mere passing along of the referential meaning (Silverstein 1976).

In the present study, I examine how these relationships between discursive forms and functions can be used to negotiate an identity by separating an individual's past and present selves. Specifically, I examine the processes by which a Deaf man, whom I here call Mark, negotiates identities for his "selves" in an American Sign Language (ASL) narrative by contrasting his earlier oral, culturally hearing self with his later and current signing, culturally Deaf self. Specifically, I will demonstrate Mark's use of the unique spatial capacities of the medium of sign to "represent [him]self as a complex, emergent, and many faceted cluster of identities" (Graham 1994, 724).

THE NARRATIVE

This study results largely from ethnographic work I conducted among the Deaf population along Utah's Wasatch Front during the summer of 1997. I analyze here an account given by a Deaf man — who has taught ASL and Deaf culture in a community college's interpreter training program and is generally thought of as a skilled performer, storyteller, and teacher — as part of a workshop he taught at a biennial symposium for Deaf members of the Church of Jesus Christ of Latter-day Saints (LDS), the "LDS Deaf Symposium," in Salt Lake City. The workshop Mark taught was titled, "Is There an LDS Deaf Culture?" Attracting at least 150 participants, this workshop was by far one of the better-attended workshops at the conference.

The brief segment I examine here is something of a digression from the main presentation, which occurred about halfway through the hour-long presentation. As will become apparent shortly, this digression was immediately preceded by a discussion about Deaf people's varying backgrounds. These differences were presented as having been largely the result of the environments in which people are raised and the effects of these environments on the kind of exposure deaf individuals have to other deaf people. As the basis for Mark's discussion, he presented a Venn diagram representing four different kinds of deafness. The center was labeled "Deaf ethnicity," which Mark loosely defined as the "most culturally Deaf." The next level was "Deaf culture," which included a somewhat broader range of individuals, specifically, those who communicate primarily with ASL — although some of them may have acquired it later in life. The third level was the "Deaf community," which he defined roughly as including not only the inner two groups but also those who have some form of significant contact with the two inner groups but for whom hearing ways are a more significant part of their lives. Finally, the outer ring represented "Individuals in isolation," who are those audio-logically "impaired" people who have little or no contact with the sign-ing Deaf population and who communicate primarily by means of oral language.

Immediately following this outlining of distinctions among various deaf people, Mark turned to some distinctions between the social prac-tices of Deaf and hearing congregations (i.e., wards or smaller branches) in the LDS church. It was at this point, that he digressed into the nar-rative considered here, which is an account of his first introduction to a Deaf branch that was also, significantly, his introduction to the Deaf community and Deaf culture. (At this point, I suggest reading the free translation of the narrative provided in appendix A.)

Negotiating an Identity

To demonstrate some remarkable differences between hearing and Deaf LDS meetings, Mark gives an account of his own first visit to a Deaf branch. But in doing so, Mark must reveal some potentially damaging information about himself: he was raised orally — as a deaf person in isolation. This information stands in opposition to the identity of a signing, culturally Deaf person that Mark presents on the stage. In revealing that he was not exposed to ASL or other Deaf people while growing up — but, instead, was trained (as opposed to educated) under a philosophy that prevented his early enculturation to Deaf ways and language — Mark presents referential information that challenges the identity he currently asserts.

In their book *Deaf in America,* Carol Padden and Tom Humphries (1988), who are Deaf themselves, write that in the DEAF-WORLD "when one wishes to say something of note about someone, terms like 'Deaf' and 'hearing' are obligatory" (13). They go on to explain that the normal usage of the English word *deaf* refers to "one's inability to speak and hear" whereas the ASL sign DEAF,[3] in contrast, "is a means of identify-ing the group and one's connection to it" (39). Likewise, Padden and Humphries define the ASL term ORAL not simply as audiologically deaf people who speak rather than sign, as with the English word *oral*, but as representing

a misaligned center, the results of having made wrong choices in life; it is an unacceptable insinuation to someone who considers himself deaf. The sign ORAL incorporates a long social and political history of the role of the school in the community. "Oral" schools promote ideologies counter to those of deaf people.... ORAL individuals are stereotypically represented as members of the establishment, as coming from hearing families that are inflexible about their children's behavior. (1988, 51)

Identifying himself as (having been) oral puts Mark in a difficult situation. Being oral means Mark's "personal identity or social position is somehow insufficient as a guarantee of a statement's truth or authenticity" (Hill and Irvine 1992, 6). It is not merely a statement that he used to speak and did not sign; rather, it is a statement that puts at risk his claims to the position of authority as a culturally Deaf person — a position he now actively asserts.

The distinctions among Deaf, hearing, and hard of hearing people are ranked,[4] and they "emerge as particularly salient when people end up in the 'wrong place,' as outsiders in a community" (Hill and Zepeda 1992, 206). The remainder of this study examines the ways Mark is able to counteract the referential message he has revealed through formal aspects of his discursive performance, which is made possible because the "locus of identity and continuity of self [is situated] in processes of semiotic communication rather than within the human organism" (Graham 1994, 725). I will demonstrate a number of ways that Mark skillfully draws on the repertoire of discursive resources available to him in negotiating for a "best identity" (Hill and Zepeda 1992), one that allows him to maintain his position as one having authority to speak about the DEAF-WORLD and for its (other) members. This tension is not unlike that identified by Singer (1989) in the work of Walt Whitman, who tried "to project a *persona* as a native American poet speaking a colloquial folk idiom, on the one hand, and a cosmopolitan and sophisticated journalist on the other" (244).

Although I believe there are other forms within this same narrative that may be worthy of analysis (e.g., reported speech, etc.), this paper looks primarily at the ways Mark uses the resources provided to him by ASL's medium of transmission, the visual-gestural channel of space, to depersonalize the discourse and thereby reduce his accountability for the referential content of it. Mark takes advantage of the signing space to simultaneously represent himself — or, more accurately, two of his selves — at two different stages in his life and to depersonalize a less desirable former, oral self. The first technique Mark uses is not possible with spoken language: he refers to himself using both a first-person singular and a third-person singular pronoun *at the same time.*

ASL Pronouns

To understand how Mark accomplishes this simultaneous referencing, it is important to know how ASL pronouns are formed. The singular pronouns are simply an (aptly named) index finger pointed at the object to which they refer.[5] So, in the case of the first-person singular pronoun, the signer taps the tip of an extended index finger against his or her chest. The second-person singular pronoun is produced by pointing the index finger toward the chest of the addressee.

ASL has two third-person singular pronouns, a present and nonpresent pronoun. The form of each is identical so far as the production with the hand is concerned. Each consists of a simple point. But the present and nonpresent differ with respect to the location of the point or, more specifically, to what they point at and to the nonmanual features accompanying them. The third-person present form is accomplished simply by pointing at the person or object (which, of course, must necessarily be present) while briefly glancing at the person or object of reference (see figure 1). In contrast, the nonpresent form differs by the absence of the glance and by the direction of the point, not at the person or object, but at a point in space that represents the person or object (either by virtue of its designation earlier in the discourse or by virtue of the use of the pronoun).

He and I

In the situation under analysis here, Mark launches into his narrative to give anecdotal evidence about the differences he has noticed between Deaf and hearing LDS congregations. However, as he does so, he realizes that to make his experiences understood, to make clear why the Deaf ward seemed so odd to him at first, he needs to explain that he was raised orally and attended hearing wards for nearly the first two decades of his life. It is at this point that Mark uses two pronouns in reference to himself at the same time. He points at himself (standard first-person singular) and then, as he says "oral," he also points down and left with his left hand to indicate "he" (see figure 2). This third-person pronoun is held

FIGURE 1. *First-("I") and third-("he, she, it") personal pronouns*

throughout the remainder of the line (see figure 3). In fact, the analysis of this usage is a central point of this paper. Consequently, this double pronominal reference deserves some additional explanation.

In the instance under examination here, just as Mark begins his narrative, he finds that to make a point, he must tell his audience that he used to be oral. This disclosure is potentially damaging to Mark's credibility, but the way he divulges the information serves to depersonalize the message even as it is presented. The form of Mark's pronouncement is significant because, in referring to himself, Mark takes advantage of ASL's spatial nature and the fact that he has two articulators (i.e., hands) to produce both first- and third-person pronouns simultaneously. Both of these pronouns refer to Mark at two different stages in his life. Mark uses one hand (his right) to say "I" (first person), and at the same time, Mark says "he" (third person) with the other hand. I have tried to capture this simultaneous production in the following transcription of lines 1–2.

Representing three-dimensional moving signs on paper's two dimensions is often problematic. However, the following transcriptions of lines 1–2 illustrate the specific structures under consideration in this paper. The first transcription is a literal gloss of the specific signs, and the second is the free translation as it appears in appendix A. Appendix B contains is a key of the transcription symbols I use. Note that the italicized "*PRO. 3lf......*" represents the left hand saying "he" and is aligned beneath the gloss ORAL to indicate when he formed the sign in relation to the signs (including ORAL) formed by the right hand.

FIGURE 2. PRO.1 *and* PRO.3 *used simultaneously*

FIGURE 3. PRO.3 *held while* ORAL *is produced*

Gloss (lines 1-2):

INSIDE, PRO.1 FIRST TIME ENTER IN #LA BRANCH. . . (hesitates, then steps back)
LONG-AGO PRO.1 ORAL. PRO.1 LONG-AGO ORAL PRO.1 . . .
PRO.3lf. . . . .

Free Translation (lines 1-2):

The first time I set foot in the Los Angeles Branch. . . (hesitates, then steps
back) A long time ago I-he used to be oral. A long time ago, I-he was
oral.

I have transcribed the text this way in an effort to make explicit both the
referential content of the message and to illustrate the spatial aspects of
ASL under consideration in this paper. I have also included a number of
still photographs that I extracted from the video footage recorded during
the workshop. My hope is that they will make my explication less cum-
bersome for the reader.

This potential of the signing medium for simultaneous production and
perception of lexical items distinguishes ASL (and at least some other
signed languages) from spoken languages. For Deaf people such as Mark,
it is yet another resource available in navigating the social world.

Various readers of earlier drafts of this paper, and audience members
in attendance when I presented this work at a conference some time
ago, have rightly looked for alternative explanations for this seemingly
anomalous simultaneous pronoun reference. The most common possibility suggested to me is that perhaps the third-person pronoun might refer
to something other than Mark, most commonly the L.A. Deaf Branch.
After all, pointing with the index finger can be interpreted in a variety
of ways. For example, the index pointing gesture in ASL can translate
into English as at least each of the following terms: *he, she, it, this, that,*
and (*up, down,* and *over*) *there.* Observers have often asked whether,
within the narrative, Mark ever uses this third-person pronoun by itself
(without the first-person pronoun) in reference to himself. The apparent
supposition is that such a usage would amount to prima facie evidence
that Mark is referring to himself in the third person. Such an occurrence,
however, does not appear in the narrative. Although the presence of a
third-person-only reference would give strong support, its absence does
little to settle the matter. To use only the third-person "he" would likely
result in confusion. By teaming it with the first-person "I," Mark makes
clear that he is still talking about himself. By using the two together at
the same time, Mark not only renders the narrative comprehensible but

also "depersonalizes" the narrative and mitigates its potentially negative effect.

Additional evidence also supports my analysis. First, the third-person pronoun in question begins after Mark says, "I ORAL." If the third-person pronoun were meant to refer to the L.A. Deaf Branch, it would make sense to produce it immediately following the production of "#LA BRANCH" either at the end of that sentence (to establish a location in the signing space for future reference) or at the beginning of the following sentence (to make a comment about the branch). He does not.

In fact, once Mark mentions the L.A. Deaf Branch, he hesitates, steps back, and then begins an entirely new sentence. The hesitation and stepping back is a discourse feature by which Mark breaks the frame of his narrative to give information that is out of context chronologically. That is, he realizes that to make sense of the information he is giving about his reaction to the L.A. Deaf Branch, the audience needs more background information about him (which he spends the next 113 seconds of his narrative providing before returning to his reaction). Because this information should have come before Mark mentioned the branch, he has to break the frame to add it. It is at this point that Mark produces the sentence with the double pronouns. The pronoun "he" appears after he says "LONG-AGO PRO.1" and as he begins to form the pronoun PRO.3. The PRO.3 pronoun does not immediately follow his reference to the L.A. Deaf Branch but occurs halfway through a sentence that makes a distinct break from the previous section. Moreover, it appears halfway through this sentence introducing his digression *after* he has established himself as the subject of the sentence by means of a PRO.1 pronoun and, at the exact same time, he produces the word ORAL in describing his former self. The right hand then reproduces "PRO.1 ORAL" while the left hand maintains the PRO.3 throughout.[6]

Finally, I take as significant support for my analysis the fact that Mark never objected to the interpretation presented in this paper. Mark, who has a significant level of metalinguistic awareness, has read the analysis and was present when I first presented my findings at the Deaf Studies VI conference during which members of the audience asked me about the interpretation I presented there and maintain here. Never at either of these times nor in any of the discussions about the analysis that Mark and I have had since did he say anything to suggest that the index reference produced on his left hand at this point is anything other than what I ascribe it to be. Mark did express surprise when he saw the video of himself. He told me that he was not aware he had done this dual representation at the time, nor was he consciously aware of a "plan" to do so.[7] For these reasons, I will maintain my assertion that Mark's dual indexical points do constitute the simultaneous production of two different pronouns, both referring back to Mark.

As I have mentioned, the simultaneous production of two lexical items (let alone two individual sounds) is not possible in English whose medium (and single set of articulators) requires a sequential stringing together of words. But in ASL, the production of two signs simultaneously is very common. The production of multiple pronouns is less common in ASL, although any user of the language has probably seen, if not produced, such a combination. For example, the question, You and me? can be produced in this way. What is far less frequent is the simultaneous production of two different pronouns that refer to a single referent. The questions to be asked here are What does this usage mean? and What are its functions? Mark uses two pronouns to say he was oral while at the same time detaching himself from this oralist person. The double pronouns say, in effect, "I am talking about me, but that's not who I am. I was a different person then." Mark reduces his accountability for his oral upbringing by locating that self apart from his present self. This distancing from the oral person he establishes in the signing space by use of the third-person pronoun is further amplified by Mark's stepping back, away from his oral self as he makes his confession. The result is a physical distancing between his body, representing his present self, and the location in space he is establishing to represent his former self.

Spatial Agreement

The kind of separation of selves seen in lines 1–2 also can be found elsewhere in the narrative. In lines 24–25, Mark says he thought he was the only LDS Deaf person in the world. Here again, we see Mark use the resources availed him by the spatial nature of ASL to distance himself from potentially damaging referential information that is itself important to the context. This time, however he uses more than the pronominal system to accomplish this distance. The ASL predicate Mark uses, TO-BE-ALONE, conforms to certain agreement rules that dictate that its location in the signing space must agree with its subject (Padden 1990). One would therefore expect to see this sign placed in first-person position, near Mark's chest, which is exactly what we find while he has assumed the role of his former self:

Gloss (line 24-25):
(as former self) " Huh?" PRO.1 THINK PRO.1 TO-BE-ALONE-1st #LDS. PRO.1 *(to audience as current self)* TO-BE-ALONE-3rd-rt WORLD ALONE-3rd-rt

Free Translation (line 24-25):
(as former self) [I said,] "Huh?!?!?! I thought I was the only [deaf] LDS person." (to audience as current self) [I-he thought] he[8] was the only one in the world.

The gloss of these lines shows that the sign TO-BE-ALONE is used twice but it is placed in a different location (first person and third person) each time. The first occurrence is located near Mark's chest (see figure 4), in "first-person position" (Baker-Shenk and Cokely 1980). This position is where we would expect it to be because he is talking about himself and because the sign is immediately preceded by a first-person pronoun (i.e., PRO.1, or I), as shown in figure 5. However, the second occurrence of TO-BE-ALONE (-3rd) is placed up and to the right[9] and agrees not with a first-person, but a third-person, subject (see figure 6).

The choice between these two forms is highly significant. Each instance is preceded by the same first-person pronoun meaning "I," and each of these refer to Mark, but they do not refer to the same person or, more accurately, to the same self. Between the production of these two occurrences of TO-BE-ALONE (-1st and -3rd) Mark switches roles. During the first occurrence, he is speaking as his former self (note his shocked expression as shown in figure 5), the oralist, and as such the location of the predicate properly agrees with "him." However in the second occurrence, Mark is speaking as his present self, the narrator of the story, about his former self. In this instance, the first person pronoun sets up a continuity between the two selves that is opposed by the variation in inflectional morphology. The first TO-BE-ALONE (-1st) is grammatically and indexically (by virtue of contiguity) tied to the speaker who is the former Mark. The second TO-BE-ALONE (-3rd), spoken by the narrator, is grammatically and indexically tied to the former Mark who is at this point a separate self.

At this point, we see a clear example of the intersection between performance and competence. When language is viewed from a Saussurean

FIGURE 4. *TO-BE-ALONE*-1st *signed near the chest*

FIGURE 5. *PRO.*1 *precedes TO-BE-ALONE*-1st

FIGURE 6. *TO-BE-ALONE-3rd signed up and right*

point of view with its strict separation of *langue* and *parole* (Saussure 1985), an utterance is subject to grammaticality judgments that compare instances of speech (i.e., *parole*) with presupposed structural systems (e.g., *langue*). Such an analysis, as advocated by structural linguistics, would undoubtedly deem this instance of TO-BE-ALONE-3rd to be ungrammatical by virtue of its failure to agree with the first-person subject, and would therefore be labeled a "performance error" (Radford 1988). The irony is that this usage, when viewed in the present context, is anything but an error.

Rather, this utterance is actually a demonstration of Mark's competence in using a wide range of language resources available to him that allow him to address multiple functions of language (Silverstein 1976). It demonstrates the link between language and culture. Mark uses his knowledge of the language to serve particular cultural ends — in this case, to negotiate for himself multiple identities that in turn affect his authoritative weight — even by producing "ungrammatical" but meaningful utterances.

Before moving on, I think it is interesting to note that, in contrast to the earlier observation about pronominal use (lines 1–2), in this instance, Mark does actually refer to his former self with the first-person pronoun

"I" that is not accompanied by the simultaneous "he." In the case of the first two occurrences of "I" in line 24, Mark's assumption of characteristics of his former self allows him to embed the pronouns within an instance of reported or "constructed" speech, which is essentially a speaker's direct quote presented in another context (Tannen 1988). This embedding effectively distances him from reference. As Urban (1989) explains,

> There is also, in some instances at least, a kind of "dequotative 'I'," where the metaphorical "I" of a quotation, through a kind of theatrical substitution, becomes a referential index, but this time pointing to the speaker not with respect to the speaker's everyday identity or self, but rather with respect to an identity the speaker assumes through the text. (27)

Through embedding the pronouns in reported speech, Mark removes himself from responsibility for the referential content of the sentence (Hill and Zepeda 1992; Hill and Irvine 1992). In this case, he downplays the significance of his admitting to having been an outsider to the DEAF-WORLD.

What is more perplexing is Mark's use in lines 24–25 of a first-person pronoun in his narrator role (i.e., as his current self) without the accompanying third-person pronoun as he used in lines 1–2. A couple of explanations are possible, among them the possibility that the lines separating Mark's former and present selves are somewhat blurred, even for Mark. It is also possible that the first-person pronoun is necessary here to make the meaning clear — precisely because of the third-person form of TO-BE-ALONE that follows it. If Mark were to use a third-person pronoun, the grammaticality problem would be avoided, but the reference would be obscured. We find support for this observation by continuing on to the next line (line 26):

Gloss (line 26):
(to audience) SOME DEAF THINK ALONE-rt. FEEL ALONE-rt DEAF. *"Well"*

Free Translation (line 26):
Some Deaf people think they are all alone. They feel like they're all alone.

Here, Mark immediately re-uses the third person form of TO-BE-ALONE[10] but this time in reference to the nebulous (third person) "some Deaf people." This use may well be an attempt to "cover the tracks" of the preceding "I" by attributing the isolation to unnamed people and is done by reusing the same predicate.

In any case, this depersonalization of the former self from the present self fits nicely into a common ideology in the Deaf community: although hearing people often look at deaf people as being isolated, cut off from society — particularly signing Deaf people — Deaf people themselves assert that it is the oral deaf people who try to pass as hearing who are truly isolated. The view holds that these people, such as Mark's oral self, not only are cut off from hearing people by virtue of their deafness but also are isolated from Deaf people (Baynton 1996; Lane 1984, 1993).

Calling *Him* Names

The narrative Mark presents is not completely void of direct, referential attention to the distancing between Mark's present and former selves. The final lines of the digression (80–82) illustrate this articulation clearly:

Gloss (line 80–82):
BEFORE PRO.3lf PRO.1 GIVE-NAME SIGN JABBERJAW PRO.3lf. PRO.3rt [UNCLEAR] JABBER JABBER. NONE MORE. SIGN (2H)FINE*

Free translation (lines 80–82):
Before I was called Jabberjaw.[11] I [unclear[12]] was always flapping my great big mouth!!! No more. Now I sign [fluent ASL]. Just fine!!! Through my mission.

Here Mark, through a nameless, genderless third person, mocks his former self, calling himself a name (see figure 7), and making fun of the way he communicated. A strictly dualistic Cartesian view of the self would suggest that Mark here is mocking his present self — or self conceived of in a simplistic way. However, because Mark is the one doing the mocking, he is able to position his identity with Deaf people who use this term toward oral deaf people. The fact that he can call himself this name (even in indirect, reported speech) is evidence of the separation of selves, just as one's speaking to one's self is (Peirce 1955/1940).

At the same time that Mark referentially mocks his former hearing self, he is also demonstrating his enculturation by the use of the ASL word play JABBERJAW. Mark's use of this common label for oral deaf people implies that he understands the sign's history and implications,

FIGURE 7. *A still photo of the sign* JABBERJAW

that he knows how it serves to mark off deaf people who are culturally hearing. But because the sign JABBERJAW in an iconic representation of a moving mouth, a three-dimensional physical object moving through and in space, Mark demonstrates his shift from a person dependant on primarily linear spoken language forms to a culturally Deaf person who uses spatial language.

This message of enculturation presented by the formal aspects of Mark's mockery also are restated referentially. Once Mark acknowledges the limited mode of communication on which his former self relied, he assures the audience that he does so "no more" and that he now signs "just fine."[13] Here, he indicates that his transformation from a culturally inept, oral deaf person to a competent Deaf person is complete. This final statement asserts referentially what has been implied throughout the narrative by nonreferential means.

Maintaining an Identity for One's Self

Mark's narrative is a classic example of a phenomenon identified by Hill and Zepeda (1992) who write, "In accounts of personal experience

speakers attempt to construct favorable presentation of self, and to miti-
gate representations of experiences that might tend to damage this construction" (197). I have already identified some specific means by which
Mark does this construction. However, a number of other factors also
collaborate to produce this effect. Some of them are specific aspects of the
narrative structure, such as the use of reported speech, which go even further to remove Mark from responsibility. Other aspects of the narrative
such as the chronological ordering of events, Mark's references to specific
people who are well known in the LDS Deaf community, and his selective
omission of first-person pronouns where they indexically implicate his
physically present Deaf self in the actions performed by his former oral
self (see lines 56–74 and especially related endnote 8) all indicate to the
audience Mark's competence at using ASL and his familiarity with DEAF-
WORLD norms and practices.

Other aspects of the context also support Mark's claims to a Deaf
identity. The fact that Mark is telling this story to a large group of Deaf
people in ASL serves to minimize the connection between Mark's former
and present selves on the basis that they are incompatible. In a sense,
Mark's presence as a workshop instructor fluently using ASL to discuss
issues of identity in the community helps him to establish and maintain
the depersonalized nature of his narrative. My observations during and
after the workshop compel me to conclude that Mark was largely successful in these efforts.

Another factor in Mark's favor, and it is a significant one, is that
Mark's experiences as a deaf person raised orally are not unique. In fact,
many people in the audience had shared experiences similar to Mark's.
The vast majority of deaf children have two hearing parents, and so these
kinds of first-contact stories in which a deaf individual begins the process of enculturation into the DEAF-WORLD are a commonly circulating
form of discourse within the community. Although Mark's first contact
comes later than most, this theme is familiar to everyone in the audience,
a large number of whom (perhaps a majority) have had similar personal
experiences.

Finally, although I have shown many ways in which Mark has miti-
gated his responsibility for his oral upbringing and has demonstrated
the cultural Deafness of his current self, it should not be overlooked that
Mark introduces this story for a purpose. In the context of the workshop
he is presenting, Mark gains authority to speak as an expert on the differences between Deaf and hearing congregations because he has been a

member of both. In this respect, the referential content of Mark's story is a double-edged sword: it has the potential to bring authority status to Mark as one who knows about hearing ways, but at the same time, it threatens to sever him from his authority to speak as a culturally Deaf person. Despite the dangers, Mark performs this balancing act effectively.

CONCLUSION

In this paper I have presented evidence for a dialogical conception of the self as emergent through the process of social interaction as seen in an ASL discourse. I have presented evidence that Mark negotiates for himself identities that account for his past life experiences as an oral deaf person and for his present status as an authoritative, culturally Deaf person. He accomplishes this negotiation, in part, by his use of ASL's spatial medium, which allows him to refer to himself simultaneously as "I" and "he." This same kind of depersonalization of Mark's present self from his former self is also argued for in his use of third-person verb forms corresponding to his former self. Finally, I presented evidence for more direct arguments for a separation of selves in the referential content of the narrative, specifically in Mark's assertion that he signs "just fine" now.

It is not surprising that Mark used these forms in negotiating his identity. The significance of these linguistic forms is described by Singer (1989):

> The use of the first, second and third person pronouns, and the corresponding forms of the verb, are implicated in this conception of self because they are implicated in the unified structures of human interactions, associations, and communication. (284)

As I have shown, just these aspects of language are what Mark relied on to present his conception of his identity. What is interesting is that, in ASL, the manipulation of the pronouns and the corresponding forms of the verb are both spatial in nature. In this case, the relationships between various loci in the signing space are what Peirce (1955/1940) labels "indexical icons" of the social relationships that Mark both emphasizes and avoids.

I have chosen to focus this paper on ways in which Mark used spatial aspects of ASL, made possible by its medium of transmission in part because of the absence of these constructions in spoken English.[14] Mark's skillful use of ASL testifies of one who has had extensive experience in the Deaf community. In spoken English, one cannot produce two pronouns simultaneously. The fact that Mark does so here is tangible evidence of his enculturation. My own experience teaching ASL, mostly to hearing college and university students, suggests that these spatial features are often the most difficult for spoken language users to master, which enables spatial features to serve as a shibboleth of sorts. Mark's skillful use of these aspects of the language itself, not just the referential content, distances his present authoritative self from a past devalued self by portraying his current self as being similar to the "ideal" (Padden 1996) Deaf person.

In this digression, Mark "faces problems in the management of a complex identity, and is vulnerable to accusations that [he] has not been 'responsible' in an important task" (Hill and Zepeda 1992, 198): being Deaf. The fact that he promotes his Deaf self as distinct from his oral self by manipulating the spatial medium of ASL further serves to indicate his successful enculturation. Even as the referential content of the narrative reveals that he was raised as oral, the skill with which he uses ASL demonstrates the distance between this former self and the one who now stands authoritatively on stage. In this respect, the form serves as a kind of "cultural capital" (Bourdieu 1977) and carries sufficient weight to offset the potentially damaging content of the referential message he presents.

NOTES

1. This paper was originally written as part of the requirements for a graduate class titled Ethnography of Communication in the department of anthropology at the University of Iowa. The data and analysis presented here were presented to that class as the original draft was in process. Eventually, I presented that paper (Eldredge 1999) at the Deaf Studies: Making the Connection conference in Oakland, California, on April 18, 1999. It was printed in the proceedings from that conference.

2. Considerable discussion and debate has surrounded definitions of and names for the Deaf community, the "Deaf culture," or both. In this paper, I follow Deaf people themselves in referring to the "DEAF-WORLD" (Bahan, Hoffmeister, and Lane 1996; Padden 1989). The use of small caps and the hyphenation is an attempt to record this phrase's origins in ASL.

3. In this paper, I write English glosses for ASL words in small capital letters as a sign that they are not to be taken as having identical referential content or distribution as illustrated here with the case of DEAF and deaf.

4. These distinctions are ranked in both Deaf and hearing communities, but inversely. Although hearing people value hearingness (viewed by them in audiometric terms) higher than deafness, the opposite is true among Deaf people (who view deafness largely in cultural terms). It is this opposition that created the oralist movement.

5. This description is an oversimplification because the signs involve articulators other than just the hands, for example, eye gaze and so forth.

6. Another possible interpretation also has occurred to me: it might appear productive to argue that the PRO.3 refers, not to the branch per se, but to a rather nebulous situation, a place in time. This interpretation seems a little more plausible to me, but it suffers from the same weakness of an unclear antecedent, as does the L.A. Deaf Branch reference. Furthermore, the promotion of this interpretation as an alternative position quickly disintegrates into a semantic argument over how best to interpret this instance of the sign PRO.3 into English. But Mark is not using English, and in ASL, both interpretations, "he" and "there," amount to the same thing: by pointing at himself ("he") or at the situation ("there") while stepping backwards and saying "I was oral" with his other hand, Mark distances his present self from the self ("he") that existed in that situation ("there").

7. I do not find this fact surprising given the subconscious level at which most people produce "talk."

8. The transcription is a little tricky here because I have represented the third-person reference with an English pronoun whereas, in ASL, the optional pronoun is absent and the person is indicated by the location of the verb TO-BE-ALONE. The English verb *was* does not show this distinction because it takes the same form for first- and third-person referents (e.g., "I was" and "he was").

9. Here, Mark locates himself (through the location of the verb) up and to his right, the opposite of where he placed himself using the double pronouns in lines 1–2. In fact, this position is the same location where he placed the deaf community (line 11). This placement seems to indicate that he is not really using the opposition between these spatial locations to contrast the status of the community and his oral self, although his later use of the same location casts some doubt on this interpretation.

10. The placement of this third-person location of TO-BE-ALONE differs somewhat from the one referring to "himself" shown in figure 6. It is to the right, but it is noticeably lower. I am uncertain whether this lower placement is significant. It is not entirely expected that it be lower given that it agrees with a different subject, but in my judgment and that of others I have consulted, Mark seems to use the higher part of the signing space an unusual amount. This more frequent use may be a feature of performance signing, which uses a larger signing space.

11. The sign I have labeled JABBERJAW here does not have a good English translation. It is an ASL word play in which the forearms are flapped together to

iconically represent the movements of a large mouth speaking. Although Mark does not do it here, the iconicity is sometimes taken further by men wearing neck ties who flip the ends of their ties over their bottom arm-"lip," imitating a long, wagging tongue. That sign has a more pejorative connotation than my English gloss and translation, JABBERJAW, implies.

12. From the camera angle, this sign or couple of signs is unclear. It may be THOUGHT I, but I am not confident enough to include it in the actual translation.

13. One could argue for a translation of "Now everything is just fine" for this line.

14. Although this paper focuses on the occurrence of this pronoun usage, the signer addresses the same end also by other means. The way he represents his former self through personifications in the form of reported or "constructed dialogue" (Tannen 1988) is one example. He also includes a short segment in the narrative in which he asks his parents why they chose to raise him orally as opposed to placing him in a signing school. Interestingly, by this act, he represents himself as blameless for his naive acceptance of hearing ways and attitudes and places that blame on his parents. He then absolves them by couching their response in terms that fit within Mormon values about family responsibilities: They tell him they wanted to keep him at home, keeping the family in tact rather than send him off to a residential school. There is no mention of the probability that his parents wanted him to be as "normal" as possible, which for hearing parents usually means to have him speak and interact as though he were not deaf. In this way, philosophical discussions about the rightness or wrongness of oralism versus signing are chiefly averted.

REFERENCES

Bahan, B., R. Hofmeister, and H. Lane. 1996. *A journey into the DEAF-WORLD.* San Diego, Calif.: DawnSignPress.

Baker-Shenk, C., and D. Cokely. 1980. *American Sign Language: A teacher's resource text on grammar and culture.* Silver Springs, Md.: T. J. Publishers.

Baynton, D. C. 1996. *Forbidden signs: American culture and the campaign against sign language.* Chicago: University of Chicago Press.

Bourdieu, P. 1977. *Outline of a theory of practice.* Trans. R. Nice. Cambridge: Cambridge University Press.

Crapanzano, V. 1996. 'Self'-Centering Narratives. In *Natural histories of discourse,* ed. M. Silverstein and G. Urban, 106–27. Chicago: University of Chicago Press.

Eldredge, B. 1999. He and I: The depersonalization of self in an American Sign Language narrative. *Deaf Studies 4: Making the Connection,* 293–316. Oakland, Calif.: College for Continuing Education, Gallaudet University.

Graham, L. 1994. Dialogic dreams: Creative selves coming into life in the flow of time. *American Ethnologist* 21 (4): 723–45.

———. 1995. *Performing dreams: Discourses of immortality among the Xavante of central Brazil.* Austin, Tex.: University of Texas Press.

Goodwin, C., and J. Heritage. 1990. Conversation analysis. *Annual Review of Anthropology* 19: 283–307.

Hill, J. H., and J. Irvine, ed. 1992. *Responsibility and evidence in oral discourse.* New York: Cambridge University Press.

Hill, J. H., and O. Zepeda. 1992. Mrs. Patrico's trouble: The distribution of responsibility in an account of personal experience. In *Responsibility and evidence in oral discourse,* ed. J. H. Hill and J. T. Irvine, 197–225. New York: Cambridge University Press.

Lane, H. 1984. *When the mind hears: A history of the Deaf.* New York: Vintage Books.

———. 1993. *The mask of benevolence: Disabling the deaf community.* New York: Vintage.

Metzger, M. 1995. Constructed dialogue and constructed action in American Sign Language. In *Sociolinguistics in deaf communities,* ed. C. Lucas, 255–71. Washington, D.C.: Gallaudet University Press.

Padden, C. 1989. The Deaf community and the culture of deaf people. In *American deaf culture,* S. Wilcox, 1–16. Burtonsville, Md.: Linstok Press.

———. 1990. The relationship between space and grammar in ASL verb morphology. In *Sign language research: Theoretical issues,* ed. C. Lucas, 118–32. Washington, D.C.: Gallaudet University Press.

———. 1996. From the cultural to the bicultural. In *Cultural and language diversity and the deaf experience,* ed. I. Parasnis, 79–98. New York: Cambridge University Press.

Padden, C., and T. Humphries. 1988. *Deaf in America: Voices from a culture.* Cambridge, Mass.: Harvard University Press.

Peirce, C. S. 1955. *Philosophical writings of Peirce.* Ed. J. Beuchler. New York: Dover. (Orig. pub. 1940.)

Radford, A. 1988. *Transformational grammar: A first course.* Cambridge Textbooks in Linguistics. Cambridge: Cambridge University Press.

Saussure, F. de. 1985. The linguistic sign. In *Semiotics: An introductory anthology,* ed. R. E. Innis, 24–46. Bloomington, Ind.: Indiana University Press.

Silverstein, M. 1976. Shifters, linguistic categories and cultural description. In *Meaning in anthropology,* ed. K. Basso and H. Selby, 11–55. Albuquerque, N.M.: University of New Mexico Press.

Silverstein, M., and G. Urban, eds. 1996. *Natural histories of discourse.* Chicago: University of Chicago Press.

Singer, M. 1989. Pronouns, persons, and the semiotic self. In *Semiotics, self, and society,* ed. B. Lee and G. Urban, 229–95. New York: Mouton de Gruyter.

Tannen, D. 1988. Hearing voices in conversation. In *Linguistics in context: Connecting observation and understanding*, ed. D. Tannen, 89–113. Advances in Discourse Processes 29. Norwood, N.J.: Ablex.

Urban, G. 1989. The 'I' of discourse. In *Semiotics, self, and society*, ed. B. Lee and G. Urban, 27–51. New York: Mouton de Gruyter.

APPENDIX A
Free Translation of Narrative

(Duration: 3 minutes, 33 seconds)

Note: The names mentioned here or pseudonyms.

1 The first time I set foot in the Los Angeles Branch, a long time ago, I-he was oral.
2 A long time ago, I-he was oral.

3 (*substantial pause*) Really, before that there was a knock on my door.

4 I opened the door and saw a missionary (*as missionary — big grin*) with hearing aids in
5 both ears with wires running own from them to a box on his chest. (*Takes on friendly*
6 *expression*) Another one on the right, deaf, his ears protruded straight out from the
7 sides of his head from wearing hearing aids.

8 (*pause — as current self*) I looked back and forth at them and noticed the name tags they
9 wore on their chest pockets. I looked at them and my jaw fell to the floor. That one
10 [on the left] was signing ASL. I had no idea! It went right over my head.

11 (*to audience*) Oh, I recognized that this was deaf people's[1] sign language. But — I stared

---

1. This statement is intriguing and somewhat problematic given the assertions I present in this chapter, although my translation does not make it apparent. The gloss before is more revealing:

Gloss:
RECOGNIZE DEAF POSS.3rt.up SIGN-LANGUAGE

Free Translation:
I recognized that this was deaf people's sign language.

I find this statement significant in light of Singer's (1989) discussion of "us" and "them" distinctions. He writes, "In all these cases the speaker uses 'we' to refer to the group with which he identifies and 'they' to refer to the group with which he disidentifies" (252). My only suggestion to account for Mark's failure to conform here is that he fails to use this means of disassociating himself. I think perhaps he does so because he has just been "acting" as his former self, although he is clearly not doing so here.

12 at him in shock — I wasn't against sign language. I wasn't warning people about it.

13 I'd never seen it before. This was the first time!

14 I opened the door. He stood there signing ASL.

15 (*look of amazement*) I looked at him and said, "Come ... Are you Mormon missionaries?"

16 He [the one with the box aid] answered, "Yes."

17 (*to audience*) He could talk. He was hard of hearing.

18 (*as former self*) "Oh. Fine. Fine. Come in." I grabbed them, hauled them in, and sat
19 them down. You two are members.

20 "Three members. Me, you, and you. Three members. Incredible!!!"

21 (*as missionary*) "There's a branch, all set up. It has 200 members."

22 (*as former self-shocked*) "Huh?!?!?! (*pause*) What?!?!?!"

23 "In Salt Lake they have over 300."

24 (*as former self*) [I said,] "Huh?!?!?! I thought I was the only [deaf] LDS person." (*to audience as*
25 *current self*) [I-he thought] he was the only one in the world.

26 Some Deaf people think they are all alone. They feel like they're all alone.

27 (*Answering unrecorded question from audience*) I was 19.

28 (*Sudden shift to former self*) "You two missionaries ... more out there ... Are you using
29 made up signs, putting me on?" (*to audience as current self*) No. No. They
30 communicated using fingerspelling and signs. It was long ago.

31 (*as former self, perplexed, addressing self*) "My father told me nothing about this." (*Turns up*
32 *and right*). I got my parents' attention and asked, "Mom, what's this?" (*motions back*
33 *left, toward missionaries*).

34 (*as mother*) "I know. I know. We didn't want to send you to the Riverside School for
35 the Deaf to stay there. We cherish you too much for that. You have a sister."

36 (*to audience*) Every day I went back and forth between home and school.

37 (*as former self*) "I see. I understand."

38 (*to audience*) Do you understand? I have my own ... If [I] were separate, to stay [my
39 parents] would worry. [Their] son staying there? [They would] worry a lot.
40 Families should be strong. You know, LDS families are strong. We cherish our
41 families and keep them together.

42 (as mother) "Taking one out and putting him there while the rest of us were still
43 together? I don't want my son there."

44 (to audience) That's a conflict, uh-huh. [Having him] there … It doesn't fit [with our
45 LDS family]. Families should be strong. Do you understand? My mother felt the
46 same way. Do you understand?

47 (as former self to mother) "I see." (to audience) I experienced that personally. (assumes
48 characteristics of former self but doesn't appear to be quoting) I saw no Deaf culture, no Deaf
49 people. None. (to audience as current self) Imagine what that was like.

50 So I went and went into the, uh, Deaf branch. The first time! I was shaking in my
51 boots!!! The missionaries saw me walk in. They were signing away!!!! With no
52 sound!!!! Just signing away!!

53 (as former self) I turned and started walking away, but the missionary ran after me and
54 grabbed my shirt on the back of my shoulder. He pulled me back in.
55 "Come on back."

56 (as former self) "Rats!" I went in.[2] It was so strange! I walked up the aisle and sat
57 down. There was a lot of commotion around. The lights flashed on and off a
58 couple of times. I looked up at them; they flashed several more times. Time to
59 start. Everyone took a seat.

60 I sat looking around. It was so quiet. When it was time to start a song, I picked up a
61 hymn book, straightened my tie, and flipped to the page. Just as I opened my mouth
62 to begin singing I glanced up. There was no voice. The chorister was signing the
63 song and everyone else was copying the signs.

64 I looked around in disbelief. I was stunned. I didn't know. I looked back at my
65 book and opened my mouth to sing. Some hearing kids looked at me. I began
66 singing with my voice, just a small, quiet voice. The hearing kids looked at me for a
67 minute and then stuck their fingers in their ears and wiggled them around. I closed
68 the book and put it down.

69 I looked toward the front and saw this woman standing there signing this song. She

2. This part of the translation (lines 57–75) includes several occurrences of the first-person pronoun "I"; the actual text, however, includes none of them. In keeping with ASL storytelling conventions, the signer assumes the role of the person in the story in telling it — a phenomenon identified by Melanie Metzger (1995), borrowing from Tannen, as "constructed action" — and in doing so here, he includes no pronouns. I think it is important to note that he could have used them; they are optional in this situation. Significantly, not using them serves Mark's purposes in two respects: first, it avoids repeating the connection between the former and present selves and, second, it allows Mark to demonstrate his ability to use ASL grammatical features and ASL storytelling techniques. This demonstration of competency indicates his successful acculturation into the DEAF-WORLD.

70 signed beautifully. Sister Andrews. That's who she was. She's hearing. She
71 smiled and signed [the song]. I was dumbstruck. I just stared at her. Beautiful
72 signing!!! She was friendly and nice … It was interesting.

73 The Sunday School teacher … I went in and sat down, thinking "I hope I can
74 understand." I looked [at him]. He was very animated in his gesturing and signing.

75 (to audience) Do you know who that was? Yes, that's right. Don James. Yes. Yes. I
76 couldn't believe [his signing]. I just stared at him with my jaw hanging to the floor.
77 After that, what did I do? I went every week, to the Deaf branch. I just kept going. I
78 learned a lot, and then they called me on a mission. A Deaf mission. I really
79 improved.

80 Before I was called Jabberjaw. People [unclear] [I was] always flapping my great big
81 mouth!!! No more. Now I sign [fluent ASL]. Just fine!!! (looks to audience) Through my
82 mission. (nods)

83 (steps back, looks at overhead projector, steps forward) Now, inside a ward … (picks up original
84 line of thought comparing Deaf and hearing congregations).

APPENDIX B

Transcription Key

small caps	English glosses for ASL words (meanings similar in some instances)
(hyphen)	The meanings of phrases in which the glosses are connected by a hyphen (or hyphens) are expressed with a single sign (e.g., TO-BE-ALONE and LONG-AGO)
PRO	Personal pronoun
POSS	Possessive pronoun
.1 or .3	indicates direction or location of agreement on pronouns, for example, PRO.1
-1st or -3rd	indicates direction or location of agreement; attached to verbs, for example, TO-BE-ALONE-1st.
rt or -lf	Indicates direction or location (i.e., right or left), for example, PRO.3rt
[ ]	Information not explicitly included in the text, provided for clarity
(small italics)	Gestures and role shifts; indicates to whom talk is directed and who is signing
GLOSSES	(Glosses in italics) signs produced with the nondominant hand; their temporal relation to the action of the

	dominant hand indicated by their vertical alignment with the line above them
#	Fingerspelled loan sign
fs-	Full fingerspelled item
*	Emphasis
(2h)	Sign done (optionally) with two hands
" "	Reported, quoted, or constructed speech
' '	Gestures
. . .	(Dotted line) when used with glosses, indicates sign is held during production of signs on the other hand
,	(Comma) when used with glosses, indicates slight pause
.	(Period) indicates sentence boundary

The punctuation of the free translations is used according to conventional rules for written English with the intent of aiding clarity.

Contributors

Jean F. Andrews
Department of Communication
   Disorders and Deaf Education
Lamar University
Beaumont, Texas

Antonella Bertone
Mason Perkins Deafness Fund
Rome, Italy

Michele Bishop
Department of Linguistics
Gallaudet University
Washington, D.C.

Marion Blondel
Le laboratoire en Sciences du Lan-
   gage DYALANG
Université de Rouen
Mont-Saint-Aignan, France

Jeffrey E. Davis
College of Education, Deaf
   Studies, and Educational
   Interpreting
University of Tennessee, Knoxville
Knoxville, Tennessee

Bryan K. Eldredge
ASL and Deaf Studies Program
Utah Valley State College
Orem, Utah

Della Goswell
Department of Linguistics
Macquarie University
Sydney, NSW, Australia

Sherry Hicks
American Sign Language
   Department
Santa Rosa Junior College
Santa Rosa, California

Trevor Johnston
Department of Linguistics
Macquarie University
Sydney, NSW, Australia

Susan Mather
Department of Linguistics
Gallaudet University
Washington, D.C.

Christopher Miller
Departement de linguistique et de
   didactique des langues
Université du Québec à Montréal
Montréal, Quebéc, Canada

Jemina Napier
Department of Linguistics
Macquarie University
Sydney, NSW, Australia

Anne-Marie Parisot
Departement de linguistique et de
  didactique des langues
Université du Québec à Montréal
Montréal, Quebéc, Canada

Juanita Rodriguez
Special Education Department
University of Puerto Rico
San Juan, Puerto Rico

Yolanda Rodriguez-Fraticelli
State Department of Education
San Juan, Puerto Rico

Rita Sala
Universita' degli Studi di Padova
Padova, Italy

Adam Schembri
Deafness, Cognition and Language
  Centre (DCAL)
University College, London
London, United Kingdom

Index

Page numbers in italics denote a figure or table.

discourse analysis, 71, 77–78, 98, 132–33

discourse-based approaches, 5, 7–9, 125–36

dissertations, 101

distance learning, 82–88

doctoral programs, 17

educational interpreting, 100

ESL curricula, 50

ethics, 31–32, 99

evaluation, 50, 50–51, 57, 60–61, 86

expectations of interpreters, 29

field observations, 14. *See also* practicum

Fullan, M.G., 51

Gajewski, P., 87–88

Gallaudet University BA program, 1–21

gender differences, 129, *159*

gestural communication, 102

graduate programs, 10–12, 24, 27, 69–74, *70, 73*, 98–103

Hatch, E., 127

healthcare interpreting
  about, 23–26
  basic components, 25–28
  course sequence, 38–42
  interpersonal skills, 25–26, 28–29
  language-specific courses, 31–32
  needs assessment and SLOs, 34–35
  principles of, 32–34
  problem-based learning, 35–37
  program descriptions, 101
  setting-specific skills, 25–26, 29, 80
  sociocultural aspect, 25–26, 30–31
  video resources, 130, 135

HIHAL (University of North Texas), 24, 27, 35

idiomatic expressions, 129

Ingram, R., 126

Internal Discussions (Bowen-Bailey), 127–28

internship, 14. *See also* practicum

interpersonal skills, 25–26, 28–29

interpreter roles, 40–41, 46, 80, 101

interpreting techniques, 98–99

Kautz, U., 118

Kennen, E., 27

Kurz, I., 114, *115*

language enhancement, 31–32, 39–40

languages of limited diffusion
  action research evaluation, 60–61
  challenges, 57–59
  curriculum design, 51–53, *54–55*, 56–57, 64–65, 107–13, *109*, *113*
  materials, 113–16, *115, 117*
  rationale for training programs, 47–49, 105–7
  teaching methods, 116, 118–20, *119*

legal interpreting, 81, 100, 130–31

Lewin, K., 50

Life in Parallel (Williamson-Loga), 133

linguistics, 98

Mackintosh, J., 118

Macquarie University. *See* Auslan/ English interpreting program

medical interpreting. *See* healthcare interpreting

mentoring, 56–57, 58–59

Metzger, M., 128, 132

Monikowski, C., 134

motivation, 33–34

multicultural education
  about, 141–42
  competencies statements, 153–56
  curriculum design, 142–51
  video resources, 160–65

NAATI (National Accreditation Authority for Translators and Interpreters), 48–49, 74–75, 84

UNIVERSITY OF WOLVERHAMPTON
LEARNING & INFORMATION SERVICES